Spiritual Training Wheels

SPIRITUAL
TRAINING WHEELS
Keeping Your Soul in Balance

Gloria D. Benish

CITADEL PRESS
Kensington Publishing Corp.
www.kensingtonbooks.com

CITADEL PRESS BOOKS are published by

Kensington Publishing Corp.
850 Third Avenue
New York, NY 10022

All Kensington titles, imprints, and distributed lines are available at special quantity discounts for bulk purchases for sales promotions, premiums, fund-raising, educational, or institutional use. Special book excerpts or customized printings can also be created to fit specific needs. For details, write or phone the office of the Kensington special sales manager: Kensington Publishing Corp., 850 Third Avenue, New York, NY 10022, attn: Special Sales Department, phone: 1-800-221-2647.

CITADEL PRESS and the Citadel logo are Reg. U.S. Pat. & TM Off.

First Printing: March 2003

10 9 8 7 6 5 4 3 2 1

Printed in the United States of America

Library of Congress Control Number: 2002113402

ISBN 0-8065-2264-X

First . . . to the Presence of God, abiding within you, the reader.

To Walter Zacharius and his beautiful wife, Alice. By opening the doors to their hearts, home, and family business, they made my dreams become reality. As people are healed through me, I am often asked, "How could I ever repay you? How can I put a price on a life?" I am now in that same position. How could I ever repay Walter for giving me a chance to express my ideals? And what price do I place on a dream? I will be forever grateful, Walter. I will do the only thing you have ever asked of me: I will just continue being who I am and let the rest take care of itself.

To my editor, Ann LaFarge. Not only has Ann done a beautiful job in presenting my thoughts and allowing me to keep my personality and "voice," but she has brought smiles to my heart in every correspondence we've had. Everyone has talents and a purpose in God's Plan, and besides being appreciated, respected, and admired by me, I trust I am in very good hands with Ann at my side through each of these projects. One person can make a difference in this world and Ann does it *just by showing up.*

To (my Knight in Shining Armor) my husband, Kirk, who supports me on all levels and demonstrates unconditional love. He believes in me, and sometimes that's all it takes for a person to keep going and growing to the fullness of her dreams.

To my children, Kerrie, Jaime, D.W., and Danielle . . . thank you for allowing me to speak about our life's experiences together to spiritually guide the world. To my sons-in-law, Christopher and Keith . . . thanks for loving my daughters. To my grandson, Colton, for being the sunshine of my life, and to my granddaughter, Taylor . . . for being the most beautiful baby I've ever seen in my life.

To my parents, Esther and Allen Hale (who, by the way, I believed were the meanest parents in the world whenever they said no). They kept me out of trouble, taught me to clean house and work hard, to be honest and have integrity, and showed morals, *by example.*

To my best friend, Linda K. (Nikki) Fudge, who was a teenage know-it-all and teenage runaway, experienced teenage pregnancy, but overcame countless obstacles and prison terms and is an asset to society. Our "spiritual family" doesn't live under the same roof, but we forever live in one another's hearts.

And last, but not least: to Matthew D. McCoy, a California state prison inmate, who inspired me to write *Spiritual Training Wheels* in this format. In return, I inspired him to write his life story. There's a "mutual admiration society" occurring between us: He thanks me for caring and I thank him for doing the hard part in our relationship. It's Matthew who sits in a sewer of constant negativity to give you and me awareness of discouraging human behavior and circumstances to help the world avoid these painful lessons.

Countless convicts have thanked me for recognizing their value, even when behind bars. Had someone seen their "innate" goodness prior to their previous choices and offered them the *truth* of their existence, perhaps their *consequences* would have been much different. There's only a single letter of difference between the words *innate* and *inmate.* Recognizing a person's virtues sooner could make prisons merely a part of our history.

May this book be a dedication to all souls, whether locked behind bars—or behind doors.

Contents

Introduction to Parents

Welcome to my heart, home, and world as a parent of four children. Join me today with your family as I give you a stable foundation to learn the balance between love and fear.

Speaking of fear, it was only weeks ago that my nineteen-year-old son, D.W., informed me that he was planning a road trip from Montana to New York State. He also told me that he had hopes that, from New York, he would just drive to Las Vegas and then back to Montana. D.W. had a *week's vacation* and he thought it would be fun to take this adventure, either alone or with a friend.

I froze. I could feel the wall of fear closing in on me. My mind raced with countless concerns for his safety.

I attempted to state my fears and cautions to him:

- Do you have any idea how much money it costs for gas, motels, and food?
- What if you were to have car trouble? (I reminded him that he didn't have a credit card.)
- D.W., you have never driven in or through big-city traffic.
- D.W., you have been overprotected living in a small town, and don't know the "Wile E. Coyote tricks" of big-city living.

I was sure:

- He didn't have any experience in attempting to pull off such a huge undertaking.
- He didn't have any idea how much money it would involve, because his dad and I have always picked up all expenses for trips.

He wouldn't listen. He wasn't going to allow my fears to be projected onto him. He wasn't willing to learn from my experiences. He believed he would be safe and that my fears were completely ungrounded.

Not only was I frustrated—remember, I had frozen. "D.W., we'll have to talk about this later—in fact, much later, because I just completely shut down. We'll talk about it again in the spring thaw when I can feel again." Maybe he was just testing me to see if I cared? He was, after all, nineteen years old and didn't need my permission to take this trip.

Having raised four children, I know the frozen feeling well. I have experienced it countless times, but at least I am aware of the resistance in my body and have learned to deal with it accordingly. Resistance is fear, which gives me an opportunity to transform it with love.

If, by the way, D.W. showed up on my doorstep today and needed to talk about the road trip *now*, I would deal with it. I honor my feelings, however, and I trust them. In this writing, I will explain why attempting to feel and express only positive emotions is unhealthy. I will teach you how to be whole and happy, and how even sadness, anger, envy, and fear can be transformed.

D.W., in my estimation, has not yet gained awareness of taking an independent step such as this. As the parent "who signed on to be Mom in this dimension," I accept the responsibility seriously for his creation.

Spiritual Training Wheels is written to give you and your children a safe and steady place to practice, as a family, how to deal with the modern-day realities that surround us. Beginning our day together, as you step over my threshold, I will offer an Opening Prayer in which I give thanks for a male convict, Matthew, and a female ex-convict, Nikki. Since 1990, I have taken every opportunity to assist prisoners in 1,104 state and federal prisons. Sometimes my assistance involves only a donated copy of one of my inspirational writings. Other times the correspondence leads to years of counseling, friendship, and deep-seated relationships.

Matthew and Nikki are the voices of experience in several stories I will be telling throughout this book. It's important for you to know that these are real people and true experiences, and that some of the information is graphic. It may cause you, as the parent, "to go numb." That is natural, and there is no need for alarm. If you are pre-reading the book for its informational content before passing it on to your child, you get an A+ *and an E for your efforts to help your loved one.*

The information that you may randomly read is not for shock value. It is given to teach how to make responsible choices. Just as I was attempting to inform my son of the possible "roadblocks" he might encounter or need to consider before making such a trip, I am here offering awareness. Our children are blessed with free will. They can, however, make choices more easily if given the tools and opportunity to learn how to do so. In this book I will attempt to teach your child the art of making healthy choices.

Where your child may turn a deaf ear and not listen to you, perhaps he or she will listen to a stranger. Many times our children will listen to someone else because there will be no resistance to doing so. A stranger's neutral, nonjudgmental, nonthreatening advice can be heard.

If, while you're reviewing this writing, your emotions temporarily freeze, it's okay. Give yourself some time away from the book and allow the information to penetrate, and I promise, you will thaw. I have written in a format that Teen Angels/Adult Children can relate to.

As a minister, I get countless e-mails and phone calls daily requesting help. Just today, a woman called and asked me to pray for her nineteen-year-old daughter who is addicted to drugs and alcohol. Unfortunately, this isn't a unique request. Mothers, fathers, and the kids themselves feel that I'm approachable and safe. They feel secure. Thus the purpose for *Spiritual Training Wheels*. You have support . . . for now, or as long as you need it.

For all those things you've wanted to discuss with your children and didn't know how or couldn't—yes, even sex— I am offering to be your voice and mediator . . . a bridge between you and your child.

For the (young) women, I will be gently introducing the facts of life in a nonthreatening, safe atmosphere. I will explain the complications and choices that await you—the parents, the daughter, and the relationships with friends and others. I will also teach how to deal effectively with peer pressure.

Concerning the (young) men, the guidance will speak of gangs, peer pressure, dating, and general intimidation and manipulation by the opposite sex. Whether a father or son reads this, the information is valid and helpful. From father to son or son to father, there may be a fear that he doesn't think he can talk to you or if he could, he's not sure what to say.

Among sensitive issues, I will also be teaching self-esteem, self-confidence, and self-love. I hope you will listen to the messages, as well. We have loved the Lord God with our hearts, minds, and souls. We have been guided, and attempted to love our neighbor as ourselves . . . living those first two and greatest commandments we were given. However, no one ever taught us *how to love ourselves.* This book is a tool to use to discover how to do so.

Thank you for accepting the invitation into my heart, home, and experience. We will take those first steps together, as your family and I learn how to achieve and maintain balance between love and fear in your heart and in your soul . . .

Always,
Gloria D. Benish, Ph.D.
(alias Dr. Glo-bug—just here "to lighten things up")

Introduction to Teen Angels and Adult Children

I am a third-generation motormouth and have been saying for years, "I have so much to say if someone will just listen to me." I think it's funny that bumper stickers say, HIRE A TEENAGER WHILE THEY STILL THINK THEY KNOW IT ALL, but it's my generation who isn't listening. I feel like a mutant at times, stuck in yesterday's memories with my photographic mind of how it feels to be a teenager while my age group wishes I would just grow up. Adults who have read enough books think they know just about all there is to know about their chosen subject. Without keeping an open mind, they want to waste time debating with those who know just a little bit more. Being a peacemaker my entire life, it's never been easy for me to have confrontations with people.

I don't go out of my way to throw sticks or stones and, most assuredly, never words, for they can break a person's heart. But knowing and seeing the results of the Teen Angels/Adult Children on the planet today and your desire to correct your ancestors' mistakes, you find yourselves not knowing who to talk to (if they would listen) or *how* you can regain what we have lost.

I received an e-mail a few weeks ago from a woman who was concerned about the latest shooting in a school. Although the first widely publicized shooting was at Columbine High School in Colorado, these things have been occurring for far longer than we all want to admit. This woman mentioned her fears, and the fears of her children.

She is seeking a spiritual understanding of why this continues to occur. Her question was, "If there's really a God—how could He allow this insane situation to occur?" God responded simply, "I'm not allowed in schools."

I recently told my husband, Kirk, "Those who don't want God in the school system should be the ones to leave." He looked at me, first surprised and shocked, and then bewildered as he understood my innocence of the fact that it's the majority who don't want God in the schools. Now, I'm not saying that prayers should be mentioned each morning before the students stand to pledge their allegiance to our flag, but hello . . . is anyone listening? God is not a far-off entity to be worshipped and read of. The Presence of God comes in the form of attributes of love, peace, goodwill, sharing, consideration, kindness, courage, faith, hope, and the list, of course, could go on endlessly. Saying that God is to be taken out of the schools is suggesting that only the druggies, gangs, and negative behavior be allowed within those hallowed halls.

Your generation and those that follow are the children of this world who are being affected. I will give you the tools to heal your lack of self-esteem, self-confidence, loneliness, and the multitude of feelings you have. Once you have those tools and incorporate them, I will continue to inspire you to go beyond what surrounds you, encouraging you to proudly and courageously make a difference in this world with your presence.

Although I'm a minister, I'm not here to shove God down your throat. My outlook is more spiritual than religious. I'm not here to change whatever beliefs you now hold concerning the Higher Power/God/Holy Spirit. I am only offering an avenue for you to learn how to open yourself to a higher calling. That Source, within you, will be what guides you on this journey.

To the Teen Angels/Adult Children for whom this book is written, I will introduce myself with who I once was and who I've become.

Past

- Shy.
- Insecure.
- Felt inferior.
- Felt invisible.
- Wasn't popular.
- Didn't have self-esteem or self-confidence.
- Scared of everyone and everything.
- Scared to try, because I was sure others were faster, smarter, or more popular.
- Afraid to say no.
- Afraid to say yes.
- Wanted my parents', friends', and world's approval (and became a people pleaser).
- Feared I would disappoint my parents.
- Spent my life saying "Why me?"
- Felt rejected in personal relationships.
- Wanted to be liked.
- Wished I had blue eyes, bigger boobs, and to be tall.
- Felt stupid.
- Couldn't "stay in my body" and spent my life day-dreaming because reality felt icky.
- Couldn't think of what I wanted to be when I grew up.
- Had a relative try to put the munch on me and didn't know it was okay to tell my parents.
- Had my confidences/secrets betrayed twice, which was not only embarrassing but also taught me I couldn't trust to tell my feelings or I would be exposed.

- Felt like a loser, although friends and relatives thought I was a bubble. I was an optimistic airhead, actually— hiding my fears, thoughts, and real feelings. (Lived in "De-Nile," which is more than just a river in Egypt.)
- Shoplifted.
- Lied. (Most often to myself.)
- Always chosen last for a team game, which was so darned embarrassing.
- Feared having to grow up and make decisions. I didn't know how to make choices. My parents and teachers made them for me, and when I turned eighteen, deemed an adult by society, I was expected to know how. I was also raised being told, "You aren't smart enough to pound sand into a rat hole." Well, I guess I really was stupid because *I didn't get it.* Why would anyone want to pound sand into a rat hole?
- Didn't believe what was being taught in church.
- Thought about committing suicide.
- Thought about running away from home—once as a child and once as an adult—but didn't know where to run to.

Wow. As I look back at who I was, or thought I was, no wonder I felt stupid or like a loser. I didn't have a very positive self-image, did I? Being a kid and a teenager isn't always easy.

My parents, of course, thought they were showing me their love by putting a roof over my head, food on the table, shoes on my feet, and vacations, gifts, and advice (bossing me around). Those were things that provided for my survival, gave me an education by seeing something other than the TV, or filled a temporary desire. But as a pre-adult, a teenager, I didn't see it as them showing me their love. I felt starved for love. I wanted to be called "honey" or "sweetheart." I wanted my parents to sit and (actually) listen to me and the feelings I had, and I wanted to be kissed and hugged tenderly. Those things I felt I wanted and needed, as a child, were what I silently vowed to do when I grew up and became a mother.

It's not that I had bad parents or a bad upbringing. My four siblings and I were left with loving, and most often nurturing, baby-sitters who played games and gave us fond memories. My point in sharing these things is only to express that my parents were so busy providing the basic needs, along with their own individual desires, that they probably didn't have energy reserves to do what I thought their roles should be.

Did any of my Past list spark a feeling in you? Do you have those same feelings, but believe (somewhere inside yourself) that you're the only one who feels this way? Do you think others are confident and you aren't?

Do you need someone to talk to, someone who will really listen?

Let's make a deal. I'll write who I am, at present, and then after you read this book, maybe we can help each other. I'll explain more of that later.

You've seen who I thought I was, but all of those feelings and experiences helped mold who I am now.

Present

- Successful housewife and mother to four children (and many who wish they were mine, taking every opportunity to stop by to eat my cookies and meals and to feed their hungry souls).
- Grandmother to two grandchildren (so far, but am hopeful of many, many more).

- Author of (fourteen) inspirational/self-help books.
- Ordained minister of (nonprofit, nondenominational) Miracle Healing Ministry, created to help convicts and charitable purposes nationwide.
- Spiritual healer.
- Founder of Miracle Publishing Company.
- Ph.D. in religious studies.

You can see that I placed my parenting role at the top of my list of life's accomplishments. I have a passion for life, to help, and to serve, to inspire, or give hope to the hopeless and encourage the discouraged. But for me personally, the role I play as a loving wife and mother speaks highly that I'm willing to share those experiences and leave them as a legacy to the world as my greatest contribution of love and life, well lived. Money, fame, medals, or honors are just "things" that can fade with the passing of time. Love, being eternal, will live on and on, from one generation to the next.

Not that our family is so perfect that we don't have conflicts or growing pains, too, but we continue to reach new levels of understanding of one another and of ourselves. I am an honest writer, candidly relating examples from our lives, demonstrated and proven successful—which I'll be sharing with you.

How was such a loser, in my own mind, able to overcome all the lack of confidence and esteem issues? It's a miracle, in itself, to stand before the world of you Teen Angels/Adult Children (as well as your parents) and to comfortably be able to say, "I love me." My goal, through simple, actual experiences, is to give you awareness and permission to say those same words, if you choose to.

Fair warning: Although I'm forty-nine years old, I'm very childlike (and child*ish* too, at times). Plus you just never know what's going to fall out of my mouth. Be prepared. When you least expect it, I'll throw a "zinger" in, just to see if you're paying attention.

I already love you, whether I can see your face, hold your hand, or listen to your heart. Lesson 1 is called Unconditional Love. That means, "No matter what you say, no matter what you do . . . I'll always love you."

How can I love you if I don't even know you? That answer, Teen Angel/Adult Child, is exactly what you're about to learn. . . .

Always,
Gloria D. Benish, Ph.D.
(also known as: Dr. Glo-bug)

Dearest Family,

Greetings, good morning my precious, and welcome to my world. Across the miles you've come, along a safe and well-traveled road. Please step across the threshold and enter our humble abode. Welcome everyone! Hang your hat 'n' rest your feet. C'mon in, make yourself at home . . . it's so nice to finally meet.

I love kids (of all ages). Years ago, while living in Texas, I offered to baby-sit for two of my friends' children. I picked the four-year-olds up from their Christian preschool and seat-belted them into my backseat. I got behind the wheel and they began talking about me as if I wasn't even there.

The little girl excitedly said, "Oh, I just love to go to Miss Gloria's home! One time I had an earache, and my mom took me to Miss Gloria's house. She laid her hand on my ear and shared her love light and my ear didn't hurt anymore."

Having to top that one, the little boy said, "So what! One time I was throwing up real bad and my mom took me to see Miss Gloria. And, when I just walked into her house, I didn't throw up no more."

Outside our home, the wooden plaque says, THE BENISH FAMILY LOVES HERE. As we spend our day together, I trust you will feel it, too.

It was five years ago when a woman from a nearby city called and asked for a private healing appointment. Her scheduled time was so close to the lunch hour, I decided to surprise her with homemade hot sauce, home-fried chips, burritos with a green chili gravy sauce . . . with tiny diced pieces of pork chops and topped with sour cream. Guacamole on the side and a small salad seemed to be just what the meal needed. After we had eaten the food, made with loving hands, she startled me with her comment. "You can't keep doing this, Gloria."

"I can't keep doing what?"

Sternly she replied, "You can't keep inviting strangers into your home and doing healings and feeding them."

I was confused. I had just fed her. Why couldn't I feed other strangers?

I know she thought she was being helpful and saying this for my benefit, but I was still confused. How could she enjoy a meal one moment and scold or prevent me from doing it for another? We discussed the situation at length. In fact, I don't even remember getting around to laying hands on her for her scheduled private appointment.

Her solid advice was this: "You can't bring the entire world into your home and kitchen like this."

Well. You and I both know what happens when someone tells us we "can't do something." It's like waving a red flag in a bull's face and expecting it not to charge. I, of course, had to prove her wrong.

So I wrote the book, *Go Within or Go Without,* a hands-on guide to healing body, mind, and spirit. In it, I invited the entire world, if they chose, to come into my home and spend a day with me as a housewife, mother, author, and spiritual healer.

After its third printing, I had a woman call and say, "I've read that book three times and have gained five pounds from all the food you serve the reader in it." At the level it's been made available to others, it has successfully fulfilled its purpose. That's why, through this sequel, I'm reinviting you into my home for a "second helping" of spiritual food. Take all you want because there's plenty for everyone. Those things you don't like, feel free to pass by.

Before we begin our day together, allow me to introduce my family and myself.

My titles and roles are various. Proudly, I am a housewife, mother to four children, and grandmother to two grandchildren. Professionally, I am an author of inspirational/self-help books, ordained minister of the nonprofit, nondenominational Miracle Healing Ministry, founder of Miracle Publishing Company, spiritual healer, and Ph.D. in religious studies.

My husband, Kirk (also referred to around the house as "Handsome Hummer," "Hunka Hunka Burnin' Love," and "Knight in Shining Armor"), and I have now been married for ten years. Two years ago we realized that I needed to take eighteen to twenty-four months away from the daily routine of the family's care to promote my inspirational books and teach spiritual healing workshops across the nation to help the masses. I felt fear. I had waited a lifetime for this sensitive, caring man, and as much as I wanted to do service for God, I feared the loss of my personal relationship with Kirk.

One evening while I was expressing my concerns, he said, "Hon, when the wars were being fought, men sometimes had to leave their families for two or three years *to serve our country.*" He continued, "I believe if I was off serving our nation in war and had to be gone that long . . . I trust you would remain a faithful wife." I assured him I would. In an extremely loving tone, he said, "I knew when I married you that you had something very important to share with the world. So I guess if you're out for eighteen to twenty-four months, setting it in motion . . . *serving God and humanity*, I don't think I'll leave you, either." As you continue to read this book, you will know the depths of my husband's love, loyalty, honesty, integrity, and support.

Together, Kirk and I have four children. My stepdaughter, his eldest, Kerrie (age twenty-seven), dreamed of working with NASA's Houston Control, and we encouraged her to reach for the stars. Three years ago she graduated from Purdue University. She is an astronautical/aeronautical engineer, calculating the jet propulsion for the shuttle missions, fulfilling her dream in Houston, Texas. She married Christopher two years ago.

Kirk's second eldest, Jaime (age twenty-five), is the mother of our five-year-old grandson and eight-month-old granddaughter. She and her husband, Keith, live about ten minutes from our home. Jaime is one of my dearest friends, as well.

Our third child, D.W., is our only boy and has just turned nineteen. Kirk's girls were teenagers when I arrived on the scene, and they helped prepare me for what would be following with my own two children. It still wasn't easy, experiencing D.W. taking driver's education. I remember sitting in the passenger's seat while he acquired his seventeen hours of parent–child driving time. If I thought that was difficult, it was nothing compared to him purchasing his own vehicle and driving to a nearby city for the first time. Alone. In the dark. I wasn't easily prepared when he moved into his own apartment, either, but he returns weekly to do his laundry and raid my cupboards.

Danielle, my baby, now at seventeen stands beautifully at five feet six, towering over me by seven inches. She's active in school, talented in gymnastics, basketball, and volleyball, and an honor roll student. Getting used to my "babies," who overnight grew into toddlers and teens, having opinions and learning to make choices was not easy.

As a columnist and writer of self-help books, I don't gloss over daily lessons that can afford others inspiration. Our family, as perfect as it appears on these pages, has problems and growing pains like any other family. I'm an honest writer and made a deal with my family long ago. When I married Kirk, I forewarned him and my stepdaughters, "Be careful what you say or do because it just might end up in book form." He laughed and said, "Okay, but just don't write about our sex life." (He didn't tell me I couldn't talk about it, though . . .) I believe that people should speak, act, and live their lives as if they would want to see it in print. Doing so would prevent countless regrets and guilt trips.

We don't need to *become perfect* before we can see the face of God or experience that Presence. In 1985, this was one of the first lessons I ever learned from Spirit. I was severely depressed and couldn't get out of bed except to care for my two toddlers. I had no strength and when I showered, I would have to sit and rest before I could have the energy to stand and rinse. By the time I got out of the shower, I would be sweating and exhausted. I was anorexic, weighing in at about eighty pounds and wearing little girl's size twelve slim jeans. I had lost every hair on my head due to alopecia totalis, and three doctors' doom-and-gloom reports promised it would never grow back. I was severely codependent and attracted every alcoholic who could find their way to me. My spirit was broken, without hope.

On October 5, 1985, I had a revelation. *God called.* I heard the Voice of Spirit: "Write a book to awaken millions and millions of My children from their past slumber of negative beliefs and fears, healing the minds of humankind." I thought He'd asked the wrong person. At that time of my life, all I could think was, "Why me?" He didn't say, "When you get all better, Gloria . . ." He said, instead, "Begin now." Each time I willingly reached out a helping hand to another, a loved one or stranger, I began being healed, as well. For nearly two years, I "tasted and smelled purity," and people were being healed through me. I was not religious, or spiritual. I didn't understand what was happening in my world. I had no conscious control. Sometimes with a slight touch, or no touch at all, I watched as miracles occurred through me.

The message itself that I've been asked to give is simple: You, too, can and will become aware of how to transform your fears into love, and the effects will be miraculously profound.

I answered (the individual call) and books began immediately. *He speaks and I listen.* Never searching for a word or phrase, I wrote the dictation that followed. Countless miracles became the contents of the writings. This goal, to teach the world's people how to heal their lives, was not prompted by human desire or I would have long ago given up.

He guides and the universe demands that I continue to grow. *I take physical action.* I willingly teach all who will listen—a neighboring passenger on an airplane, a child on the street, a man behind prison walls, in a church, an auditorium, and sometimes a bar.

Although I respect and actually admire skeptics, there is a fine line between someone who truly wants to learn how spiritual healing occurs and one who just wants to have a meaningless debate.

For those who have found painful lessons in an experience of spiritual seeking, I patiently empower a person to no longer have dependencies on others who falsely promise health or answers, *if the price is right.*

For those who don't really want to hear the message, I honor them and judge not that they haven't opened their mind to receive. Debating, however, is a waste of my time. It takes time to argue or stand in defense, and I could use that time and energy more wisely. I choose, instead, to allow God to love through me, as an instrument, to heal ten people, mop my kitchen floor, and answer the countless calls I receive daily to encourage the discouraged and give hope to the hopeless.

Everything I share in columns, books, or while standing before groups in workshops is the truth . . . to the best of my ability.

Teachers came to me, first in the form of my daughter Danielle, who at age three, *taught me how to give others a little extra love.* God, appearing in the form of Jesus, is also my teacher via example and revelations. *Miracles happen:* cancer being dissolved overnight or broken arms healed in

three days. Divine experiences aren't always easily understood or accepted.

This book is an opportunity to learn how you personally
can experience the Presence of God so you can begin enjoying miracles every day of your life. The Bible teaches,
"Seek ye first the kingdom of heaven and all else will be
added." Jesus explained, "The kingdom of heaven is within." As a spiritual teacher, I will be teaching you *how to go
within,* as well as the inspiring effects that occur as you do.
It's that simple. Please don't make life harder than it needs
to be.

I have a silly sense of humor, I must forewarn you. The
incredible experiences I have, coupled with daily (Stepford)
chores of being a housewife and mother, tend to place people in awe when they hear the miraculous mixed with what
others term "mundane." Describing a typical day in my life,
I replied to an e-mail from a woman on the East Coast. She
had just one question: "Where is your cape?" I responded
simply, "In the laundry."

Before we begin this day together, please get a Journal
or lined notebook to write your thoughts and feelings in.
Also, please follow me and look into the mirror. What do
you see? Who do you see? Be honest. Don't tell me what
you think I would want you to say . . . or what someone
else would see, God forbid, if they picked up your personal
Journal/notebook and read what you have written. I want
to know what it is that *you* see, looking back at you. Are
you ugly? Zits? Too pointy a nose? Yellow teeth? Nice
smile? Pretty eyes?

How are you feeling right this moment? This day (and
book) is between just you 'n' me 'n' God. There are no right
or wrong answers to any of the questions I'll be asking you,
so I would prefer you to be honest with yourself and me as
we explore this life and teachings together.

Following each chapter are Journal questions and a personal affirmation for you to meditate upon. I am asking the

questions, which will help you to learn to know yourself and what you desire out of life. You can use your separate Journal to privately answer these questions so others can't see what you've written. If you lend the book to friends, they can use their personal Journals to write their thoughts and feelings.

After you have looked in the mirror and written down what you see, how you're feeling, and what just occurred to make you feel that way, feel free to move on to chapter 1. Your personal Journal for this book is for you, alone. Answer the questions I have asked, and end it with the affirmation I have offered. Write your heartfelt thoughts and concerns, and release them. Letting go/surrendering fear allows a Power greater than yourself "Its" natural expression. Love knows how to figure out all the details of your life.

As this day begins, let's all join together, here, in my living room. Can I offer you a cup of hot cocoa? Or perhaps a glass of juice? And you just have to try one or two of my warm, fresh-from-the-oven cinnamon rolls.

As you're enjoying your snack, let me tell you what we'll be doing today. I'll begin by talking to you as a family, and taking you through a meditation together. I'll make sure each of you is comfortable and busy while I speak to the girls privately, then the boys, and then the parents. We'll rejoin as a family, for lunch. Depending upon your special needs, we will have a question-and-answer time, and none of you will leave without knowing that I gave all I have to give.

Let's begin and see how I can best serve all of you today . . .

OPEN YOUR JOURNAL AND ANSWER
THESE QUESTIONS

1. I looked into the mirror and this is what I see:
2. This is how I feel right this moment:
3. This is what occurred that made me feel this way:

Write your heartfelt thoughts in the Journal and state this affirmation aloud. *I am always doing the best I can with the awareness I have.*

Opening Prayer

We begin this day, together, in deep gratitude to a man named Matthew. Had it not been for him writing to me, we would not be enjoying this time together. I will read you his first letter and you will understand why I encouraged him to write a book. This man is extremely gifted. Because he sits within a prison cell and has no access to a typewriter or computer, I have offered to edit and type his book. My attorney has agreed to work on his behalf, and I am willing to help him find a publisher when that moment arrives.

He has a remarkable style of writing and deserves an opportunity to be heard. If the experiences he is writing of can help even one man, woman, or child avoid the life he's lived, then he has served society well. We give our thanks that God continues to manifest His blessings, mercy, and peace today and always. Amen.

Dear Mrs. Benish,

My best to you and yours. My name is Matthew. I'm writing to you from Pelican Bay State Prison here in Northern California.

The reason I'm writing to you is that a copy of your book Go Within or Go Without found its way into my hands. At first I looked at the cover and said, "Aw, man! Another one of those people trying to 'self-help' me!" Believe me, the prison is flooded with holier-than-thou literature. So without even cracking the cover, I sent it on the first thing smokin' back to the guy who sent it to me. He

22

told me, "Man, that was quick! You're either an Evelyn Woods graduate or you didn't even check it out." I responded, "Whoa! You must be psychic," and continued on my way. Yeah, I'm a smart-ass sometimes. Okay. A lot of the time. Anyhoo . . . about two weeks go by and another one of the residents here asks me if I had a book I might want to trade with him. Now, being the kind of guy I am, I haul out the heavy armaments. I sent him a nine-hundred-pager, horror, by a new author, the next Dean Koontz! A real spellbinder from start to finish. I mean, in prison, these types of books are gold! Destined to be a convict classic!

I'm "knowing" that I got a "blockbuster New York Times best-seller" coming back at me, ya know what I mean? I send him the "bomb" (I like that word), and he sends me his offering. So this book slides up under my door and lo and behold, your smilin' face once again is gracing me with its presence.

I go to my cell door and give a holler down to the guy who sent it to me. I say, "Hey, I got that book you sent and 'yo,' you gotta be [bleeping] kiddin' me!" It probably was my imagination, but I could have sworn I heard him let out a snicker or two. Well, let me tell you, at the time, I was pretty P.O.'ed about the exchange. He was most definitely coming off my Christmas list, let me tell ya.

I tossed the book on my shelf with about a five-minute tirade of explicit instructions on ways that the guy could abuse himself. A couple of days go by and as I'm not allowed to have a cellmate and having read everything in my cell, I was pretty much bored. I happened to glance at my shelf and, sure enough, there you were, still smiling at me. (At this point, I would like to praise Nikki on her artwork. Outstanding!)

So I say to myself, "Self! The lady has got to be grinning like the cat that ate the canary for some reason or other." I picked up your book, stretched out on the bunk, fluffed up my pillow, and cracked open your book. Now, I have to confess, I was still pretty much peeved over the swapping of books and when I'm in that type of mood, I tend to get overcritical. So I settled in to nitpick your book.

Mrs. Benish, as they say in the cellblock, "You ain't right!" (Smile . . .) Not only did I read the entire book in one sitting; I have since read it two more times. You not only taught me something while at the same time making me laugh, but you really made me feel like you care about us "Dungeon Dwellers."

Now, don't get me wrong. I'm still not able to see the Light, although I've tried and will continue to try, but I honestly believe that if a person only reads your book for that purpose, then to an extent, they would be missing the point. You are touching people's lives just by who you are. It's hard for me to put into words, exactly, but I believe that even if you did not have the abilities that you have, you would still be touching people's lives in some way. And I think your true message is that every person should take the time to care about one another.

Thank you, Mrs. Benish, for a wonderful, uplifting experience. By the way, the book trade is now a done deal. I'm keeping your book!

There is one thing I would like to know. How is Nikki? I was once on parole and know it's not easy. I also lived the same life as her former life. A child of the drugs and streets. I'm hoping and praying that Nikki did make it. Every person who walks out these gates and does not return adds one more spark to the flame of hope.

Well, Mrs. Benish, I just wanted to let you know that you brought lightness of heart and put a smile on this old convict's face. You and yours take care of yourselves and may you stay in the Light.

Very respectfully yours,
Matthew

Nikki, to whom Matthew refers, is my best friend. We met when she was in a California state prison and wrote asking for spiritual guidance. We teamed our talents—her artwork and my written word—and continued a friendship for six years, with her behind bars. Nikki is a *heroine* in my eyes, and please don't get that confused with her past addiction. She is one of the strongest, bravest women I've ever had the pleasure of meeting. She recovered from a lifetime of addiction and dysfunction. Her mere presence has created a ripple effect throughout her entire family.

I am currently attempting to get approval for a self-awareness class in the prison system. In Nikki's reflection of our meeting, she wrote the following letter, on my behalf, to the warden of Chowchilla State Women's Prison:

> I've been asked by my dearest friend and mentor, Gloria D. Benish, to write a letter summing up the effects her teachings and books have had on my life. I was asked to do this a week ago and have just begun.
>
> Gloria's goal is to be granted the opportunity to teach life-altering knowledge to women in Chowchilla. My goal is to have the right words to illustrate just how amazing and realistic an opportunity Gloria's goal is. After running hundreds of ways to present this letter through my mind, I've, as usual, fallen back on what I've learned to be true. "Open your heart, don't think about it, and let the truth speak for itself."
>
> I believe my public record is easily accessible to you, the person reading this letter. It might give you a greater sense of the miracle my life has become to have that black-and-white printout before you.
>
> When Gloria came into my life, I was hopeless. I was sitting in Avenal Prison with a broken back and wrists I'd acquired while in the Sacramento County jail. A heroin addict, in withdrawal, waiting to be sentenced to twelve years for drug sales. Third sentence. IV drug user for over twenty years. Hooker. Dealer. In my thirties, with no hope for anything better. I jumped backward off a top bunk and tried to break my neck or crush my skull. Time to stop. Believing the only way to stop was to stop.

A trip to U.C. Davis Hospital, where the emergency room physician refused to look at me once he was told I was in heroin withdrawal. (Another junkie trying to get drugs.) A pissed-off officer, who'd previously been kind, dragging me bent over through the hospital by cuffed and broken wrists. Throwing me into the van because I could only drag my legs, unable to lift them to step up. Once back at County, no treatment because I'd been medically cleared. To shorten this end of the story, I "twentyfolded" the usual heroin withdrawal humiliations.

Two months later, out of County to Elk Grove, awaiting transport to C.I.W., I received an X ray. I was diagnosed with a compression fracture of the spine. Three or four months later, while in Avenal, awaiting transport to the brand-new Chowchilla Prison, X rays showed broken wrists, as well.

At this point, of course, I was not happy that I had not succeeded. I existed in a place with cold, numbing rage. Worse, I was too weak to physically strike out at anyone. I used words and strong women close to me to ensure that no one would strike at me in defense. In all of this . . . pain. Pain. Inside and outside pain. No end. No soft place for relief.

One of the strong girls, Madeline, had attached herself to me in County jail and had been moved with me at every stage. Madeline, a first-termer, still scared. Me, a third-termer who didn't give a shit. Madeline, with a mother who made sure she had every possible thing she could have in prison to make it easier. Me, who'd burned out the hopes of anyone who'd ever tried and was now left with no one. I had succeeded in becoming dead somewhere after all.

Madeline's mother, Paula, knew Gloria. Paula had sent her daughter a letter Gloria had written, concerning Madeline. In a nutshell, it said, "Madeline is doing what she's supposed to do in her life right now and she'll be fine." A little background on Gloria, from Madeline, sent a small fissure cracking through the darkness I'd blanketed myself in.

No judgment. Can that be possible from a "straight" person? She wasn't saying Madeline needed to do anything to be a worthy or deserving human being. "She's perfect just how she is."

You may not understand the magnitude of that. Do you see my judgment in that last paragraph? In my world where "The Good Guys" were clearly not so good and "The Bad Guys" were not clearly so bad, I'd judged the ones I'd assumed were always judging me. In my mind, my one redeeming quality was that, at least, I wasn't a hypocrite/liar. I didn't need to look down on anyone's life to feel more powerful in my own. I'd never be "one of them." But I'd done just that, hadn't I?

To reestablish my comforting belief that "The Good Guys" were all some other species other than the species I belonged to, I wrote to Gloria. I dumped on her the curt facts of my life, and invited her to fill a role: Judge me.

Almost twelve years later, I've long since given up waiting for that judgment to come. Having no clue at all about my lifestyle, except what I told her and others warned her about, Gloria never flinched or wavered. In return, she gave me a gift to give. I lost the division between "them" and myself.

When there are no "Good Guys" or "Bad Guys," there is only us. We, the people . . . all struggling toward or away from something. We, the people . . . no one less or more than the other, regardless of circumstance, beliefs, backgrounds, strength, or weakness.

If you can see for yourself that twelve-step programs work, then take your sight a step further. A program where the people graduate without needing a program to continue staying healthy, happy, and productive. A program where people learn to "know" they are perfect and have plenty to offer. What would that be worth?

My name is Linda Kay "Nikki" Fudge. I am not ashamed of the life I had because it brought me to the life I have. Because of who I am, innumerable lives have been changed.

I am forty-nine years old, a miracle in itself. I am written about and cherished by one of the most amazing people you will ever meet. I've traveled with Gloria as an inspirational speaker, but am most blessed by the people Gloria and I touched while I was incarcerated. I am respected and depended upon in the job I have now held for nearly four and a half years. I have become the center of strength and unity for my family. My mother and I recently bought a home together. In February, I became a grandmother for the first time. I deem myself valuable, therefore, I am. I always have been. I always will be.

This is only one of the things Gloria can teach the women. This, and more, is what they can pass on to others in their lives . . . who, in turn, can't help but pass it on to others . . . in a continuing and growing cycle of love.

Once I got Nikki paroled to Montana, to live with my family, she and I enjoyed two wonderful years as inspirational speakers together. She now lives in Sacramento, California, and is a healthy asset to society and living her dreams. It was Divine, unconditional love that brought two such uniquely different women together and gave us the honor of passing on the miracles to others. We remain best friends, speaking several hours a week. Yes, Nikki is a heroine in my eyes, and please don't get that confused with her past addiction . . .

Countless convicts write to me, but only a handful of male convicts have reached out to me. Maybe that's what makes Matthew so special to me. He reached out his hand. I was smart enough to take it.

May every blessing you receive from this book return full

circle to this man and woman—my source of pride and inspiration.

And now that you've met my family and those who have and are directly affecting my life, allow me to focus my full attention on you. *You* are my priority today. *No one* except you matters. I'm giving you a safe place to just be you, because I'm just going to be me. I don't know how to be anything else. Let the fun begin!

Spiritual Training Wheels

1

I.O.U. the Right to This Knowledge

Be patient with me, please. I have so much fear in me to use our day together to write this book. I always try to practice what I preach, though, and before crowds of audiences or in my other books, I inspire people "to feel their fear and *do it anyway*."

For years, others have asked and begged me to write books and teach workshops for kids and to write books for the entire family. I resisted. It's apparent that what we resist, persists. In the last few weeks, those requests have been numerous. It seems we ask and pray for guidance and as it appears, we don't want to listen and acknowledge it as the answer to our prayers. Probably because it's not the answer we thought we wanted to hear.

I also believe if I hear the same thing, even if it's only three times within a seventy-two-hour period, it's the "Unseen World" sending me Divine Guidance. So why would I hesitate to take action to write a book for your family? Why would I drag my feet, today and yesterday, with excuses of "I need to clean house first, send out book orders, complete the taxes, think about it, meditate and contemplate?" Or fall to the easiest of all the excuses to avoid such a project: "I don't have a title yet, don't know what to say, and what gives me the right to think that anything I have to say is important?"

The answer to those questions is: *Fear.* Plain and simple.

Are you surprised to hear that I (as an individual who has *a Direct connection to God*) have fear, too? Did you think that emotion was reserved only for you?

What is the fear that attempts to prevent me from writing information that *I know* can inspire the young and young at heart? To name a few: fear of failure, fear of success, fear of rejection, and fear, of course, that some parents would believe I'm the twenty-first-century Pied Piper, leading their children astray. I'm also the first to admit that I don't know how to be a good parent. Those who see the results of our family believe I have some secret formula and beg me to share it. If there were a secret, it would be this: God is the parent, I'm merely the "stand-in."

The attribute I display, not only with my family but also with anyone who touches my life, is His Presence, demonstrating Itself through me. I am loving, consistent, dependable, courageous, and I say what I mean and I mean what I say. The consistency of those ideals builds a trust in a family or friend. They never question whether I will fluctuate or fall short. Anyone who knows me knows that I am doing the absolute best I can with energy, intentions, and actions.

The courage, of course, especially in parenting, is to do what is right, which sometimes includes the word *no* whether the children are going to be mad at me or not, or perhaps even hate me temporarily. Three of our four kids did a good job following orders, but one challenged every breath. It was she who became my greatest teacher. Thanks to her, I learned how to express my real feelings and to understand that I had been born with my loving nature, but my courageous nature needed to be developed. Generally speaking, kids don't want to lose the approval of the parent(s). But imagine this: Parents don't want to lose the approval of the child, either. Unconditional love is a two-way street!

Human beings are unique. No two kids (or parents) are alike. What works for one person in a given situation may not work for another in the same situation. Before I had children, of course, I was one of those people "who had all the answers." It took only minutes after my first child was in my arms, and me shouldering the responsibility for another life, for me to realize I didn't know anything.

You may ask, "Well, ol' Dr. Glo-bug, if you're the world's largest Chicken McNugget and if you have so many fears, why bother?" I can only answer, "Because I love stronger and deeper than I fear and I owe you the right to the spiritual knowledge I incorporate daily."

The wisdom I have to share and the experience of love was not earned by the ministry certificate, the B.A., master's degree, or Ph.D. diplomas that take up an entire wall in my office. Their presence in matching frames, and the years of acquiring them, are for me to look upon, but they do not grant me any right to speak with authority.

In reality, no school or university could take the credit for what I know as a love(r) of humanity and have experienced as the core curriculum of my teachings. Of course, I could quote various books giving the "correct" answers so I could maintain a perfect grade point average. But the wisdom of leading a fulfilled life on all levels has never before been written. All books give pieces of life's puzzle as "how-to," "self-help," or "inspirational" works, for their respective purposes, but none has totally fulfilled that simple element for which this book will be written. It may only take a few hours to read, but it will take a lifetime to live.

Now perhaps you understand my initial fear. Without

having a clue what I'm going to write until I see the words flow forth from my pen, I have declared that I'm offering you a book, filled with wisdom that will give you Divine Guidance so you can experience a totally fulfilled life. I will be counted among the students here, for I will learn as I teach.

I know love, through experience, and am willing to teach you how to recognize it, how to allow it to guide you, and how love, though invisible, appears as your needs and desires. I am not speaking about the love you feel when you read a card filled with loving words, or as you open a gift from a friend or loved one. Most of those feelings we experience are conditioned with guilt, them wanting something from us, or the love that is withheld if we don't do things the way the person requests. Those feelings are human love and their various expressions.

I choose to teach you how to feel Divine Love, that love that fills your being with an icy hot, tingling pure Presence. Divine Love says, usually without words or thoughts, "No matter what you say, no matter what you do . . . I will *always* love you."

To human understanding, with all the judgments we hold against ourselves and one another, unconditional love is just a far-fetched, unrealistic, unreachable dream. But I tell you, "It" is within reach, for It (already) is within you and I am willing to teach you how to open yourself to that Presence.

Once you (re)discover It, you'll arrive at a point of acceptance where you can voice your fears, without shame, and love yourself in spite of them.

When I was fifteen, I stood before my dad and said, "I could marry any man because I love them all." He replied sarcastically, "You don't know the meaning of the word." I apologize to my dad here in print for the first time before I tell him how I felt then (and couldn't express) and how I still feel *now*. He was wrong. I did meet four men in my life I didn't like, but I was still willing to allow God to love them *through* me.

We look to parents and teachers, doctors and attorneys, and others who can and do speak with authority. We become intimidated or rebellious by nature, at times, to force change. I, being a "peaceful warrior," would prefer to allow transformation in our world through love and acceptance. That can't occur on a global scale, however, unless it begins (with)in each of us individually.

With a few alterations, I would like to share the famous Serenity Prayer that I heard in a speech given to a group of convicts, by my friend, Mr. Robert Peck:

> May God grant me the serenity to accept the
> *people* I cannot change,
> The courage to change *the one I can,* and the
> wisdom to know *it's me.*

When I see or experience things in my personal life that I don't like, think are unfair, or judge as "bad," I realize immediately that the problem is within me—within my state of consciousness/awareness. I am not a victim of chance, nor are you. We, of course, would like to think we're right and others are wrong, that we have closed-minded parents who don't understand, kids who won't listen and learn from our experiences, teachers who should have retired before they became older than dirt, or employers who drive us nuts. But each of our experiences is based upon our belief systems, and those ideas we hold from programming.

As an example, I was raped in high school. I wondered for years what I had done wrong to attract such a frightening experience. I was a *good* girl, but maybe I flirted too much. "Why me?" When I was thirty-two years old, I spiritually awakened. Through countless unsought and unasked-for mystical experiences, I received the answer to that question and many others I'd had throughout my life.

I created the experience. As a teen, I read romance novels and cheap teen magazines. As I read, I fantasized about being taken without my permission. The subconscious/imagination, which creates, doesn't judge the thoughts we hold. It merely acts upon our suggestions and doesn't say, "Gloria, I don't think you're going to like this." It sees our thoughts and assumes we know what we're doing, and is thus set in motion to create what we pay attention to. We can attract this and other frightening experiences because we judge them as bad or wrong, and we also attract those situations we fear. My goal is to give you awareness of how to heal your fears.

In my case, this fantasy went forth and came to rest in the consciousness of a young man who probably fantasized about taking someone against her will. I wasn't a victim. The rapist and I were co-creators of the experience. I could forgive him, as well as myself, "for we knew not what we did."

As I explained to you earlier, my education was not always gained in school. This life experience afforded me the ability to counsel others. My soul needed this expression of discomfort to help me be able to help others more effectively.

I am not attempting to minimize the severity of a rape, because along with this experience, terrific amounts of anger, rage, hatred, and helplessness are felt. I was able to experience those feelings quietly because I didn't share the attack until I was an adult. When my destiny brought me to awareness of my spiritual healing gift, however, I was grateful for that experience the very first time I could say, "Been there, done that . . . I know just how you feel. And this is how we will work together to heal your pain."

Can you begin to understand the damage done to our world and individuals, through the media, writings, television, songs, or violent movies we are all watching, listening to, and absorbing? With this awareness, perhaps we'll want to select more carefully those people, places, and things we invite into our lives.

In 1986, my mind opened to a sort of wide-screen TV within my inner vision, and I was shown an immense golden sphere of light that I knew, intuitively, as the Mind of God. On the outside of the sphere, there were black strands that appeared to be spiderwebs.

For just a moment, I'm asking you to visualize a golden light surrounding you, a golden light around your home, a golden light surrounding your city and state, and a golden glow around all of Mother Earth and every possible infinite universe. Everything you just saw, surrounded by that golden light, *is already within the Mind of God.*

In the beginning, He created the heavens and earth and looked upon it and called it "Good." He didn't call it "good and bad."

The spiderwebs on the outside of the golden sphere (within my inner vision) were symbolic of the cancer, AIDS, greed, selfishness, and so on that we experience in this dimension. However, because they are on the *outside* of the Mind, these imperfections or negatives have *no reality.* I will teach you throughout this day (and book) how to easily dissolve these situations from your experience.

The love, acceptance, approval, pride, and fulfillment of dreams you seek already exist within the Mind of God. Layers of fear, in the forms of "I'm not good enough," "not worthy," "too stupid," "too fat or ugly," "can't find the right mate, job, or direction"—or whatever you feel in life—have covered the real you. The core of you, however, is goodness, and you don't have the power to change that; nor do any of the limitations you have superimposed over that goodness. I'm willing to teach you how to peel those layers away so you can experience a wonderful life, filled with love for self and others, and to experience the added things that we call miracles, success, prosperity, and joy.

One evening in meditation, I found myself as a single audience to a lighted, empty stage in the Hall of Wisdom on the etheric level. The voice of an unseen messenger told me to place the person I hated most on stage. Going through my memory bank, it didn't take but a millisecond before I saw *myself* on stage, dressed in a little black skirt, white blouse, and black bow tie . . . it was my first-grade band uniform. I came out of the deep meditative state, racked in tearful sobbing. I thought I loved everyone. Throughout my life, I would never knowingly hurt anyone, and because of that and lack of boundaries, I had endlessly hurt myself by trying to be nice all the time. How could I possibly love everyone except myself?

All those years of shyness, thinking I wasn't good enough or smart enough, no self-esteem or confidence, and my best friend, fear, flooded me. I was overwhelmed with self-hatred. Anger that I could never stand up for myself or another, or for anything I believed in, made me feel weak and cowardly. I felt shame. Abandonment of God and earthly parents for never teaching me *how to love myself* crept in.

I was going to go to God to have a bitch session for not sending "instructions," but I found myself surprised as I opened my consciousness to Him. At first it annoyed me that I didn't even know how to pray right. There I stood, in my inner vision, calling out to Him to remove my pain and I discovered, instead, that I was there to serve Him. The pain had been a tool I could use later to help others. Had I been protected from sadness, loneliness, insecurity, inferiority, and all the other situations I listed in the introduction, I couldn't honestly help you or anyone. My self-help for you would have had to come from an education in book form, which isn't bad, but because I can speak from my heart you'll be able to hear me, understand, and *know* the truth.

The thing that amazed me the most, when I made direct contact with God, within my individual consciousness, was that He didn't mind that I felt angry with Him and life. He only knew me as pure love, because He created me. We are told we're created in His Image. We are held within that golden sphere, His Divine Mind, within His Imagination.

God's Spirit, within each of us, doesn't measure us by how many times we've screwed up. Or how many times we've been selfish when we should have been giving, how many times we say no to someone in need, or how many times we say yes when we should say no. God is constant and never changes His Mind about us.

We have free will. We are free to choose to entertain or plant any seeds of thought we want into our subconscious/ imagination. However, once we find ourselves tired of the painful experiences and reruns of disappointment, He gives us new opportunities to grow, and when we take that knowledge and make it wisdom, through experience, we find an easier way to live our lives.

Today is a good day to begin anew. No matter where you are or what feelings you have—and even if you feel overwhelmed because you have so many weighty problems to deal with—understand that the first step, which is willingness, can take you where no one has taken you before.

Take a deep breath, count to seven, hold it to the count of

seven, and release it to the count of seven. Let's continue our journey as we transform our fears into unconditional love.

OPEN YOUR JOURNAL AND ANSWER THESE QUESTIONS

Journal—Chapter One

1. Name as many of your present fears as you can think of. (After you finish the book, look back over the fears, seeing and understanding that they no longer have any power in your life. They will no longer control you, because you've become aware "they have no reality in the Mind of God"—which is where you really are.)

2. What statement or teaching had the most profound effect on you as you were reading? For what reason did it touch you so deeply?

3. Write down your weaknesses, habits, addictions, or personality traits you most dislike about yourself.

4. Name an experience you can recall that you feared happening—then later occurred. Do you remember dwelling on it prior to its occurrence, or fretting a lot before it happened?

5. Name an experience you excitedly awaited, which did manifest. Do you also remember how much energy and attention you put into thinking about it before it happened?

6. What is your biggest frustration, or anger, concerning your personal world? What is your biggest frustration and anger concerning the entire world?

7. Do you feel abandoned by God or parents? Why? What is it you would like to experience concerning each?

8. Do you question if a God really exists? If you were in God's position, what do you think you would want us to know?

9. Write of an example of conditional love from your personal experience. To spark your memory, did anyone ever say, "After all I've done for you . . . and you can't even do this one little thing I'm asking, for me?"

10. Name at least one person who has demonstrated unconditional love for you. Write about the experience.

Write your heartfelt thoughts in the Journal and state this affirmation aloud. *I am an answer to God's Prayers.*

2
Stairway to Heaven
(Meditation)

As I stood on stage in Boise, Idaho, a few years ago to introduce a spiritual healing workshop, my attention was drawn
to a young man in the audience. Because I'm empathic, I
literally felt his stomach pain. Most of those who read this
book also have the same "gift," but, unaware, they believe
everything they think and feel "is theirs."

I said to the young man, in front of the crowd, "You
have a tummyache." He responded, "Actually, I do." Teasing, I said, "You had too much pizza for dinner," and the
crowd laughed as he replied, "Actually, we did have pizza
for dinner."

I asked him to come up on stage so I could heal him in
front of everyone, demonstrating how healing occurs. He
agreed because he didn't feel very good.

I sat him in a chair and began rubbing my hands briskly
together. As I did this, I explained why hands-on healing is
effective. Because there are countless pores in the hands,
energy can be transferred quickly and easily.

Just before I placed my warm hands, which radiated now
with love/energy/electricity (whichever you feel most com-

fortable calling it), upon his stomach, I had the thought to ask a little girl in the audience to join me on stage.

As the eight-year-old child joined the young man and myself before the crowd, I asked her to rub her hands together and kneel before the boy. I then asked her to scan his stomach, about an inch or so away from the body, feeling the energy and sensing if any areas were hotter or colder. I taught the guests that hot is *too much* electricity in the energy field and cold *is not enough*. Both are an imbalance, and when you lay hands on those areas, until it doesn't feel hot or cold but "just right," the balance of the energy field is restored. Harmony and healing naturally occur.

The girl noticed a cold area and was advised to lay her hands upon the young man's stomach in that area. I asked the girl, who was being used in this experience as an instrument for the Divine, to go within. I explained this term in simple wording: To go within just means that we close our eyes and open our mind.

"With your eyes closed," I told her, "I'm sure it's just dark in your inner vision. But in just a few moments, you may begin seeing tiny pinpoints of white light. They may appear for only a millisecond and then fade, almost like a Christmas tree light, glowing and then burning out."

The child validated that she was seeing the little white lights, as her individual mind began to open to the Presence of God. I replied, "Although your inner vision continues to be dark, it will begin to lighten up to a shade of gray and then turn to a possible dirty yellow or dirty green color." I advised, "The colors may start turning pretty, perhaps to a pink or blue or green. Can you tell me when you start seeing the pretty colors?"

She immediately responded, "I am seeing pretty colors already."

The instructions continued, "Soon you'll start seeing a

violet light. Can you tell me when you see that purple light?"

This eight-year-old, her first time ever attempting a spiritual healing, proudly said, "I am seeing the purple light," and the young man immediately startled the audience by exclaiming, "And my stomach doesn't hurt anymore!"

To the group of people present that evening and to you, I beg you—*please don't make this harder than it needs to be.*

When you close your eyes and see darkness, it is for two reasons:

1. Your third eye, in the middle of your forehead, which is your spiritual vision into the imagination/subconscious, and other dimensions, is closed.

2. You are looking directly into a state of consciousness/awareness that believes in two powers or—easier to understand—the world of duality. The world believes there is rich and poor, health and disease, sad and happy, and, religiously speaking, Light and darkness, God and Satan. Our world validates two powers daily in your life. You can be happy one moment and sad the next. You can have health today and tomorrow a headache. Life under these conditions is a roller coaster with ups and downs, emotional highs and depressing lows.

When you go within and begin opening yourself to the violet light, within your individual mind, you are opening yourself to the pure and perfect creation of the Divine. Remember the golden sphere of light we talked about earlier? In the beginning, when God created you, He created *everything* you would ever need. Every slice of pizza you eat, every shirt you wear, every answer you seek is already established within His Mind. When you open your individual mind and begin seeing the violet light, His creation of your spiritual good begins to flow into the outer world of form.

In the world of dual powers, you struggle for good grades, acceptance, success, respect, power; you strive to be healthy (or stay healthy) and to keep peace in your home. Kids try to follow the rules that you must abide by if you live under your parents' roof, and parents try to follow man-made laws. Laws, by the way, of parents, city, state, and government, as well as commandments and shoulds or shouldn'ts, attempt to make our life easier. Instead, sometimes they consume us, and we wonder if we'll ever get to an age where someone isn't bossing us around and telling us constantly what to do or how to do it.

When you see the violet light, God's Law, which is the Law of Love and One Power (rather than good and bad), begins to govern your life. As you continue to open to that Presence, you'll find every level of life becoming easier—your grades will improve, you'll feel more peaceful, users will fade from your life, doors of opportunities will open, and your health will automatically improve. Not because you earned it, but because it's your birthright.

Seek not for worldly things.
Seek this state of consciousness and you'll have the earthly things as a result.

Once you have attained this state of consciousness, you don't have to think about being loving, because you *are* loving. You don't have to try to have morals, joy, peace, because it's your nature. You realize you are transforming in endless ways . . . ways, however, that don't take human effort to accomplish. Your energy level will naturally and effortlessly be higher and you will gradually become aware that you are experiencing self-esteem and self-confidence. Your human fears are transformed into Divine Love.

The violet light is a Divine State of Consciousness (or God Consciousness). As you visually view the violet light, you are within the kingdom of heaven. While opening yourself to the Presence, you will find yourself filled with peace and harmony. You experience a state of grace as you find yourself back in the heart of God. Within that Oneness, you no longer feel separated from your family, friends, strangers, a leaf, a cloud, your destiny, the junkie on the street, or even the food you eat. In Oneness, all things are made anew.

In the introduction, I professed my love for you, although we have never met. I am One with you, for we are all *in* the Mind of God. You are just another "aspect of me" in the totality of All That Is.

A neighbor knocked at my door in an emergency situation one afternoon. "Gloria, I have a problem and you're the only one I could think of who can help me." As we rushed next door, she explained the situation.

She had two of her grandsons visiting, and they had gotten into an argument. The older boy had punched his younger brother. Through the pain of the punch, the twelve-year-old went into shock and either couldn't or wouldn't speak.

I had no training for this type of situation, but love is natural to me. Without thought of how I would "fix" this kid, I held the boy in my arms and gave him permission not to speak. I told him I was taking him on a quiet journey, within his mind. If he could visualize what I was saying, that was okay. If not, that was okay, too. Following the meditation, he if wanted to speak, that, too, would be okay, and if not, I would honor his choice.

Remember: What we resist, persists. To break through resistance/fear, we give permission (which surrenders judgment). Whenever we have an illness or uncomfortable situation, we "want it to go away." Therefore, the illness or problem remains and we feel hopeless and helpless. When we give the "dis-ease," discomforts, and fear permission to just "be," they naturally transform to love.

I spoke the meditation you are about to experience in a very soft voice, speaking lovingly from my heart. The path he and I took was Divinely given, not a rehearsed meditation. In the quiet time together, with me voicing the visions and thoughts that spontaneously were shown and given me, I introduced the boy to all aspects of himself—his anger, abandonment, fears, and love.

As the meditation ended, he quickly began chattering in excitement to his grandmother, telling her all he'd seen, heard, and felt. His soul was healed, and his grandmother was back at peace.

I'd like to take you, as a family group, to that heavenly state of consciousness through this simple meditation. Let's go within by closing our eyes and opening our mind where peace, on all levels of our being, awaits us.

Get comfortable and take a deep breath, counting to seven, holding it if you comfortably can to the count of seven, and releasing it to the count of seven. Ask your toes to relax and go to sleep. Move on up to your ankles and ask them to relax and go to sleep. Move on up to your knees and ask them to relax and go to sleep. Now your hips, relax and go to sleep.

At your waist, while asking it to relax and go to sleep, take another deep breath, counting, holding, and releasing to the count of seven.

Move up to your rib cage and chest, asking them to relax and go to sleep. Talk to your shoulders, down the arms to the elbows, the hands and fingers, asking them to relax and go to sleep. Ask your neck and face to relax and go to sleep.

Take a third deep breath to the count of seven and slowly release as you clear your mind by silently stating, "Peace be with me." Those words are the only words I'll ever ask you to memorize, until they begin to become habit when you're in a stressful or frightening situation.

Your mind may wander during your meditation; you need not be concerned. The mind is greater than we are and cannot be humanly controlled. However, once you're aware it's wandering, gently reaffirm, "Peace be with me." It will wander again and again, but remind yourself of peace.

Eyes closed, body relaxed, you may begin seeing small pinpoints of white light in your inner vision. Whether you can visualize or imagine the following, let's begin taking the steps on the stairway to heaven.

The staircase stands before us in a rainbow of colors. A brass handrail appears before us, which is cool and silky to the touch as it guides us upward on our journey.

The first step of the stairway is red. Breathe in this color. It is the color of blood, your life force, linking you to the heart of God. Already you feel reduced emotional and mental stress. You are willing to begin anew.

At your own pace, step two takes you on the stair step of orange. Breathe in orange as you feel the color erase your limitations, giving you courage, integrity, selfless service, joy, and spiritual devotion. You will emerge as a spiritual leader.

The third step on the stairway is yellow. As you breathe in yellow, you will know and understand faith. "Belief in those things not yet seen." Stress dissolves in this breath of color, and you become aware of a heightened sense of intuition. Your personal growth will be accelerated.

You trust as you take the fourth step onto green, breathing in this color. You feel yourself filled with love and kindness, tranquility, balance, healing energy, and more patience. You find you possess deeper spiritual insight.

The fifth step on the stairway is blue and as you breathe in this color, you realize you have clarity of thought. No more confusion. It's as if the gift of pure love has poured out from heaven, for you now have Direct communication with your Higher Power.

The sixth step on the stairway is violet, and as you breathe in the color it's as if your soul is being bathed and purified. Your personal transformation has begun. You feel calm, strong, and protected. Divine Love and pure inspiration are your birthright.

Still holding the handrail, you take the final seventh step, which is white. As you breathe in the white, you begin remembering who you are, in your purest essence. Your mind, body, and soul are purified on all levels. No negativity is remaining. You feel only spiritual goodness as you take another breath. The weight of the world has been removed and you are pure in Spirit once again.

At the top of the stairway is a door to your left. Embedded in the door is a heart made of colorful stained glass. You reach out to touch the golden knob, and the door to your heart opens and you step into the chamber before you.

Surrounding you are full-sized mirrors, as if you're in a department store. As you view the images of yourself before you, you see yourself in the mirrors, one by one. In one mirror, you are happy, safe, and loved. In the next, sad. Lonely in another. Angry in one. Scared in another. Still you turn, to see yourself as selfish, greedy, kind, caring . . . and still the images present the mirrors of your mind and actions.

Rage. Contempt. Envy. Revenge. Compassionate. Giving.

Honest. Liar. Thief. Drug user. Innocent. Sharing. Smart-mouth. Shy.

All the images you see, you look upon without judgment. They are all aspects of everyone in the earthly dimension, but you know the images are not who you are. They are only effects of your present belief system and level of awareness. After all, you are an innocent and Holy Child of God and the core of you is goodness. For the moment, you accept these aspects of yourself wholly and completely, loving yourself in spite of them, for the healing has begun.

To your right, your attention is drawn to an open window. You are aware of a bird on the windowsill, and he has a saddle on his back. You become miniature as you climb upon his back, fasten the seat belt, and he spreads his wings.

Higher and higher you soar through the sky, lifting higher and higher through the clouds. A kingdom of golden light awaits you; double doors to the entrance open for your expected arrival.

Souls of all ages rush to greet you. Saints, sages, and seers . . . visionaries of ages gone by. Angels and spiritual guides surround you, willing to answer your countless questions. Within this dimension, there are no dual powers, only God Who is the Power of (unconditional) love. Within this state of spiritual consciousness, there is no more sickness and health. Only health, for that is all God knows. No good and bad, for God is only good. No rich and poor, for God is only abundance in all things. And with this awareness, you know how to rise above the human states of consciousness and miscreations of insanity, pain, and heartaches, to return at will to this spiritual state, to begin helping yourself as well as one another.

Hand in hand with your chosen spiritual guide, you are ushered through the grassy field to a waterfall that cascades to the canyon down below in misted colors that have never yet made their way to earth.

Ask your guide to place your spiritual symbol in your mind. It may be a flower, a bird, a cross, or any number of things you can identify with on the physical level. You will know, in your daily life, that you are Divinely guided as your awareness and attention is drawn to your symbol. Ask your guide for an inspired message—that which you most need to hear at this time. Trust the unspoken thoughts, realizing the words are not your imagination.

Ask your spiritual guide and/or angel for his or her name, so you can call upon this being in moments of need.

Before you is the river of life. You look into the waters, to the left, and you can see your past. In the clear water before you, your present mirrors itself in your mind. As you turn to your right, you watch the natural and graceful flow of life. With your spiritual awareness and spiritual vision, you can also see those things that have yet to come into physical expression in your life; that are in the days to come.

You feel filled full and fulfilled, with wisdom and love as well as peace. But now it's time to return to the earthly dimension and bring these gifts to others. As above, so below. On earth as it is in heaven.

Knowing that you no longer walk alone is comforting. You become miniature once again as you climb onto the back of your bird, fastening your seat belt as you descend lower and lower, feeling the effects of gravity . . . down, down through the clouds and back to the windowsill where the journey began.

Stepping down from the windowsill and becoming full sized, you turn to thank the bird, and he disappears right before your eyes.

You gaze one last time into the mirror, no longer self-hating or judging yourself as bad for having those secret,

silent aspects. You have felt your fears and now you take another nice, deep breath and release them. And as you take
the steps back down the stairway—white, violet, blue, green,
yellow, orange, and red—you understand that the transformation from human to Divine happens one step at a time.

OPEN YOUR JOURNAL AND ANSWER
THESE QUESTIONS

Journal—Chapter Two

1. Are you aware that you have felt another's pain, sadness, embarrassment, love, or fear through empathy?
Were you aware that it's a spiritual gift? Name an example.

2. Have you ever been aware, when you closed your
eyes to sleep or meditate, that pretty colors could be
seen? Have you ever seen the violet light and wondered
what it was or if it meant something? Are you able to see
it?

3. Have you experienced something that seemed good
but ended up having a negative outcome? Name an experience.

4. Have you experienced something that seemed negative but ended up having a positive outcome? Name an
experience.

5. Has anyone ever given you "permission" to feel your
feelings? Are you aware that you're "not bad" if you feel
negative feelings?

6. Do you have someone you can talk to, about anything, and not be judged "wrong" to express yourself?

7. While taking the "Stairway to Heaven," could you

feel your body relax and your mind become still? What was the best part of the experience you enjoyed?

8. Could you visualize the steps being taken? What were some of the strongest pictures you saw while doing this meditation?

If you couldn't see anything during the meditation, get comfortable in a chair and try this instead:

- Rub your hands together briskly, and, using your right hand, wipe across the top of your head/hair, from your forehead to the back of your head, three times. Shake your right hand sharply to your side (as if trying to shake off a sticky piece of paper).
- Wipe across your forehead with your right hand three times. Shake your hand sharply at your side.
- Wipe your hand down the back of your head and hair toward your neck three times. Shake the energy sharply from your hand.
- Wipe from your chin, down your throat, three times with your hand. Shake your hand sharply at your side.
- Wipe from your upper left chest, above the heart, across the heart three times with your hand. Sharply shake your hand.

Close your eyes and ask yourself a silent question. Your body will now speak to you, from your subconscious level. If the answer is a yes, your body may feel like it is floating in a front–back motion. If the answer is no, your body will feel like it's swaying from side to side.

You may also begin seeing visions while doing this exercise. As you sweep your hand across the five places, you are clearing the energy fields of your spiritual centers.

Now, with your energy cleansed, try the meditation again and "see" if you get greater results.

If you were successful on your first attempt with the meditation, please answer the following:

1. Did you see spirit guides and/or angels?
2. Were you offered a name for the guide or angel?
3. Were you shown a spiritual symbol, so you'll have reminders in your day-to-day world "that you're on the right track" when you see it? If so, what was it?
4. Were you given a spiritual message? (If so, write it down.)
5. Did you see your past?
6. Did you see your present?
7. Those things to come?
Write it down.
8. Did you have a spiritual experience? Please document it (and any future ones you may have).
9. Did you feel peaceful and loved? (Realize you can go back to this quiet place, within yourself, anytime you choose. There you can be refilled with love and given answers, as you need.)

Write your heartfelt thoughts in the Journal and state this affirmation aloud. *I love and accept myself in spite of my weaknesses, inferiority complex, insecurities, addictions, and fears.*

3
Gifted Children

When I first learned we would have this day together, I took a poll from parents and Teen Angels/Adult Children, asking what should be included in this writing. Fear-based adults asked me to mask the sensitive issues by not discussing them at all. Teens concluded that if I chose to deny their needs, teaching them only how to *think all day about getting good grades,* they wouldn't be interested in what I have to say. To quote their "voice," I was told, "We don't only think about getting good grades. We think about sex, running away from home, drugs, sometimes even suicide. If you want to help us, *we need someone who feels safe enough to discuss those issues."* As delicately and as neutrally as I am able to do so, I will address these needs.

You are not here by accident "as a family," you are here by Divine Right. You appear to be separate, physical individuals, but in spiritual reality, you are One unit. Every story I speak and the spiritual principles I teach will touch each of you on some level, for you see, even adults have a child who lives within.

My generation was taught to respect our elders, which I

believe was good advice. But as a child and adult, I think it is a good idea to respect children as well.

When I was growing up, my parents would entertain visitors. Upon their arrival, we were sent out to play. I'm sure their grown-up talk centered on gossip they wouldn't have wanted repeated, as well as adult topics that little ears shouldn't hear. It was understandable that parents needed their time just as children needed theirs.

However, somewhere along life's path, the respect for people of all ages diminished. TV commercials and movie topics became bolder and even embarrassing to those of us who had been so protected from the issues of the world.

Viewing programs on TV or in movies, where disrespect was apparent and approved of, began molding a sick society. It seemed we were given permission to degrade ourselves and loved ones with hints of sarcasm or outright rudeness. Canned laughter on TV sitcoms gave us permission to laugh along, although an initial hesitation from our heart and conscience told us otherwise.

Once in grade school, I chased a girl home with stinky blue cheese that reeked of smelly socks, from our refrigerator. Other kids from my class had invited me in on the behavior and, afraid to say no or to be as disliked as the classmate, I joined in. I still remember her name and the day. I'm sure she does, too, although we never caught her. Just as in every movie today, *where the girl always falls down* in the chase scene to add to the drama and excitement, I fell that day. Probably planned unconsciously on my part, because even at that age I knew that what I was doing was wrong.

That day changed the way I would deal with people in life. I didn't want to follow the crowd, especially when I knew better. I didn't want to be part of something I knew, deep in my heart, was wrong and harmful. I was tested once in high school, as well. An overweight, supposed nerd, wearing glasses and sporting zits, was the topic of some rank conversation. The reminder of my earlier years and the blue cheese incident gave me an opportunity to atone for my behavior and actions.

Never normally bold, I made an honest attempt to stand up in this classmate's defense. "If you girls would look with your heart, rather than your eyes, you would see _____ as a sensitive, brilliant, warmhearted guy." The gossip and put-downs halted immediately. As it turned out, one of our friends ended up marrying the guy, having a lovely family, and living happily ever after.

I think kids of all ages are one of our greatest gifts from God. They are brilliant, unless they're hypnotized into believing they're stupid. I believe today's kids are strong and smart and as your present spiritual teacher, I'm going to stretch you, if need be, to be all you can be. You are not weak or ignorant. You are fully capable of running circles around me. I'll give you the foundation and you can build your dreams and destiny upon it. Being honest, I need you and all you can teach me far more than you might think you need me. I need your help to make a difference in this world.

When my son was in second grade, a friend of his came to our home after school one day. I've always been the "friendly neighborhood priest," and people of all ages felt comfortable telling me their stories. On this day, this second-grader confided that he heard voices. The prior evening, he was sitting in the family living room when the voice of Spirit spoke, telling him to go to his bedroom where he'd be safe. It was revealed that his father was going to beat his mother. The boy went into his room, as guided, and it was only a few minutes before his unseen guardian angel/spirit guide asked him to run next door and call 911. The child did, which probably saved his mother's life.

Chris N. (age ten) and I recently met in Los Angeles while I was doing a private healing at the UCLA Medical Center. We spent only a couple of hours together, but he became one of those who helped inspire me to write for kids and teens. As we stood talking, he mentioned that he's capable of seeing visions without going to a quiet place within himself. He can be in a mall or out in public and gaze at people, knowing those things that are to come. "Not all of them are very pretty, either," he said.

Chris also revealed that he can hear voices from unseen messengers. As I confirmed that I do, too, a look of relief and understanding appeared on his face and a deep sigh escaped his lips. In fact, I believe that the younger generations are being born with a more advanced state of consciousness than the parents now have, and this is what is partly leading to discord in the homes.

That afternoon, in the presence of Chris, I asked if, while he was looking at me, he had any visions of things to come for me. He replied immediately, "Yep. Ya wanna hear what it is?" In response to his question, I immediately began "seeing" this same vision as he projected it, as our minds melded.

"I see an open field and in this field is a rose garden, a small waterfall, and a running brook." Chris could not have known that the rose is my personal spiritual symbol. Whenever I receive a rose, a card with the flower, or see a rose in any form, it's Spirit's way of saying, "You're on the right track. Keep going."

As Chris described this beautiful, serene place for me, he added, "A message awaits you in the rose garden, Gloria."

"Since you are clairaudient, Chris, and can hear Spirit speak, do you also know the message I'll be given?"

He smiled and replied, "Yep. Ya wanna know that, too?"

As I nodded my head, he proudly said, "You're going to do something very important for humanity, Gloria. In the next year or two, you're going to write a book for kids that will be widely accepted in schools across the nation." Looking intently at me, eye to eye, this little prophet said, "You're going to teach us kids self-esteem, self-confidence, and how to love ourselves as well as one another."

Chris isn't the only ten-year-old prophet I've met. Jordan knocked at my door one midafternoon. I was on the telephone, and my kids ushered him into the kitchen where he stood quietly waiting. I explained to the caller that I needed to get off the phone and see what my little visitor wanted, assuming he was selling Boy Scout popcorn or something for one of the local schools or church programs.

Jordan held his hand up and said, "Oh, no . . . I can see you're busy. You don't need to get off the phone. I'll just stand here quietly and wait for you." I assured my caller I needed to end our conversation. "He's got manners, too," I said.

As I walked toward the boy, he extended his hand, introducing himself along with his age. He stated the reason for his visit with his first words: "I'm here for Book II."

I asked, "Book II?"

He smiled and replied, "Yes, I read Book I and it works, so I'd like to read Book II."

Jordan explained he was riding his bike, fell, and skinned his hand. He sat on the pavement, closed his eyes, and saw the purple light as taught in my *Go Within or Go Without* book. His hand stopped hurting and he wanted to read what else I had written.

I expressed to Jordan that I'd donated my books to the local library and if "Book II" *(Spiritual Life Savers)* wasn't available, I'd make sure he got a copy to read.

As I was walking this friendly chatterbox to my front door, he noted that although he's a kid and I'm an adult, we were standing eye to eye in height. Shocked, he remarked,

"Ya know, you're a lot shorter than you look on your book." And thinking it was a compliment, he added, "And your hair doesn't look as doofus-y, either."

I walked Jordan outside and as I turned to go back into the house, he asked me to promise if I ever moved, would I please make sure to give him my forwarding address? His reasoning was, "Someday, someone is going to make a movie of your life and I want to go to the premiere of it with you." Out of the mouths of babes . . .

Again, our generation was taught so long ago to respect our elders. Therefore, you "old souls" deserve our complete respect and admiration. Children these days are wiser and more evolved consciously. I believe that each of you has something very important to teach us, and I'm definitely willing to listen.

My Seattle hostess, Rondi, brought me to her area to teach a spiritual healing workshop. She had read my book and was in awe of my experiences. She complimented me on how wise she believed I was. I laughed and replied, "You think I'm wise. My best friend, Nikki, thinks I'm an ass. So I guess that makes me a smart-ass." I'm sure many of you have been called that, also.

Do you, like Chris and the other children I mentioned, see visions or hear voices that you don't feel safe to share, for fear of being put in an institution? Do you feel like you're "different" and don't fit in? Do you wonder why people treat others the way they do? Do you find yourself feeling very strong emotions and not knowing how to deal with them? Do you have the sense you're here on this planet to help, but don't know how?

The consciousness, that unseen spiritual substance that creates our physical world, has been rising due to prayers and meditations. Each one of us who closes our eyes and opens our minds, allowing the Presence of God/violet light to use as an avenue of spiritual expression, helps the world evolve into a more spiritual planet.

Each meditation aids the world through one less child going to bed hungry tonight, one less woman being beaten, one less bank robbery or crime.

However, as the consciousness rises, purifying the world's awareness, it brings an increased energy field that tends to make those who are confused, more confused. Those who are already negative, become more agitated. Those who are depressed, become suicidal.

The rising of consciousness also makes it easier for children to be born into this dimension with increased intelligence and more sensitivity. In fact, I am witnessing more and more children who are highly intuitive, telepathic, and more gifted as healers.

These incoming souls, born into families with very little spiritual awareness, become out-of-control children. Unaware of their telepathic abilities, they read their parents' minds and become confused because the words and actions don't match what they spiritually perceive as incoming data. Even in Lamaze classes, we are taught that newborns are highly telepathic.

Children, adults, teachers, and society must become aware of the spiritual talents they have in their midst. With this understanding, perhaps God, as a principle, can be readmitted into the environment where children spend the majority of their time. Classes on self-esteem and group meditations would replace drugs and guns.

Politicians and world leaders seek the answers to these violent and dangerous situations in school settings. It is not stricter gun control and laws that are needed. Instead, it is necessary to heal the cause for the drugs and violence, or the need for numbing/desensitizing substances.

A mother read one of my inspirational books and telephoned me one day to seek my help. Her child was worshipping Satan and asked if there was anything I could do. Not knowing what I would say, I asked if she could listen in on another extension. In the background, I heard the teen cry out, "I don't want to talk to her." Following her opposition to discussing this situation with a stranger, I then heard a meek "Hello" on the other end of the line.

I laughed and asked, "So you didn't want to talk to me, huh?"

Quietly she responded, "I don't know . . ." afraid the truth might hurt my feelings.

I surprised myself with my honesty. "I'm not sure what I'm going to say to you. It appears you don't believe in God and I've never believed in Satan." I also explained to the teen that I had lived a very overprotected life, asking for her to teach me, and she agreed to answer my questions.

"Are you in a cult?" I asked. She responded, "Yes" without hesitation and explained that there was a cult leader. Still allowing her to guide the conversation, getting comfortable with sharing, I asked if the cult leader wanted his followers to do negative things and asked her to name an example. The girl affirmed the negative guidance, telling me that one of her friends had been asked to commit suicide. She had tried to fulfill his request, but the attempt failed.

Knowing her mother was on the other line and listening to the child's confessions of using drugs and having unprotected sex, my heart ached.

I explained my connection to an ex–heroin junkie, a friend I made across the miles while she was serving time in a California state prison. I told her how Linda K. (Nikki) Fudge and I became best friends over a six-year correspondence. She became the illustrator for three of my books, and I now call her my "(con) artist."

I advised the child, "When I was writing to Nikki, I once

shared my belief that people use drugs for two reasons: to have mind-expanding experiences to remember God, or to numb and forget the pain that life sometimes brings.

"You worship Satan and say you don't believe in God, so I assume you're not seeking mind-expanding experiences," I said. "Can I assume you have pain you're attempting to numb?"

She sighed a relieved, "Yes . . ."

Knowing intuitively that the child didn't feel safe saying these things outright, at least not in the present moment, I asked if she would be willing to read my book if I mailed it to her. I also asked if she'd be willing to begin corresponding and relating her pain to me. To both questions, she replied she would, and actually welcomed the opportunity.

I believe drugs can be used for entertainment or experimental value, but the chief cause for today's teens is as a tool to numb themselves. Years of corresponding with Nikki helped her understand how empathic she was and had been her entire life. Dealing with not only her pain and confusion as a teen, but also the fears and stresses of others, only served to compound the problem. Later today, I'll be teaching you how to deal effectively with your gift of empathy, as well.

One of the meanings of the word *respect* is "to pay attention to," and I believe it's time to give children of all ages this courtesy. You are commanding our respect and attention to your problems, and I'm sorry we haven't listened. At any rate, I apologize that spiritual understanding is not always available to you.

With awareness, you are (already) gifted healers, prophets, seers (visionaries), empathic, telepathic, intuitive, and sensitive. You are highly evolved spiritual beings and with the guidance of your gifts, you can begin now helping yourselves, your families, and the world. I'm willing to teach you everything I know to help make your lives better on all levels. And I'll be grateful if you'll continue teaching me, as well.

OPEN YOUR JOURNAL AND ANSWER THESE QUESTIONS

Journal—Chapter Three

1. Have you ever followed the crowd, even when your heart said not to? Write about an example.

2. How would you handle the same situation if you had it to do all over again?

3. Was following the crowd a life-changing experience? If so, write down the deepest message of how it has affected your life.

4. Have you ever been able to stand up for a friend or family member in a situation where he or she was being verbally or physically attacked? Please describe what happened.

5. Have you been able to stand up for your beliefs, a cause, or yourself (besides to a parent)? Write about a time when you were willing "to right something that once went wrong."

6. Have you ever had a psychic/spiritual experience, vision, or dream that came true?

Document it.

7. Do you feel that you're "different," and that you don't fit in? In what ways?

8. Do you get confused that people treat each other the way they do?

9. Do you have strong emotions and not know how to deal with them?

10. Do you have the sense you're on this planet for a special purpose, but don't know what it is (yet)? Write down the "bits and pieces" you feel and might know, but don't fully understand yet.

I heard a cute story about drugs many years ago. A man, seeking spiritual enlightenment, met a wise, old soul who had attained a Conscious Oneness with God. The seeker used drugs for the mind-expanding, soul-searching revelations. He offered a sample of the drug to this spiritual teacher. The man cautioned the Wise One about the strength these drugs had and advised him never to take more than one. He also stated how expensive they were. The Enlightened Soul took the entire bottle, dumped them all into his hand, threw them into his mouth, and swallowed. The seeker of Truth was shocked, concerned, and frightened about the forthcoming overdose. He explained those fears to the teacher.

Time passed and the man watched for the teacher's behavior to change. It didn't. Confused, he questioned, "Why has this massive amount of drugs not even affected you?" The teacher smiled and replied, "If you're already in Cincinnati, you don't have to take a bus to get there."

Please understand: Once you have achieved the awareness of how to reach the higher states of consciousness, you will never again need a foreign substance to take you there.

Write your heartfelt thoughts in the Journal and state this affirmation aloud. *I am One with God, and within that Oneness, Infinite, pure Power stands behind me . . .*

4
Natural Course of Life:
Bliss 101A

Last night, after I had cooked dinner for my family, did dishes, and emptied the trash while Danielle did homework, I went for my evening walk. As I walked under the Montana Big Sky, looking at the stars, I became inspired to write another love song for Kirk. I returned home and went into the home office to type it into the computer.

I completed the lyrics and joined Kirk in the living room. We snuggled closely as we talked about the day's events and my writings.

I began to empath a friend's feelings across the miles. By ten-thirty, I couldn't stand her pain any longer and went to bed to open myself to the violet light, performing an absentee healing long distance.

I rubbed my hands together briskly and reminded myself that she and I are One with God. Both of us, appearing individually, with her in California and me in Montana, is only physical geography. In spiritual reality, we are both held within that golden sphere of light where her perfect health already exists.

We are never in an airplane, on a bus, in a house, or in a body. We are in God.

Realizing our Oneness, I lay on my side and propped a teddy bear under my upper arm so it wouldn't get tired from being in this position. I rubbed my hands together, "turning on the electricity," and placed both hands over my eyes.

Everyone in the world should be aware of this technique, of course, but especially those who know empathy for another. Those of us who find ourselves listening to and uplifting others must take every opportunity to have the energy before we give it. Otherwise, we will "spiritually bankrupt" ourselves, becoming depressed, with no energy or with various body parts hurting or becoming diseased. In fact, most people's pain or disease isn't even their own. They have *taken it on* through their gift of empathy. (Which I do consciously many times. Since I *know how to dissolve it,* I remove it from another by free will. When I no longer feel it, neither does the other person.)

My mom used to always call me long distance with names for my prayer lists. During one of these calls, she said my sister Vicki had been diagnosed with intrauterine cancer. Mom's voice cracked as she cried, begging, "Oh, my God, Gloria, do something." I did. I called my sister and talked to her for an hour, willing the energy into myself. I knew she'd be safe, which she was . . . getting confirmation from a doctor, plus she was no longer hemorrhaging. I was. I bled heavily for three days while doing private healings in the Pacific Northwest. By the third day, *I'd had just about all the fun I needed.*

I lay on the bed and said, "God, I've really gone and done it this time. I need a little extra help here." A very strong electrical pulse started down at my ankles, pushing stronger and stronger as my legs were being forced apart on the bed. When my legs were in a V, the "electrocution" shot up through my crotch. I didn't bleed a drop following this experience.

I don't recommend you to take on another person's pain or illness until you feel secure enough about how to dissolve it.

We must have the energy, however, before we give it. Love thyself. Give first to self so you can freely give to others.

Having your hands over your eyes, with your palms themselves resting gently, you feel the warmth as the heightened energy dissolves negativity you've taken on or unknowingly created during the day. The eyes, being the windows to the soul, with this simple teaching, are the fastest way to get energy into the body. And the body can heal, but it needs energy to do so.

A few years ago, on Danielle's birthday, she had a sleepover for eight fourteen-year-olds. They were very good that evening, and the only time I lost my sense of humor and "nice mommy voice" was at three in the morning when they awakened Kirk and myself having "caterpillar races" in their sleeping bags on the kitchen floor.

The following morning, I was making breakfast pizzas and the smoke alarm went off. One of Danielle's little guests started freaking out, body trembling, voice shaking with fear as she cried out, "Oh, my God, what's that sound?" Danielle, well trained, grabbed a magazine to go fan the smoke alarm to silence it. She replied, "It's just the smoke alarm. Doesn't your mom set yours off every time she cooks?"

I was embarrassed. Following breakfast and delivering the eight children to their respective homes, I returned to my kitchen where I remained for the next eighteen hours. I sprayed the oven and while it was dissolving the burned-on residue, I decided to clean the refrigerator and small freezer above it.

As I finished that task, my attention was drawn to the big freezer, realizing I hadn't rotated the meat in a very long time. From cleaning the freezer, I went to the pantry; it was evident that "pigs live here" and I cleaned it. I straightened and cleaned above the laundry facilities and made my way from floor to ceiling, cleaning cupboards and drawers.

I vacuumed the flour bin and cleaned the microwave and ended up back at the stove where the cleaning had begun. All the yecchy black goo had dripped down into the broiler and onto the floor. So I cleaned the stove and oven and finished the kitchen by mopping and waxing the floor.

I was so tired from eighteen hours in the kitchen that I could have sat and cried. If I went to bed exhausted of all energy, I would have tossed and turned, and my body would have been uncomfortable. Instead, I went to the living room and lay upon the loveseat.

I rubbed my palms briskly, placed them over my eyes for fifteen minutes and Da Da Da Da Ta Da! Charge! I was fully reenergized and went to clean the hall closet and underneath the bathroom sink. My day ended, comfortably in bed, reading until it was time to go to sleep.

Last year, I taught forty-six workshops from sea to shining sea. These 460 hours qualified me for my teaching credentials through Emerson Theological Institute in Oakhurst, California, as well as earning me a Ph.D. in religious studies.

In those workshops, I teach the participants the importance of rubbing your hands and placing them over your eyes several times throughout the day. It only takes two to ten minutes to achieve results; you can do it longer, of course, because it feels so danged good. Although I have taught the following information in one of my other writings, I believe repetition and reminders are necessary. You will be amazed at the results if you will follow this simple technique.

- In the morning when you awaken. Doing it at this hour of the day reenergizes you. Just because you slept eight or ten hours doesn't mean you got a good night's sleep. Sometimes we work harder in dream time than we do in the physical world. Placing your hands over your eyes, with your fingers up on your forehead, also helps you to open the third eye so you have clarity of thought and are able to picture Divine Guidance easily. Your gift of telepathy is heightened as well.
- After you eat lunch. Because it takes energy to digest your food, you tend to feel sluggish. Instead of taking a nap, which you aren't able to do because you have afternoon classes, appointments, or meetings, or a million tasks to perform, a few minutes with hands over your eyes will reenergize you quickly and easily.
- When you're falling asleep at night, reviewing your day of "What ifs?" "If onlys," "I shouldn't have said this," "I shouldn't have done that," or creating fearful scenarios within your imagination . . . with your hands over your eyes, you are dissolving negativity, heightening your consciousness, and raising your energy field so you can carry more light (electricity/energy). Even if you go to bed late, getting only a few hours of sleep, you'll feel as refreshed as if you've gotten your full rest.
- I encourage those of you who inspire others through a loving, listening ear (bartenders, hairdressers, or those of you who work near the public a great deal) to perform this technique often throughout the day. If you

are surrounded by "energy vampires" (and I mean that in the nicest way), they usually come in the form of best friends and family members: those who feel comfortable around you, telling you their problems. After they have dumped their pain and problems, however, they walk out uplifted and you feel hammered. Give them the time, energy, attention, advice, and love they need and seek from you, but before they leave—teach them this technique. Empower them to seek within themselves rather than relying on you any longer. After they depart, rub your hands and put them over your eyes, "beefing up your energy field," and get ready for the next one.

- And finally, I suggest that when you're sitting "on the throne"—unless you're reading one of my books— what better thing do you have to do with your hands? Rub and place them over your eyes. Take every opportunity to keep your energy field as high as possible. Place a small note above the toilet paper to remind you, "Hands over eyes."

**Love yourself. Give first to you,
and you'll have it to give to others.**

While your hands are over your eyes, you may begin feeling what I call "shifts" or "electrocutions." For a moment, think of a regular garden hose kinked in half, which prevents the water from flowing. Tension, stress, fear, or injuries create "kinks" throughout our body. Pain is a sign of lack of love or energy. When you place your hands over your eyes, you may or may not see the violet light. Sometimes I do. Sometimes I don't. However, the warmth from your hands tingling through your body, or the sensation that someone has lifted the world from your head and shoulders, will be validation that the technique is working.

"Shifts" will be felt in the body. It may occur through a heavy sigh, a slight, moderate, or unexpected twitch, which can be physically felt. Each shift in consciousness from human to Divine will be physically felt (in the body). Each shift will also affirm that "one more kink or block in your energy field has been dissolved"—Like a garden hose opening so the water can flow easily. As the shift occurs, energy will naturally flow freely again.

Healings on physical, emotional, mental, moral, financial, or spiritual levels will begin to manifest in your world— usually spontaneously, and if not immediately then within a seventy-two-hour period. By daily placing your hands over your eyes, you will no longer carry another's pain. Love can travel for miles, entering the hearts and homes of loved ones, but so can pain. If you continue to carry and feel the pain longer than seventy-two hours, it's because it has become deeply embedded within your consciousness. Continue to do this exercise until your consciousness is purified and the violet light heals your mind. Because consciousness creates matter, the outer manifestation of change is your validation that the human state of consciousness has been transformed into the Divine state of consciousness.

The "electrocutions," as I call them, you've felt before. Some night as you were drifting off to sleep, your body "spazzed" uncomfortably, nearly knocking you out of bed. You may have thought of a variety of reasons for this occurrence. You may have thought that your muscles had just relaxed. In reality, you have plugged a 110-volt human into the "Omnivolt" Supreme Being. You have risen your consciousness above the world belief in good and bad, sickness and health, or life and death. You have spontaneously plugged into One Power of health and goodness on all levels of your being. When you feel an "electrocution," your consciousness has been purified and either you or someone across the miles who was merely thinking of you, or praying, received a healing or Divine blessing through you.

When Danielle was a toddler, we were playing "Three Little Pigs" together. If I was in my "brick house," she would huff and puff, but she couldn't blow me over. If I was in a "straw house" during our playtime, she would huff and puff and when she blew on me, I'd roll into a backward somersault. Hearing her little belly laugh was worth repeatedly playing the game.

One morning we had played a very long time and during one of my backward rolls, I threw my neck out of whack. I made an appointment with a chiropractor. She was quite a bit bigger than me, and as she crossed my arms over my chest and pushed on me, she put my neck in, but threw my back out. I was too embarrassed to tell her she'd hurt me, so I left her office with as much pain as I had come in with.

Upon returning home, I lay upon my bed and silently said, "God, you just saw what happened. Now I need a little extra help." I levitated a few inches off the bed and was "electrocuted" quickly and immediately, which felt like my midsection had been twisted. I could feel it snap (shift), and I was gently placed back upon the bed. All that occurred in far less time than it just took to say it. However, the "electrocution" immediately stopped all my pain. My body was completely back in balance and I silently said, "Thanks, God. Next time I'll just come to you Direct!"

For the most part, I do go Direct, but that's not to say that I dislike doctors. I don't encourage people to stop going for medical care or to discontinue the use of their medications. Doctors and medical testing can also reveal the recovery and miracles. I don't see doctors as separate from God, which is shown through the example of the following joke.

A man died and was standing in line to get into heaven. St. Peter, one by one, was checking off those who were being admitted through the Pearly Gates. A guy in a white doctor's coat cut in line and walked past all of those patiently awaiting their turn. Confidently, he just went straight into heaven. The gentleman who had waited his turn asked St. Peter, "Hey! What's the deal here? How come that guy can just walk straight in?" St. Peter looked to the new arrival and said, "Oh, that's just God playing doctor."

During Easter last year, I was in Phoenix and while in church, my new shoes began pinching my right foot. It was very uncomfortable, and then I realized immediately that I had made a separation between God and my shoe. Silently I stated, "My foot isn't in a shoe, it's *in God*," and it felt like my shoe had expanded to an infinite universe. I could wiggle my toes comfortably; there was no more pain. As you take on this awareness, it will become daily practice to recognize how many people, places, and things you are separating from the One Power. As you reidentify the situations with the Truth of spiritual reality, you will notice the side effects of living a much easier life.

I was driving to Spokane to perform three days of individual healings and found myself driving across two mountain passes, alone for the first time. I felt fear. What if I broke down? I didn't have a cell phone; nor did I know how to change a flat tire. Realizing I felt fear was my first clue that I had separated myself from God.

Silently I asked, "God, I'm asking for a conscious realization of Your Presence." Immediately, a little thunderbolt of electricity started down at my ankles and shivered its way up through my body. I silently said, "I'm *not* impressed." After all, I was still feeling fear. So a second time, I asked, "God, I'm asking for a conscious realization of Your Presence." No sooner did I think the question than I "heard" Spirit say, "I appear in many forms." Along with that one-liner, I felt the rock 'em, sock 'em, knock-you-off-your-barstool Thunder of Silence/Intuition fill me with complete knowingness that the van surrounding me, the pavement beneath me, the trees I was passing on the right, and the vehicles passing me on the left were all God, but appearing in many forms. No longer feeling fear, I silently replied, "Thanks. Now I'm impressed!"

During this past Christmas season, I was taking my evening walk. It had snowed, then rained, then froze. Our streets were sheets of ice. As I was walking, I felt a hint of fear fill me, thinking I'd better be cautious or I was going to fall on my keester. Dang it. See how easy it is to separate everything in our day-to-day world from God? As soon as I realized fear and the belief that ice could be separate, I stopped walking and realized the Truth. I am One with God, which constitutes my Oneness with all spiritual beings, ideas, and creations . . . which includes ice. There isn't ice *and* God. There is only God, appearing as ice. Fear dissolved. It felt like someone had put football cleats on the bottom of my snow boots and I walked without fear.

You know those days when you feel "in the flow"? Your energy is high and you're proud of yourself for getting so much accomplished, and no one can rain on your parade? I feel that way every single day of my life. *Unless I choose to feel otherwise.* Sometimes it just feels good to have those human traumas or dramas. I feel happy 99 percent of the time, for no particular reason. Just simply because. The 1 percent of the time I choose to feel sad or another earthly emotion, how long is completely within my control. People wonder if I have more hours in a day than the rest of the world because I am able to accomplish so many things and live my life to the fullest. It's just because I have "plugged in to the Source Who can see the Whole Plan." My minutes, hours, and days are organized, and I'm in the natural flow of life. A Natural Course, which I am teaching you.

And by the way, thank you for attending Bliss 101A.

OPEN YOUR JOURNAL AND ANSWER
THESE QUESTIONS

Journal—Chapter Four

1. Do other people feel comfortable telling you their problems?

2. Do you feel tired and empty after they have been with you?

3. Make a list of those who make you feel that way. (Listing them will remind you to place your hands over your eyes after your visit with them.) You can teach, if they're willing to listen, but don't force your information on anyone. Give everyone the courtesy of learning at his or her own pace.

Also, if people call you on the telephone to dump on you close your eyes as you're sitting there. Open yourself to the violet light and you'll find you're not exhausted after you hang up. You'll be pumped.

4. Are you depressed, now or often?

Rub your hands together and place your palms on top of your head. Allow your elbows to rest on the table. This is the most comfortable position to do this exercise. With your hands on top of your head, close your eyes and see the purple light. In fifteen to thirty minutes, depression is dissolved. Your energy field will be purified and you won't feel so heavy or like you're carrying the world around on your head and shoulders any longer.

5. Practice placing your hands over your eyes, throughout the day and evening, for at least three days and write about how you felt doing this simple exercise. Did studying and remembering come easier? Did you feel lighter? Did you notice others are more attracted to you? People will unconsciously sense your Light/energy and be attracted to you. Also, they will consciously be aware of your shift in attitude and wonder what your secret to happiness is. Tell them.

6. With your hands over your eyes, especially at night, did you feel shifts? If you're sleeping with a sibling in the same room, or a mate, you may witness the other person shifting and electrocuting, also. They, being within your state of consciousness and energy field, will also experience the heightening of energy and purification of consciousness. Your home and atmosphere will be healed of negativity. Write about a sibling or mate shifting where you felt the shift within your body.

7. Have you ever felt a spiritual "electrocution" when you were falling asleep? Now when it occurs, you'll know what it is. If you are aware of the miracle that followed, write it down.

8. Practice this technique and write about your first experience of feeling a shift and being aware of a pain that instantly disappeared. Write, too, about being conscious of a shift and no longer being afraid—aware that, following the shift, your "human" way was made easier.

Perhaps you were offered something that you had no idea how to purchase or get. Write about this manifestation.

9. Ask God for a conscious realization of His Presence. Did you feel anything in your body? Warmth, tingling, electric pulsing? Peace? What is your individual body sensation or experience? Write of your experience as you become aware how it feels. Also, if you're in a frightening situation hereafter, and feel the adrenaline/ pure God Power, you'll be conscious that He is working in and through you. Doesn't it already feel better to know you no longer walk alone?

10. Just looking around your immediate surroundings (and within you), name as many "things" as you can that God is appearing "as."

11. As you practice the Presence, return to your Journal and write about an experience of being "in the flow." A day in which you felt on top o' the world and felt pride at how much you energetically accomplished. A day that no one had the power to ruin with a sour attitude.

12. Can your attitude shift dramatically if you're around a "grumpy Smurf butt?" Name an example when you allowed your attitude to change from positive to negative.

13. Is it common for you to be easily manipulated by someone else's attitude?

14. Does a friend, child, parent, or teacher easily push your buttons? Name these people. Becoming honest and aware of such people and situations will help you rise above the now established pattern of *allowing* others the power to disturb your inner peace.

If you have a button that keeps being pushed, be aware that it is being shown to you for a purpose. *Heal the judgment* or you can guarantee that you'll keep attracting more of the same. (Refer back to chapter 2 to review how to heal resistance/fear.)

Write your heartfelt thoughts in the Journal and state this affirmation aloud. *No longer does any person, place, experience, or appearance have the power to disturb my inner peace. I am peaceful.*

5

An Act of Love

Before I begin taking the daughters, followed by the sons, and then the parents into my home office for private time, I want to tell you of my greatest desire. Throughout my life, all I could dream of was to have a close and loving family. My "dream family" would stand by one another through thick and thin.

My "physical family" enjoys the close and loving ties I dreamed of. You—my readers—are my "spiritual family," and nothing is as priceless to me as knowing that, as one big happy family, we're all here for one another.

I haven't told you this before, but one of our family's entertainment favorites is watching movies. Love stories and comedies are my choices, but sometimes I enjoy a drama, a thriller, a sad movie, or a high-excitement film.

Since kids, and many parents, are so visual, I would like to use an analogy of words to show you something about all of us.

Remember Matthew's letter? He wrote so clearly that you could almost "see" the cell door as my book was slid under it for him to receive. You could picture him "sending it on the first thing smokin' back to the guy who had sent it to him." You could visualize the book arriving a second time; and couldn't you just *hear* the "snicker" that Matthew described from the man who had just conned him out of the nine-hundred-page thriller?

I'm sure you could see him throw *Go Within or Go Without* up on his shelf . . . and couldn't you just feel his frustration? He'd gotten rid of it once, and here it was "in his face" again. I'm not even sure how that copy grew legs and walked its way into a maximum-security prison and ended up in solitary confinement. (God does work in some serious, mysterious ways!) And how about the days that passed before he became bored? By visually picturing someone in solitary confinement—with no TV, no general population to hang out with, and living in a small, enclosed cell without a window—you could *feel/imagine* his desperate boredom.

Although you have never seen his face, you could actually visualize a man standing at his bunk, fluffing up his pillow, and getting comfortable to nitpick the book. Did you smile when you heard his words that the book trade was now a "done deal" and he was keeping the book?

All through Matthew's letter, you could *imagine* what he was saying. You experienced his emotions, as well. Now I'm going to show you a "movie," titled *An Act of Love,* using the written word as Matthew has done.

It's a drama of your life. You are the "*lights,*" the director, producer, the projector, the actress or actor, the financial backing, the writer, and the extras. You are all the credits, shown before and following. It's all about *you.*

Now, while you're writing the script, you recall you're the "good guy" and the "bad guy." You are the victim and the victimizer. In the movie, if someone hurts you or your feelings and you don't choose to be harmed, you can "write them out of the script."

The life you're now living as a family or as an individual is a movie. You have chosen the cast carefully. But remember, they are still *you*. Poetically speaking, we could say that they are a *camera*, showing you a reflection of the images you look upon. They are also a reflection of your hopes and dreams, as well as your expectations and judgments. They reflect your loves and fears. Your mind projects these images in your physical experience.

Does it feel selfish to have it all be "about you"? What resistance do you feel if you think you're selfish by placing yourself first? (Remember—if you are already giving until it hurts, you have to place yourself first and have the energy before you can give it.)

In your life movie, you have created the characters that will show you the judgments you hold. Perhaps one of the actresses or actors is withholding love or something you want. There isn't anyone "out there" in another form keeping anything from you. The "other person" is you. Only you can keep something from yourself. What are you withholding from you? Listen carefully and pay attention to what your feelings (through these outer-appearing aspects of you) are saying to you. If you feel resistance/fear of those things you're hearing, remember to give your "voice" permission to speak, even though it appears to be spoken through another individual. It's all about *you*.

In the movie of your life, you channel-surf constantly. Sometimes you're in a drama; later in a comedy, a love story, or a sad movie. If you don't like the story line—remember that you're the writer!—change the script. You even have permission to show reruns of the same story lines, if you choose.

We have all walked around, acting like we don't know what we're doing on this planet, and I suppose we all created that story line just to make it all more interesting. I think God is a pretty smart cookie, though, because once you become aware of Oneness, there's a happily-ever-after ending.

When you realize "It's all about me," you view your entire life differently. You become conscious that *each* person, book, or movie you see or feel attracted to has a message just for you.

As an example, there is a movie called *The Divine Secrets of the Ya-Ya Sisterhood.* A friend invited me to go to an afternoon matinee. I didn't know what the movie was about, but Julie had asked me *three* times. (Remember, when you hear something three times, it's a message for you.)

I met her at the theater and was only into the movie about ten minutes when I whispered, "I absolutely *love* this movie." I knew it was one I'd want to own, as well.

The movie, for me, was Divine, just as the title had promised. I won't give away the story, but at the end of the movie when the mother gave her closing speech to her daughter, the "Light" turned on within me. Aha! I got it!

The mother lovingly stated, "I always prayed to God to be strong and famous, and I am . . . through you. He answered every single prayer of mine, through you."

I came away from the movie with a knot in my throat that begged me to give it a voice through the sound of a sob. I had teased (or so I thought) throughout my entire life that I wished to be tall, sleek, and sexy rather than a four-foot-eleven "elf." *I am, though.* In fact, I'm stunningly beautiful . . . through my daughter, Danielle. I always wished I could be silent at times, rather than a raging motor-mouth—and through my son, D.W., *I am.*

My point in sharing this analogy of Lights/Camera/

Action is to teach that there is no one outside of self who is doing anything "to you." No one is keeping your goodness "from you." And no one—when you realize the judgments you hold against yourself or others—can change it, *except you.* The life movie is clearly showing you the beliefs and images you "entertain" and always giving you choices of love or fear. You are the writer. You can write repeated *Acts of Love, Acts of Faith,* or *Acts of Fear.*

Remember, from this moment forward—watch, look, and listen for the messages you are always receiving. Each day gives you a piece of your personal puzzle for growth and understanding. There are no chance encounters. Each meeting is Divinely orchestrated. Each experience is an opportunity for you to "see yourself." Stand tall on this worldly stage in the light of your own spirit!

You are a powerful, spiritual being, and you have the God-given ability to *create* anything you choose. You do this, simply, by *imagining.*

Being aware that imagination is the source of your creations allows you to responsibly begin feeding it with new images, putting your thoughts and energy into what you do "want," rather than displacing them in fear.

Once you can imagine what you choose to experience, *it already exists,* and we, as humans, allow the imagination to figure out the "how." Imagine the possibilities! If we are already in the Divine Imagination, we can draw from It, actually doing anything and everything with no limitations. Imagine creating a game and imagining how it is played. Imagine a doctor telling you that an illness has dissolved overnight. Imagine anything you choose and then imagine that it is already manifested in your world.

You, children, are wonderful! You imagine everything and *have no doubts* (unless an adult tells you there is no way for it to occur).

Can you imagine perfect health, freedom from addictions, good grades, experiencing successful relationships, achieving dreams? You can allow your imagination to find your lost set of car keys, or arriving on time for scheduled appointments that you appear to be running late for.

The human body is electromagnetic energy and thoughts become electric impulses, which are seeds, planted in the fertile magnetic field of emotion. The Natural Law of Attraction brings into our lives these and other experiences that we turn our attention/imagination onto. We must remember, always, that what seeds of thought we plant is totally a personal choice.

To begin with, attempt to remove the word *want* from your vocabulary. Be aware and replace it with the word *choose*, whenever possible. When you say "I want," the word *I* is the key to setting thoughts and words into *action*. The word *want* tells your subconscious/imagination that you fail to presently possess what you seek or desire. The word *want* symbolizes lack of, depriving you of necessities.

To replace *want* with *choice* means you have an alternative, to freely choose a preference. Don't *want* grades, *choose* good grades. Don't *want* healthy-minded friends and mates, *choose* them. Don't *want* to be happy, *choose* to be happy. Don't *want* to become a better parent, *choose* to be one.

I choose how long I wish to experience earthly emotions. So can you. Your emotions don't have power over you. You are not a victim of them randomly coming and going whenever they feel like it. Until I became aware, I acted like a victim, and there were times that I look back on when I acted weak, acted powerless, and acted happy when I really felt sad. I probably should get the Academy Award for all those years of acting like a martyr. Wow. That one was a biggie for me. I think most of my personal healing occurred when I was no longer a doormat.

Being happy all the time can be a real drag. There are some days I just choose to be grumpy for no particular reason. Just because it's "in the air." When I deny myself permission to express one of the earthly emotions, I deny a part of myself.

I was misinformed as a child. I thought to be Godly meant to be nice all the time. Those who profess to be happy all the time are only hurting themselves. (I know this from experience.) I was once teaching a workshop and looked into the audience. My attention was drawn to a woman. I had an immediate flashback of my past as I saw my reflection in her. Not even caring if I embarrassed her or myself, I said, "I'm not leaving this city until you become a bitch." She giggled and said, "Then I guess you'll be here for a very long time, because I'm not a bitch." She emphasized, *"Because I'm nice all the time."*

I shook my head in sadness for her and for my own past. I couldn't force her out of denial. I could only teach her that she was hurting no one but self. No one can be nice all the time without becoming very ill. To *be spiritual* means to be yourself and honest with your feelings. Not just the good ones, but all of them.

I was honest with the woman and said, "If I lived here, you couldn't be my friend because I couldn't trust you. You're not real, not with me or yourself."

Even Jesus wasn't nice all the time. He felt frustration at the scribes and Pharisees, calling them hypocrites. He got angry with the money changers in the temple and threw their tables over.

A friend of mine once said, "I want to travel with you because people treat me nicer when I'm with you, and everyone likes you so much." She then threw in a dirty dig as she sarcastically added, "But of course, they like you *because you're so nice all the time.*" Not expecting my comeback, she was shocked as I raised my voice and screeched, "I'm *not* nice all the time. I can be a real bubble bitch at times." I continued, "People like me because *I'm real* and if you would be, people would like you, too."

People aren't stupid. They sense when a person is shallow, overly sweet, or pretentious . . . pretending, not genuine. Your desire to please may be just the way they like you, because they can use and misuse you, without feeling guilty. Besides being abused for your kindnesses, you're getting something out of the behavior, too. They like you. You want them to. It's a win–win situation until you see how much energy you have to give, in order to be liked. (And there are bazillions of people out there who will like you even if you're real and get angry, upset, have boundaries, or say no. Think about it.)

I know the results of trying to be something I'm not. Being a people pleaser and giving beyond my means as a human, energy wise, nearly killed me. The stress of attempting to be superwoman led to alopecia totalis, and every single hair fell from my head. (How to heal the loss of falling hair is taught in *Go Within or Go Without.*) I became bulimic and then anorexic. I was so emotionally empty at one point because I had given more than I had gotten. The teaching, "It is more blessed to give than to receive," was the root belief that almost buried me. Giving and never receiving is not in balance. If you gave everything in your checking account without making deposits, your money would run out. The same balance in giving and receiving energy through daily living is just as important.

Had it not been for God appearing as Keebler Graham Crackers—which were my diet through my emotional starvation period (aka: anorexia)—I would not be here today to write these words. They were one of the only foods I could get down or keep down. They helped maintain my life when I dropped to eighty pounds and wore size twelve slim girl's jeans. I, of course, wore baggy clothes so no one could see the bag o' bones I truly was.

Anorexia wasn't a conscious death wish. I had no clue, at the time, why I was doing this to myself. I just hurt so deeply in my solar plexus (above the navel and below the breastbone). I didn't know then that when people hurt as if they're hungry (and nothing sounds good), they're "low on Light/energy." Food, and the thought of it, almost made me gag—and sometimes did. Thank God in those moments for Keebler Grahams.

Infinite energy is available, so *why* are millions and millions of people starving, emotionally or physically? Unawareness. Can you even begin to imagine how many people need this information?

When you rub your hands together and place your right hand on your solar plexus and lay your left hand atop the right, you are filling and healing your emotional (power) center.

The right hand is the power hand—unless, of course, you are left-handed. We can easily remember this because we shake hands with the right hand. It is also the hand that pats people on the back for an "Atta boy—good job."

With your right hand on the solar plexus and left hand atop it, I would ask you to close your eyes and open yourself to the violet light/Presence of God. Fifteen minutes a day, or longer if you choose, will be the greatest gift you can give yourself. Those who are anorexic will find recovery. Others will find and have the energy to enjoy life.

Do I think you're going to do this for yourself? No. And I'd be kidding no one except myself if I believed you'd take fifteen minutes a day and devote it to yourself.

Putting on makeup, fixing your hair, trying on one outfit after another, watching TV, shopping, working on your car, reading magazines, playing on the Internet, or yakking on the phone for hours . . . we can find and make time for those things. But we can never seem to set aside fifteen minutes to do the most loving thing we could possibly do for ourselves. Why?

By the way, I'm not ragging on you. I'm saying "we" as in "you and me" because I wouldn't do it either, not even when I knew the benefits of this simple exercise. That's why I already knew you wouldn't want to do it. (And you thought I was either psychic or a know-it-all, huh?)

The only way I can take the time, at this stage of my life, is to do it for another. I take a piece of paper and place my name at the top of the list. (Gosh, who among us would think to put ourselves first?) It's all about *you!*

The next names I place under my own are those loved ones I'm willing to love across the miles. I also write the names of any I might be having problems with. Those who seemingly deserve it the least are the ones who need love the most. If I have a human problem with any folks and find it hard to like them, let alone love them, I open myself for God to love them through me. This removes the ego from the picture. Add to the list your school, strangers, or any situations you are aware of that need to be transformed.

I place that list of names on my solar plexus, rub my hands, and place them on top of the paper. Right hand first, left hand on top of the right hand. I close my eyes, seeking only God's Presence/violet light. Because I am One with God, this constitutes my Oneness with every person, place, or thing on my list. By opening myself, I am raising the consciousness of everyone and everything I've written on that piece of paper.

Because I am the instrument through which the energy travels, it must first fill me. Because there is only "One Mind" and "One Body," the peace and reenergization that I feel, those on the list feel, as well. Cool, huh?

Once we realize our Oneness with other individuals, it helps us understand "unconditional love" a little easier, doesn't it? The unconditional love I've felt for Matthew and Nikki is natural. I'm not saying, of course, that in the beginning of our relationships we humanly weren't expecting to get something out of it. With Matthew, in the beginning, I was a security blanket. My letters and photos had a calming effect for him. For me, his letters "called out to me from my mailbox," letting me know they had arrived. In the beginning of Nikki's and my relationship, I wanted her to be my illustrator. I'm sure she wanted quarterly boxes, free stamps, and collect phone calls made to me. But during both friendships with these people, we all realized that we had no expectations or judgments of one another. The friendship was the gift itself.

Before I begin telling you how Nikki and I found the true, unconditional love, freedom to be who we are, to go where we need to go, and do the things we need to do, I'd like to take a brief walk down memory lane. (Just because I think it's time for ol' Dr. Glo-bug to lighten things up.)

After writing for six years, while she was in prison, and knowing of her past negative behavior and lifestyle, you might think I'd have been prepared to understand our huge differences. Nope. It wasn't until Nikki was living under my roof that she told me this particular experience from her past: *being the only one of several women to survive a serial killer's attack in Sacramento.*

The story itself is bloodcurdling; I'll be sharing it later today. In deeper detail, at some time in the future, it will appear in our book *Between Saint & Sinner,* which she and I coauthored. I am mentioning the terrifying experience here only to describe my reaction to her telling me of the incident.

I burst out laughing. Of course, I felt her terror as she told the story and wondered if I would have had the courage to do as she had done.

Why the laughter, then? Because when she said "serial killer," it made me think of my favorite, Cap'n Crunch, breakfast cereal. You know . . . you eat it, and it scratches the roof of your mouth (if you eat if before it gets soggy), and "it's a killer." Life is just a matter of perception, isn't it? Until Nikki came into my "movie," I didn't have a "serial killer" awareness.

Until that moment, I had only known that Nikki and I lived in two different states—she in California, and me in Montana. More than that, she and I lived in two different states of awareness.

We learned of more differences. She liked black, I wore white. She liked night. I love day. We were two completely different personalities, extremely polar, and we loved each other deeply. She had lived an extremely negative past—I was an overly optimistic airhead. Together, we were "the saint and the sinner." We needed one another desperately to bring balance to one another's lives. (Ha! I just realized as I wrote those words—Nikki and I were Training Wheels of support and balance for one another.)

I joined her in Seattle, as support, when she spoke about drugs before five hundred troubled teens. She joined me on stage, teaching workshops. Our dreams together were becoming reality. But then one day, Nikki said she didn't want to be part of the dream any longer. She enjoyed the miracles and inspiration in the moment, but couldn't stand the repetition of me telling the stories at workshops. She comforted me every way she could. "You're the teacher, Gloria.

You have to say it over and over, but I just can't listen to the stories any longer."

My heart was broken the day she left Montana. April 15 . . . I'll never forget. When Kirk returned home from work that night, he asked how my day had been. "Not very good. I just sat on the couch all day and looked out to the mountains. I thought about walking deep into the heart of the forest and digging a deep hole, but I couldn't think of how to get the dirt in on top of me so no one would ever find me again."

Shocked, Kirk replied, "Gosh, hon, I'm very concerned that you're entertaining thoughts of suicide." (Wow. Kirk feared I was going to *"walk out of the movie early."*) I said sarcastically, "Right, Kirk. I'm going to physically walk into the woods, carrying a heavy shovel, dig into rock-hard dirt, and jump into a hole that might have worms or bugs in it. *I don't think so.* I'm just telling you how deep my despair is that Nikki left my life."

I took the entire day to grieve and fully gave myself permission. The many emotions I felt and experienced, I actually welcomed. I felt used, disappointment, anger, frustration, and hate . . . actually every emotion I'd never allowed myself to feel or I wouldn't be a good person. I gave everyone else the right—in fact, full permission—to feel their feelings. But as a human and teacher, I never allowed myself the same courtesy. My greatest healing came through Nikki. I experienced unconditional love so I know it's possible.

My deepest fear that day was, "Can I go on alone, without her, and accomplish my dream?" The answer was yes. By letting go of previous expectations and promises, we were both free to be, to do, and to enjoy our lives. I gave her heartfelt permission and blessings to follow her path, wherever it would lead—even if it was back to prison someday. I trusted Nikki's Divine Guidance. I also trusted that if she reverted to her past lifestyle and got her third strike against society, she would at least be able to teach others behind bars. I was at peace.

When we released one another to go on to our greatest good, our friendship in fact became stronger. We became equals. We were both teachers, on different levels.

I always said I had faith in God, faith in Nikki, and faith in myself. But the *Act of Faith* itself was just a parroted, meaningless phrase until Nikki. I prided myself on being her caretaker and friend as well as spiritual teacher. But in reality, she was the Master Teacher. Not that I'm glorifying sex, or drugs, or prison time as the tools that molded Nikki and her form of teaching. We, as society, could call her a slow learner or bad for taking the path she did. But I believe that where Nikki walked, God walked with her. I don't believe that's a hard act to follow, do you?

Enjoy your Journal!

OPEN YOUR JOURNAL AND ANSWER THESE QUESTIONS

Journal—Chapter Five

1. Being aware now that you have choices/preferences, let's establish some new boundaries. List twenty *new* choices you would like to incorporate into your life. As an example, "I choose to live my life in love, rather than in fear." Or, "I choose happiness."

Begin writing each sentence with the words *I choose* as a reminder when you hear yourself saying *I want*.

2. Are you nice all the time (or pretend to be)? Write about why this is harmful to you.

3. Are you aware of a friend or family member who is attempting to be nice all the time? Describe that person.

Does their behavior confuse you, because their actions don't match how you feel when you're around them? You, being empathic, find it hard to *trust your feelings* concerning these situations. Outwardly, you are hearing them say, "Oh, yes, I would love to do that for you," but inwardly you feel their hesitation.

4. When I was growing up, I might say, "I'm cold." An adult would say, "Oh, you're just being silly. It's not cold in here." Even that simple example was teaching me I couldn't trust my feelings. My feelings weren't validated. I *felt* cold . . . but if an adult said I wasn't, well, then I must be wrong. Write about an example of how you felt one way, but were told to feel another.

5. Do you have a friend, family member, or yourself whom you can't trust because the words and actions don't match? I once had a close relative who *constantly* told me of his love. It drove me crazy because *I couldn't feel it.* Therefore, I placed blame on myself for not being able to accept his love. Write about a time when the words and actions didn't match.

As another example, a close friend's daughter was once selling her vacuum cleaner. Upon hearing of this much-needed item, I immediately wrote and handed the check to her. She promised on her next visit to the area that she would deliver the appliance to her mother, to forward on to me.

Weeks passed and I knew the daughter had been to visit her mother several times. I asked if the vacuum had been delivered. My friend said, "Oh yes, weeks ago, but I decided to keep it for myself." She proceeded to write me a check to reimburse me. I was shocked.

I said, "Excuse me, best friend, I hope you'll forgive the pun, but our friendship really 'sucks.' Your actions just helped me realize that, to you, our friendship means less than dirt."

Unaware that I had a choice, I remained constant and loyal to someone who didn't recognize the best friend she had. Continual harsh and hurtful situations occurred.

Now that you're aware you have the choice to consciously no longer place yourself in hurtful relationships, I hope one of your new choices is, "I choose friends who treat me honestly, with integrity and love."

Describe an example of any person (friend or family member) who disrespects you as an individual.

6. Are you afraid to be honest with friends or loved ones, fearful you'll lose them, if you tell them how you really feel (concerning any situation, even if it's trivial)? Write to these people, telling them how you really feel. *Do not give them your letter.* Remember: This is for *you.* Writing it down will give you practice, until you can feel safe and courageous enough to say it aloud to them.

7. Are you bulimic or anorexic, and attempting to hide it from others? Do you feel emotionally starved?

When you don't eat, you feel energized and powerful after the initial deep pain. I'm sure you like this feeling. I did. You are, however, in a physical body that needs to be maintained or you are going to croak—graveyard dead. Be aware that by practicing the Presence, you can continue to experience those natural/super highs without endangering yourself.

We need to get some meat on your bones, because the physical *and* spiritual must be in balance. I know you get a lot of attention because you're so thin. The comments "feed you" because you're so hungry for attention. Been there, done that—you can't trick ol' Dr. Glo-bug. I know exactly how you feel.

Write about your need for attention. Write down how long you've been feeling this way. What is your favorite reason for being anorexic or bulimic? Is your life so out of control that you feel empowered to at least be in control of this situation?

Do you think you *are* in control of the situation? Are you in denial, believing you don't have a problem? Are you scared that you can't stop this behavior, that it's gotten out of hand? Until you begin being recharged and eating normally, would you please promise me that you'll eat at least a half—or more, if you can—of a peanut butter *and* honey sandwich and get some Keebler Graham Crackers to help ease the nauseousness you feel? It's hard. I know. But you can do it. I'll walk every step with you. You don't need to be afraid; I'll be your friend. Any comments?

8. Have you ever thought of *"walking out of the movie early"*? Write about the feelings and thoughts that made you consider doing this.

9. Nikki's past lifestyle appeared negative and self-destructive, which on a human level, it was. She helped countless convicts with her growth, as well as family and friends. She lives in a new home—the first she's had in forty-nine years of her life. She is a valued employee and an asset to society. John Walsh lost his son to a kidnapper/murderer. He went on to create a children's program that has relocated and saved countless children. A mother who lost her daughter to a drunk driver founded Mothers Against Drunk Drivers (MADD). Those three people have taken negative situations and transformed them into positive, helpful services for humanity. What negative situation has occurred in your life that could be

transformed to enlighten or help humanity on a global scale?

If you can't think on a global scale right now, begin smaller. How can your experiences help others in your school and workplace? Or maybe even someone you meet on the street in passing. Every experience we have is an opportunity to serve at least one other, if we're willing to share compassionately and openly. Write about this.

Write your heartfelt thoughts in the Journal and state this affirmation aloud. *I trust myself and my feelings. I receive constant validation that what I'm feeling is real.*

6
Birds 'n' Bees 'n' Facts o' Life
(for Daughters)

Mom and Dad, I'd like to borrow your lovely daughters for a while and take them into my home office to speak privately with them. You and the boys can remain here in my living room or kitchen and just make yourselves at home.

All right, girls. I want you to know that I feel honored that your parents trust me enough to allow me to discuss these sometimes sensitive issues with you. At any point that you feel uncomfortable, just let me know and we'll rejoin your parents. I think I'll begin with a few warm-up stories before I spring the birds 'n' bees on ya.

When my eldest stepdaughter, Kerrie, was a junior in high school, she was required to attend a band festival in a neighboring Montana town. Being an avid straight-A student, she was concerned about missing her English class because of an upcoming test. She asked if I would attend in her absence and take notes. I had never heard of a parent doing this for a child, but I agreed to do so, with the permission of her teacher.

Mrs. Stewart gave her approval, and I showed up for Kerrie's first-period class looking more like a student than an adult. I wore a pair of Levi's, a sweatshirt, and, of course, the bells on my tennis shoes. As I walked into the classroom, Mrs. Stewart said, "The school needs an emergency substitute teacher for freshman English today and you're it." Totally unprepared for the offer, I declined. She said, "But we need you." I still attempted to avoid the task. "Kerrie asked me to take notes." Mrs. Stewart promised she wouldn't cover anything my daughter didn't already know.

Making one last stab at convincing her I wasn't the right person for the job, I said, "Look how I'm dressed. This isn't very professional clothing." Mrs. Stewart dismissed it as unimportant. She notified the office that a replacement was available and escorted me down the halls to the classroom of fourteen- and fifteen-year-olds who awaited me. I wrote my name, "Mrs. B.," on the chalkboard and waited for the morning bell.

Assigning them quiet time to read for the first quarter of their period with me, I noticed one of the girls in the front row in obvious pain. Being empathic, I knew the problem: She was having cramps on the left side of her abdomen.

Whispering in her ear to avoid any embarrassment, I advised her to quietly remove her shoe and massage her left foot under the inside anklebone. As she pushed on that area of her foot, she found tenderness. She gently massaged, and within just minutes, her pain and cramping were gone. I explained the foot reflexology technique simply to her and a few girls surrounding her. If the cramping was on the right side, they would massage under the right inside anklebone.

Following the quiet time, I had the students move their chairs into a circle, taking turns reading aloud. We were interrupted by a neighboring teacher, who asked our group gruffly, "Why are you in here alone? *Where is your teacher?*" Intimidated by his tone, I slowly raised my hand and replied, "I am the teacher." Embarrassed, he responded, "I thought you were one of the kids." (This is a perfect example of why I wanted to grow up to be tall, sleek, and sexy! Adults have treated me like a child my entire life due to my small stature and youthful appearance. I understand how adults can disrespect and intimidate teens . . . because I'm nearly fifty and they still do it to me!)

The last few minutes of the class, one of the freshmen approached me and said, "Mrs. B., if you'd just put a *big ear* on your sweatshirt and roam these halls, the kids would come out of the woodwork to talk to you. You'd make such a great counselor."

I replied, "You don't even know me . . . what makes you think that?"

"Just a feeling I have," she said. "In fact, better yet—go downtown and rent an office and we'll find our way to you. We just need somebody to talk to."

The bell rang, dismissing the kids, and I sighed heavily as they departed because I still wasn't sure why I was there that day. Surely they could have found someone to supervise a classroom of kids in the teacher's absence. Why me?

The next incoming group of teens entered. Somehow, following that first class, word spread throughout the school about the temporary emergency substitute teacher, Mrs. B. The students that day opened their hearts and told me who was pregnant, who was drinking, who was abused at home, and where the parties were being held. For some reason, even as a parent, I wasn't a threat. These kids wanted to talk to a grown-up and they sensed I was safe—and I was. It's my nature to be neutral, nonjudgmental, and nonthreatening. I came home that day with far more knowledge than I ever thought I was going to learn by going to school to take a few simple notes for Kerrie.

A few weeks later, I received a call from a freshman girl.

She informed me that the school counselor had referred her to me to discuss her problem. Surprised, I asked, "The *school counselor* wants you to talk to *me?*" She affirmed it again. When I asked, "Why would the counselor send you to me, rather than counseling you herself?" the teen responded, "She said you would be very easy to talk to . . . Also," she added, "legally, she can't advise me on this problem or she'll have to call in my parents and the authorities."

At that time, I still didn't get it. I wasn't an ordained minister then, nor did I have a Ph.D. I was just an inspirational writer and mom.

Compassion kicked in, because I could feel the child's fear, and I arranged for her to come by after school to talk. In moments, she felt comfortable in my presence and addressed the issue. She feared she was pregnant and if she was, her parents were "going to kill her."

Never having dealt with this personally, I could only relay the sequence of events, logically, that I thought would be best. First of all, a doctor's appointment to confirm or deny the possible pregnancy. Perhaps she was worrying needlessly. Second, if she was pregnant, I promised I'd go with her to tell her parents. Third, she obviously needed more information about birth control and pregnancy. Luckily, when the tests were taken, she wasn't pregnant.

It hadn't been that long before that I'd given my first "mommy–daughter talk," one evening, riding in a car in the darkness so neither of us could see the other blushing or embarrassed. With today's vivid movie sex scenes and available information, I still found it uncomfortable to talk to my kids about sex.

Somehow, my opening statement escaped my lips. "When a boy kisses you, you're going to feel something you've never felt before." And then I openly shared all the information and feelings that I thought my daughter could understand. Ignorance is *not* bliss. Awareness is. The first kiss, or the first time you make love, should be exciting. Making love is an intimate act that *can* be the closest feeling of God's pure love and power that we can feel and experience consciously in our dimension. Unfortunately, in our society today, sex and love don't necessarily go hand in hand.

Two nights ago, I had a dream that took me back in time to my high school years. In the dream, my *friend* Randy gave me a kiss. Not an exciting kiss . . . and yet I knew where it would be leading. In the next scene of the dream, he and I were removing our clothing and—surprise, surprise—my mom walked in. Although he and I were both "exposed," I was trying to convince my mom how innocent it was, no matter how it looked. In my head and heart, in the dream, I knew I wasn't going "to let it get out of hand," but it already had, hadn't it?

The guy I dreamed of was only a friend, and there was no passion between us in our high school years. The only reason I could think of having such a dream was to prepare me for today and this part of the talk, reminding me of what it's like on the level of a teen or preteen and dealing with this issue. Following this example, I'll explain more on how we *allow* our experiences to get out of hand.

When I first married, at age eighteen, I was diagnosed with fibrocystic breast disease, which means "lump, with tenderness." The caffeine in coffee, sodas, and chocolate didn't help. My physician believed a shot of the male hormone testosterone would relieve the pain. Which it did. With side effects—it made me a frisky little bugger. I was merely walking through the grocery store doing my regular shopping one day when I felt the strongest need for sex. Not later, but *now*. I literally left my cart, full of groceries, and went home. My newly married husband, of course, was delighted.

The hormone wore off and my breasts began hurting again. I went back to the doctor and requested another one of those shots. He denied my request, stating that with too much of the hormone, my voice would begin deepening and I would start growing facial hair. I replied in a pretend deep, sexy, sultry voice, "I wouldn't mind . . . having a deep, sexy, sultry voice." The answer was no. (Dang!)

That experience gave me more compassion for men and boys than I'd ever had. They have that hormone flowing throughout their veins daily. No wonder they have one-track minds! So girls, let's be a little more patient and understanding with the opposite sex. Our teasing, flirting, and seductive clothing heightens their friskiness—which probably doesn't need to be heightened.

It will sound so corny but, *honest to goodness,* your body should be honored. Hopefully, this day together is going to increase your awareness of how valuable you are, so you no longer take risks toward pregnancy, disease, rejection, or being degraded.

I will teach you pride in yourself before this day ends. You do not have to give that much of yourself to be liked or approved of. You don't have to prove yourself to anyone, for any reason. Anyone who asks you to risk yourself is not honoring you.

I was a hooker in a past life(!), which Spirit showed me one evening as my mind opened to a "wide-screen TV." I was shown the vision so I would be less likely to experience judgment when Nikki appeared in my life. I'd been there, done that, walked in those moccasins, which gave me the empathy for her chosen occupation in this lifetime.

During a discussion, Nikki said, "I remember walking late-night Sacramento streets on uneven pavement and feeling terror over the echo produced by the clicking of my three-inch heels. Something new. I had acquired a new sense of fear to heap on the old, deadened fears. Late bloomer or hardheaded, who can say?

"By then, I'd been raped several times, left for dead by a serial killer, stabbed twenty-three times in an attempted gang hit, been to prison twice, and experienced innumerable other events that should have inspired 'echo fear' much sooner. Fear had finally saturated through the heroin.

"No cure. Collapsing veins trying to be fed three grams of heroin a day. Nude-colored Band-Aids covering abscesses under tan-colored panty hose. All compassion, for myself or anyone else, shrunken to Raisinette proportions. I'd accomplished a comfortable emotional zombyism just to find fear in an echo."

Nikki, being a teenage runaway, teenage know-it-all, and experiencing teenage pregnancy, didn't have job skills to rely on. Her choices trapped her in an unhealthy lifestyle, which I am using as an example to help make you aware so you can make more responsible choices.

Animal lust, which I felt with the sex from the shot of testosterone, is what guys and gals experience in one-night stands. Making love is something else: pure love. The difference between lust and love is that love involves the deepest respect for self and other. Love energy can enhance your Oneness with God, life, and one another.

Spiritually speaking, when you have a close encounter and join, you are becoming One with that person on a physical level. You, from then on, share the same energies for approximately ninety days. That means you carry his fears, attitudes, weaknesses, strengths, and ideas. If they aren't lofty ideas or you begin feeling abnormal negative feelings, maybe they aren't yours. You just "borrowed" them by sharing the same energy field through having sex.

I'm not sharing this to frighten you or gross you out, I'm giving you awareness so you can be more selective. Look at the person's overall behavior. Look at his present state of consciousness. It's not hard to see, because "it" appears physically as the way he dresses, walks, speaks, acts, and treats himself and others. Ask yourself, "Who do I choose to share my energy field with?"

Okay, take a deep breath and we'll continue. Oh. Okay, I'll take a deep breath, too. (I had to before I continue.) Kids these days are more grown up than in my generation. You wear makeup earlier, get a computer at ten, and believe you're ready to have sex by twelve. Bless your hearts. The world has so accelerated and stimulated your feelings that unless you can add excitement from sex, drugs, or frightening action-packed movies, your desensitization makes you feel numb to life.

As with most adults, you like instant gratification. Waiting, working toward a dream, or sacrificing now to save for later are some of the values that have become lost.

I'm not asking you to "save yourself for marriage." I'm asking you to look at the truth of your expectations when you become involved with a boy/man. What is it you're seeking? Just because he sleeps with you doesn't mean there will be a lasting relationship. Do you fantasize about being married to him? Some girls believe if a man shares this experience, she is special to him. Maybe and maybe not. Just because you have sex doesn't mean that a marriage and commitment will take place.

A good mother–daughter talk should include how *not* to put yourself in an uncomfortable situation that may be difficult to get out of. Avoiding it to start with is easiest. You can use your parents as the "bad guys" in a stressful situation—for example, "My parents will kill me and definitely you." Your parents don't mind being disliked. They're not playing this role in your life for a popularity contest. They don't lie awake at night trying to think of ways to make your life a living hell. *Most parents* only want what's best for you and no one in the world is going to love you as much as they do. (Except maybe you by the time you get through with this day.)

Helpful hints for preventing an unwanted sexual encounter:

- Double-date.
- If a boy wants to spend time with you, meet in a public place.
- Walk, when possible. The exercise is good for you both anyway.
- When you take a boy into your room to listen to music or talk, keep the door open. (Whether Mom and Dad are home or not.)
- Don't have a boy over when your parents aren't home. (Too much temptation.)
- Kissing and affectionate touches are normal. However, they can get out of hand quickly. It's up to you girls to be in control.

If you feel things are going too far, *act* on that feeling *immediately* or you may find it's too late. You may need to "suddenly remember" that you were supposed to be home an hour ago. Always follow your gut and if you're uncomfortable, leave immediately. Practice following your intuition. Remember that having sex is a personal decision that no one should attempt to make for you.

If you find yourself way far into the *Oh, boy, I've really gone and done it now* phase, feel safe in saying no. Say no in any way necessary to get your point across.

I know your hormones are raging, too. It's part of growing up. But remember how I told you that my parents and teachers made all my decisions and when I turned eighteen, I was expected to know how to make choices? This part of our discussion can be considered pretraining on how to make responsible, clear choices *now.*

What if you become pregnant? Would you use abortion as a form of birth control? Can you abort? Does it feel right in your heart to do so? Could you live with your decision? Could you feel and withstand the fears of raising a child alone, possibly on welfare if your parents refused to help? Do you even like kids? Can you handle the responsibilities that go with parenting?

Think about these questions and answer honestly in your Journal. Thank you, girls, for this time we've had together. Could you please send the boys in here, so we can have some time alone, as well?

OPEN YOUR JOURNAL AND ANSWER THESE QUESTIONS

Journal—Chapter Six

1. Has a parent, friend, or teacher explained the birds 'n' the bees fully to you? Not in a deep way, with words and terminology you don't understand, but simply so you can get it? Write down some of your questions, especially those you think others would consider stupid if you asked them.

2. Are you afraid to say no to a boy? Have you already been intimate? Do you experience feelings of guilt? Do

you have a reputation for "being easy"? Are you afraid you'll lose your boyfriend if you say no? Do you worry that if you say no, you'll hurt his feelings or make him angry? What about *your* feelings? (They're important, too.) Write about how saying no makes you feel.

3. If you had a sexually transmitted disease, would you be honest with a partner before you were intimate?

4. If you contracted a sexually transmitted disease, would you be willing to seek medical attention? Many kids are so ashamed or embarrassed that they fear telling their parents. Please don't put yourself at risk with needless fears. If you suspect you have an STD, seek medical help as soon as possible.

By the way, if you are thinking of running away, or have, contact a church or a state agency hot line. They will help you in your confusion, finding a safe place for you. If you're living at home now and the conditions seem unbearable, don't run to the streets. *Ask for help,* because help is available. If you don't get help the first time, keep asking. Or ask someone else. There is a safer place than the street.

5. What if you become pregnant? What is your plan?

6. Could you live with your decision? If not, write why it would be so difficult to live with.

7. Do you even like kids?

8. Have you felt unloved and think having a child would fulfill that need?

9. Could you handle the responsibilities that go along with parenting? Are you patient and consistent?

10. What are some ideals you would choose to display as a mother?

11. When do *you* think family planning should realistically begin? How many children do you think you'd like

to have? At what age would you choose to have your first child?

Write your heartfelt thoughts in the Journal and state this affirmation aloud. *I am empowered to say yes when I mean yes, and no when I mean no.*

7

Boys Will Be Boys—and
So Will Men (for Sons)

Okay, guys, we have a lot of ground to cover. Pull up a chair and get comfy. You might even want to take notes . . . Don't panic now. This won't be so bad.

I was fourteen years old and it was November 10 at ten-thirty the night I received my first kiss *on a real date*, but who's being a sentimental softie? After my invitation to a high school dance, Gary walked me two miles home from the school. On the corner lot, adjoining our home, we were uncomfortably saying our good-byes.

I guess he was the brave one who finally placed his hands softly upon my shoulders, stopping me from fidgeting from one foot to the other. He pulled me into his safe arms and only hugged me at first.

My best girlfriend, Barbara, and I had been practicing the hug and *head tilt* for this forthcoming cherished moment, for weeks, before the dance. Everyone knows that when you kiss, the guy tilts his head one way and the girl the other. She and I were both scared, because what if . . . in that big moment we'd waited for . . . the guy leaned his head to his right for the kiss and you leaned your head the same way? How silly would it be if our man and us didn't comfortably fit together in that romantic encounter? It would wreck the kiss! But here Gary and I were in one another's arms, a tickle in my tummy anticipating our lips joining. "Thank God," I thought as he tilted his head to his left and I got to tilt mine to my practice position (to the left). As he kissed me, *wow*, was he ever a great kisser. On a scale from one to ten, he went off the charts. Not that I'd had any practice to compare it to, but it felt as good as those kisses looked that Elvis gave in the movies. It was just dreamy. (And so it should be.)

Barb and I counseled one another how silly it would be to *ever* open your eyes while kissing. What if the guy opened his eyes and saw you looking back at him? Of course it would be hilarious, because we see double with our eyes open that closely. The laughter would be enough to ruin the moment.

Nevertheless, I had to do it. Even against fair warning. I don't know why I had to, I just did. But to make myself only half wrong, I only opened my left eye. I saw the moon, bright and white, and thought how romantic it was to be kissed beneath it. Our lips parted and we said our final good-byes and thanks for the wonderful evening. He walked me to the door and I watched him walk away so he could walk the last remaining mile to his home. Me? I think I probably just floated into the house.

But just think! That first kiss was so important to us that we actually practiced first. This may be silly, but it illustrates how truly important girls consider their relationships to boys. Guys don't need to try to make girls like them. They (we) already do. So there. You can relax about ever having to worry about that again.

I think, in reality, women greatly adore their males. To their (our) secret hearts, we believe you to be the magnificent creatures you are. We may not always agree with what you choose to do with that magnificence. But you don't have to try to impress us. We're already impressed.

What we need is to be able to work together. To appreciate each other's special traits. And not *just* our physical "special traits" that you males seem so particularly interested in.

Males and females differ in the ways that they think. It makes sense that combining our two ways of thinking would make our whole world a better place. Learn to problem solve and compromise.

Take two varying perspectives and meet somewhere in the middle. Bear in mind that this bit of information applies to your future, as well as every other portion of your life. You will be dealing with the opposite sex for the rest of your life. Learn now to see them first as humans—then as partners—then as a cherished loved one.

Whenever you reach the "cherished loved one" stage, it is probably the optimal time to make love. You'll note that I used "make love" instead of "having sex." That's because when you get to "cherished loved one stage," it is *making love*. (And let me tell you kids, making love is a *whole lot* better than "having sex.") And remember, intimate contact was never meant to be so difficult to understand.

To be engaged in making love, spiritually speaking, is to keep in mind the highest good for yourself and other. This is like having the magic key. Your relationships will only be able to flourish. All of your pitfalls happen when you leave the path of highest good for self and other. Sex troubles, drug troubles, all the troubles. Speaking of sex and drugs, let's move on to a couple of gang stories. These stories demonstrate certain pitfalls, but also moments of unconditional love.

When I received interstate parole approval to bring Nikki to Montana, I flew to Sacramento to pick her up. Our first day together, with her as a parolee, she took me to meet family and friends from her past. As we took the path down her shadowy past, I met drug dealers, friends on welfare, and people existing in filthy conditions. I had a million questions for her that day and by evening, I felt like someone had put blocks of concrete on my feet. "How had she survived all this?" I wondered.

Before we caught the plane back to Montana, I met her "true love." She had been writing to him from prison for years. He had shown his love by supplying her with drugs and money when she was unable to prostitute herself or care for her needs while she was recovering from a client's attack. This man—I'll call him Roach—was also the leader of a large gang. Proudly, he took me on a tour of their clubhouse, which was filled with Harleys and other bikes. I silently wondered if some or all of them were stolen; reading my thoughts, he said, "Ya know, Gloria, I never stole from anyone who didn't deserve it." He didn't want to "lose my approval."

I asked Roach innocently, "If I wanted to be a member of your gang, what would I have to do to be admitted?"

Gruffly he said, *"Anything I told you to."*

I asked, "But like what? Give me an example."

His voice became harsh as he said again, *"Anything I told you to do."*

Still not getting it, I asked a third time, "Like what? Name an example so I can see how willing I'd be to be part of your club."

Patiently, but with authority, he responded, pointing, "If I told you to drink that mud puddle, you'd better start drinking."

Like a Valley Girl, ticktocking my head back and forth and in a dumb-blonde voice, I asked, "But why would I want to do that?"

Angrily he yelled, "Because I *told you to do it.*"

I must have driven this guy nuts about then, as I asked again, "But why would I wanna do that?"

Nikki, about this time, seeing Roach's frustration concerning me and my innocence replied, "Roach, honey, I've been trying to tell you . . . all these years in letters from prison . . . this is just who she is."

It was time to go, time for the two of us to say good-bye to Roach as well as to Nikki's past with him. He was a mountain of a man, standing six feet four and weighing nearly three hundred pounds. I stood on a chair to comfortably hold him and hug him good-bye. He whispered in my ear, "I love Linda [Nikki] more than words can say and I know you love her, too. But I have to let her go because there's no way I can ever give her all you can." This man loved Nikki unconditionally and released her to go on to her highest good . . . Just think, a *gang member* demonstrating unconditional love. (You never know where love will turn up, huh?)

Roach, as the leader of this gang, served as a father figure to his followers. He made sure they were taken care of, teaching them, to the best of his ability, how to survive. I'm not glamorizing misdeeds, misconduct, and crimes against society. In God's Mind, there are many mansions . . . different levels of consciousness. Roach, at his level, was serving others in the only way he knew how. He gave boys and men a place to come when society and peers had rejected them as *misfits.*

I know this is changing the subject somewhat, but thinking of Roach and his type of life, and speaking of Nikki's parole to Montana, reminded me of the word *freedom.* Until September 11, 2001, when New York and Washington were attacked, I don't think our nation really understood the meaning of freedom. I walk around my neighborhood nightly, and following our nation's attack, each house had flags displayed, even if it was simply drawn on paper by elementary schoolchildren and taped to the front window. As I walked, I noticed, too, that TVs were turned off; through one window, I saw a family singing around a piano.

I'm going to read you an excerpt from a letter I received from Matthew. Through pen and paper alone, he expresses the reality of freedom being lost.

I went "outside" today for my daily hour of looking at the sky and to get a little fresh air. It was cloudy and raining. I love the rain. I stood under the rain and turned my face up to the sky. I got soaking wet, but I didn't mind. For a minute or two, I wasn't here. No voices. No doors slamming, no P.A. system blaring, no radios playing. Just utter silence.

But then the sounds started to come back one by one and the reality of where I am slammed back home. And I smiled. I smiled because I had escaped and there was nothing the Department of Corrections or the court system could do about it. I smiled because God had given me a few minutes to cry and no one would know if it was tears on my cheeks or raindrops. I smiled because I wasn't sure which one it was, either. I smiled because this place hasn't diminished my capacity to have normal human emotions, no matter how hard they try. I smiled because there are people in this world like you, Gloria. People who won't turn a deaf ear and wrinkle their face in disgust at the mere mention of the word *convict*. People who will try to guide a lost soul to the road home and voice words of encouragement every step of the way.

I smiled because I am still able to smile. And I smiled because I know that tomorrow, when my hour arrives, I will once again be free. Just for a few minutes, that's all I need.

It's funny. When guards see you smile, they think you're planning something ominous or you're high on drugs. They think you're mentally disturbed. But sometimes I see someone come in from his "hour," and he has a faint smile and I think to myself, "He's crazy or on drugs." Yeah, I seem to forget. I fall back into the convict mentality just that quick. I'm not perfect. Look where I'm at. But tomorrow, if it's raining, I'll remember.

Men in prison don't have the luxury of exposing their feelings or they're seen as weak, I'm told. But boys/men have feelings, too. They need more ways for it to be okay to express themselves. Boys may think that crying will make them appear weak. It's not true. Women may not want a crybaby, but neither does a man. I've never met a woman who's not truly and tenderly touched and concerned when she sees a man cry. It brings out the nurturer in us and deepens our love. If we weren't meant to cry, we wouldn't be biologically designed to do it.

Feelings, by the way, are used to get your attention. They are not meant to be blocked and rejected. They are meant to be felt and thought about. After a while, the feeling moves along to be replaced by another. Blocked feelings will store, energetically, in the body, creating an imbalance that can eventually lead to illness or pain. Feelings are meant to be felt.

Guys, I forewarned the girls to check out your state of consciousness, how you act, dress, and behave. But I'm going to give you the same advice.

If you're tall, dark, and handsome, you'd better be extremely careful because you're the first on the list they dream about—the "I want a boy of my very own!" list. Girls who are unhappy living at home are not above getting pregnant on purpose. If this occurs, remember that you are not a victim—you are a co-creator by not making responsible choices.

If you're a nerd, or someone not terribly popular, somewhat inferior feeling, you are the next level who should be aware. You will feel so grateful for a girl's attention, you'd do practically anything to get and keep it. You'll want to please, because you're so grateful anyone would have you—and girls/women will take advantage of your inferiority complex (as well as your wallet).

Someone wonderful awaits you. In fact, she's seeking you right this moment, so be patient and pay attention so you don't walk past her. Watch where your attention is drawn in a crowd of people. Watch, look, and listen to that still small voice within you . . . your heart. *Heads up, walk tall and proud* because no matter what you look like on the outside, this girl/woman is going to be looking with her heart. So now that you know there's someone looking for you, how are you going to recognize her?

Use your feelings! That's what they're for. When you meet a girl, how do you feel? As you get to know her, how do you feel? If you feel good, keep learning more about this girl. Problems arise when you *don't* pay attention to your feelings. If your feelings become negative and draining, that is your spirit trying to tell you things aren't for your highest good.

Remember: You deserve the best!

In my particular experience, when Kirk and I met, he was a single parent, raising and providing for Kerrie and Jaime alone. I wasn't expecting *to use him*. I was trying to figure out *how to be useful to him*. He worked all day, only to come home and do all the house chores. He cooked and cleaned, without the services of a maid or ever a day off.

Having been an organized and successful housewife, I could relieve him of these duties. I could serve him in various roles, making his burden lighter, not heavier.

If a girl/woman finds herself attracted to you, ask yourself honestly, "How will she make my life better?" Will she strengthen your energy field or drain it?

(Girls, if you're reading this chapter, which I hope you are, I'm asking you to do the same with the boys/men. Be honest and ask yourself these questions.)

Guys, most of all, how does she treat you? With kindness, respect, and sensitivity? Is she affectionate? Once again, go with how you *feel*. Feelings are immediate spiritual guidance.

Does she have addictions? You may think it is a marvel now if she joins you at a party and can drink you and all your pals under the table. But in real life, she'll be hiding the vodka bottle under the sink, behind the trash sacks. (She'll feel guilty as hell, of course, but guilt isn't going to make the problem go away . . . nor will your concern or nagging.)

It won't be too funny to deal with later, so if she has a drinking (or drug) problem now, it won't get any better later—unless she herself decides to do something about it. You'll know if she means it, because she will take physical action and just do it. Otherwise, please don't keep your fingers crossed and falsely trusting. *Action* is the key word. She either takes it or you are conscious of where it all goes from here.

Look at the divorce rate and the amount of pain it's caused countless children and families. Three days after I married, at the ripe old age of eighteen, I knew that I had made a mistake. I got in the truck to leave, drove to the edge of town, and wondered where I thought I was going. I turned around and went back home, and stayed nineteen more years. I'm not saying divorce is the way to go. Just because I'm a slow learner, doesn't mean you need to be one. This is my gift to you . . . to help increase the awareness you have.

I just sighed with relief that I courageously said some of these things to you. I am trying to put myself in your position, to teach in a style that won't lose your attention. But I'm also attempting to give information that your parents won't freak out about. Some of you may have noticed that it's hard for your parents to talk to you about this sort of thing. That's because *our* parents didn't talk to *us* about it. We may not talk about it "right," but at least we're trying. Maybe the divorce rate won't be so high for your generation.

My goal today is to strengthen the family unit. Were you aware that a world leader once documented in our history records that his country didn't need to attack our nation because we would destroy ourselves from within? His prophecy was that through our lowered moral standards and ethics, greed, selfishness, and self-hatred, we would eventually self-destruct. Remember how waving a red flag can make a bull want to charge? When I heard that statement about our country self-destructing, I made a vow to do what I personally could to prove that leader wrong.

The superpower of love will mend the human soul and our world. In this time we have together, I'm giving you a little extra love—in fact, take all you want, because there's plenty for everyone. It's an inexhaustible supply.

Guys, aren't you starting to feel better about yourselves? The bigger picture doesn't look quite as overwhelming, does it, once you have a little more awareness?

Thanks for this time together, but I suppose it's time to send your parents in so I can talk with them next.

Enjoy your Journal!

OPEN YOUR JOURNAL AND ANSWER
THESE QUESTIONS

Journal—Chapter Seven

When my grandfather turned a hundred years old, he was asked, "What's the best thing about being one hundred?" He responded without forethought: "No peer pressure." You just have to hang around that long, or do something about it sooner to change how others control your actions, decisions, and styles.

When my grandpa turned 101, he was knocked to the floor in the nursing home by a little old lady and her weapon, a cane. It seems he had offended her by saying, "I haven't had a piece of tail in a very long time." Good grief. You guys just never give up, do you?

1. What attracts you most to the opposite sex? Their bodies, personalities, or the feelings you experience when you're in their presence?

2. Are you afraid you must put the moves on a girl early in the relationship?

3. Write about an example of being judged, concerning sex or anything else that may have hurt your feelings.

4. What does commitment to another mean to you? Think about the perfect mate and relationship you would like to experience. Write about it.

5. Are you in a gang? If so, what drew you to join? Did you feel unaccepted/rejected by your peers or society? Did you undergo an initiation to prove your devotion to the leader? How can your gang experience serve you to help yourself and others? Write about your experiences.

6. Are you aware when a girl/woman is trying to

change you? List an example of a time when being yourself wasn't "good enough."

7. How do you handle rejection? With humor, pretending it doesn't hurt? Or with a self-assured, but false sense of self-confidence? Describe an experience of rejection and how you felt.

8. If you find you repeat the same patterns, attempt to determine what they all have in common emotionally and behaviorally. Make a list of your motivations for dating.

9. Write about how you feel when a girl says no.

10. Do you like kids? How many can you foresee choosing to have? At what age will you choose to start a family?

11. What is your idea of a perfect wife? Write your dream relationship.

12. If you could be (and you *can be*) any kind of father and husband, what ideals would you choose to express?

Write your heartfelt thoughts in the Journal and state its affirmation aloud. *I am willing to love myself as much as I have been willing to love another.*

8

United We Stand
(Words of Praise for Parents)

I'm so glad to have this time alone with you parents. Most people tell you all you're doing wrong as a parent, but today, if you don't mind, I'd like to tell you everything you're doing right. If you can stand waiting for that pat on the back for just a few minutes, though, I'd like to tell you a story.

Recently I was flown to Los Angeles to help a dying six-year-old child. A Catholic priest had heard about me. His church believes in laying on of hands and miracles, and with the church sanctioning, it was recommended that I be brought in.

The tragedy of September 11, 2001, had occurred only weeks before. Our local Farmers State Bank here in Stevensville, Montana, was selling shirts to raise money for the relief effort. I purchased a sweatshirt and a T-shirt that said, UNITED WE STAND, with the American flag on the front. Under the flag, the words read: MONTANA CARES. I packed these shirts, as well as my favorite purple T-shirt that says, EXPECT A MIRACLE.

This child had brain cancer. The doctors had told the

parents, "Fly in the little healer from Montana, but don't get your hopes up." The child, Alexandra, had already had several brain operations. One of these surgeries had cost her her vision, as she now saw double. Another surgery had cost her the hearing in her right ear. This fifth surgery, the doctors said, would leave her paralyzed on the left side . . . or dead, and neither was a good option.

I arrived on Sunday and Alexandra's surgery was scheduled for four days later, on Thursday. On Wednesday, the day before the surgery, she was scheduled for an MRI. Before the family left for the hospital, they stopped at my motel for one last prayer and healing session.

As I greeted them at my motel room door, I happened to be wearing the long-sleeved cotton T-shirt I'd purchased before leaving Montana. As I hugged Lee, the mother, I whispered in her ear, "Today, we stand united *as one mother,* under God, indivisible, unconditional, all-powerful . . . with perfect health for all."

Lee asked for a healing from her own fears and stress, as well. She had never read any of my books, nor was she aware of the violet light. When we finished the session, she asked, "Gloria, I just saw a violet light and it was coming together in the center of my vision and flowing away from me, like it was traveling down a tunnel. What does that mean?" I smiled and said, "The purification of the consciousness of this situation has occurred. Lee, we need to expect a miracle!"

I walked the family to their car, and I hugged each one of them. As I held Lee, the voice of Spirit spoke through me: "Lee, remember, today we stand united as one mother. You be My hands, and I will be your peace."

The first miracle began with the traffic. What should have taken an hour and a half to drive took thirty minutes. Lee later said that it was like an invisible Presence had gone before them and moved traffic out of their way. I even wondered, was time altered? Had we transcended the worldly and touched the heavenly realm? At any rate, thus began one miracle after another.

During the MRI, the child was to lie completely still for four sets of pictures on four different areas. During those sixteen minutes, Alexandra had to remain in the same position, without movement. For a small child, lying perfectly still for that amount of time would seem like eternity. To assist her child, Lee stood next to the table, tapping sixty counts on Alexandra's foot, and touching the other foot, following those taps, to let her know, "Okay, there's one minute."

During this procedure, Lee's back began aching. Still holding her daughter's foot with one hand, she bent over the table, resting her head on her hand to relieve the stress in her back. Normally not having a deep lung capacity, she found herself breathing so deeply that as she exhaled she was blowing the breath down across Alexandra.

As she related the experience later to me, she said, "Gloria, my hand *became the hand of god*. I couldn't have moved it if I had wanted to. I was superglued to Alexandra's foot. I was in awe that the Holy Spirit was breathing through me, as I was pulled up and out of my body, watching as Spirit used my body as the instrument to heal my daughter."

The surgery on Thursday was canceled. Even today, this child experiences perfect health.

And here you sit today, parents, united as one in purpose of getting these children raised. I chose this miracle story because I believe it illustrates a parent's devotion to a child. Although Lee had never heard about me, nor read my book, she had absolute faith in God . . . bringing me into her awareness, to do everything she possibly could to help her daughter. It is miraculous in countless ways how parents sacrifice and unconditionally love. Most kids don't have a clue until they are parents themselves.

I see that level of commitment in your relationship to your children and family. (Give me a "high five"!)

I have to congratulate you, also, because as the babies became toddlers, you never allowed a three-year-old to tell you what he or she would eat or what hour was bedtime. Their crying ended quickly, without further tantrums, when you realized that crying was actually good for kids . . . and of course, they could do it in their room. It's so important that you realized that your quiet time together was important (and necessary), too.

And I think it's great that when one of the kids skipped school, you addressed it immediately, promising to walk them to every class and sit with them, if need be. It takes soo-o-o much energy to be a good parent, and you get another feather in your cap for your efforts. In fact, for everything I'm about to mention that you're doing right as a spiritual family, you get a feather for each compliment. You're going to have so many feathers by the time I get done talking that you can make an Indian chief's headdress, plus a little feather duster, both to share.

Oh, and I really would like to remove the guilt you carry about reading papers found in your child's bedroom. I know that kids believe they should have privacy, and I hope their Journals can remain private, but it all depends on the child and what's going on around him or her. I believe I'll follow your example and know that if the behavior of my kids changed, they would lose all rights to privacy; I would make it my job to know every single thing that touched their lives.

I also appreciate your philosophy that allowing someone to be harmful to themselves or others *is not an act of love*. You never once believed that you "have to always be nice and speak softly" if the situation didn't warrant gentleness. I think you're doing a great job as parents! And don't you just *hate it* when you're doing every single thing you can, physically, mentally, emotionally, financially for your family, and some idiot tells you that you're doing it wrong or not well enough?

I knew how much courage it took for you to contact the parents of your child's friend to advise them of the misbehavior. What a tough thing that was to do, but of course if your own child was headed into some kind of destructive behavior, you would have wanted to know, too. It also took great determination, strength, and love to no longer allow that child to be part of your kid's life, unless she or he chose to change.

You are so clear with your children. You choose to know when they'll be home, who they are with, and where they'll be. Keeping all their friends' phone numbers handy sure saves time instead of having to look them all up if you find yourself calling around.

When one of my kids got upset with these simple rules, I was challenged. "I think your rules are stupid. My friends think your rules are stupid. And even some of my friends' parents think your rules are stupid." I had to laugh and I seriously meant what I said, following this manipulation: "Oh . . . my . . . God—I am *so glad* I don't need your friends' parents' approval to know that I'm doing a good job as a parent."

Holy guacamole . . . I think one of the attributes you have, as a parent, is probably one of the best that I've seen in a very long time. You aren't trying to be your kids' "friend." I know that when I introduced my children to you today, I mentioned that Jaime is one of my best friends. She's my buddy and we can talk about anything and enjoy doing everything together. In fact, together we've learned how to have no judgments or expectations of one another, enjoying the freedom to just be who we are. But when she was being raised, I wasn't her buddy—I was her mother.

We can look around us and see that some parents want their children's approval so badly that they think if they're the child's friend . . . they'll be confided in, the child will be more honest, and they'll be "accepted." Maybe you will and maybe you won't. Kids, like adults, can be great pretenders and manipulators. Kids might hate us, rebel against us, and challenge us for power, and if they do—we are "getting something out of it," too. But our role as parents is not to be their friend at the cost of fearing loss of approval, or allowing them to run the show or do things that are not appropriate.

So plain to see, you have taught your children manners and how to respect your belongings and other people's property. You have invested so much time, attention, energy, and love. From all appearances, your investment has paid off.

You don't believe it's bad for your children to work for what they want. What a great philosophy! That alone teaches them to appreciate what they have. When I get you all back together as a family, I'll have to tell you how Kirk and I "blew it" by giving one of our children too much, unearned.

Each of your kids has assigned chores to help you, and I have to agree, I think that's very important. Saying that made me snicker; it reminded me of when Danielle was fourteen and I asked her to fold a load of clothes for me. She gave me "a look" and sighed heavily as she exclaimed and complained, "I have to do everything around here." (Her "reward" for that behavior was to do *all* the laundry for two weeks.)

I left the room and dialed my mother in Colorado. My

sister Sheila answered, and I asked for Mom. She asked (teasingly) what I wanted to speak to Mom about. I told her about Danielle's attitude and explained that I was just calling Mom, in gratitude. Sheila asked why. Since Sheila is a mother of two, I didn't think it would hurt her to hear what I'd be repeating to Mom, so I went through the entire gratitude speech I had prepared. I was right. Sheila needed to hear it, too.

As my sister passed the phone to my mother, I said, "Mom, I'm going to say something and I want you to just say you're welcome. I don't want you to question why." She agreed.

"Mom, I just called to tell you thank you for all you ever did."

She asked, "Why?"

"No, Mom! I asked you not to ask *why*, but to just say *you're welcome* to the compliment."

"But why are complimenting me?"

"Okay, Mom. It's like this. I asked Danielle to fold a load of laundry for me and she rolled her eyes and gave me a look that could kill. Her words were so stupid, though: *I have to do everything*, I repeated in the overexaggerated whine Danielle had used.

"Mom, here's why I called, though. Danielle's words reminded me of me when I was fourteen. I flashed back to the dining room table heaped with towels and the load of whites and you asking me to fold them for you. Folding socks for six sucked, and please don't make me say that ten times fast!"

Still confessing: "Mom, the look Danielle gave me today is the look I gave you on that day. I even remember saying those same words. In that moment, I'm sure you considered slapping me to a peak—and knocking the point off. And now that I'm grown and have so many kids, I realize how difficult it had to be for you. You worked a full-time job, keeping three elderly people for the state, helped Dad get through college, and raised five kids. I just wanted to say I'm sorry. I apologize that I didn't support you more, and to thank you for everything you ever did to make our house a home.

"Oh, and Mom?"

"Yes, Gloria?"

"Next time I call and state, *I just called to say thank you*, would you please just say *you're welcome*, and not ask why?"

When I was a teenager, I thought my mom was a "*b/w*"*-itch*. What a rag . . . from sunup to sundown. She never let up. Parents definitely influence us to be who we are. And you as parents are just as consistent as you should be. Oh, you have weaknesses? You soften, at times? You get suckered sometimes? You get used? They've taken advantage of your goodness? That's okay . . . they're going to grow up and have children and whewie—that's instant karma for ya.

Years later concerning my mom and her "rules," I got revenge.

When I first married, my dad was being transferred from Arizona to Thailand. Mom needed a temporary place to live for a few months while my sister Sheila and brother Bill, finished the school term. The three of them moved into my first home.

Mom started going out evenings to party with a co-worker. She was a nondrinker, but she was spending too much time with a woman who had quite a reputation in town. Being responsible for my two younger siblings while Mom was out, I began to feel anger that she was acting so irresponsibly.

I waited up until midnight one evening. When she came through the front door, I asked where she'd been. Finding my comment comical, she giggled and responded, "Well,

Gloria, I am over eighteen—I think I can take care of myself."

"Laugh if you will, Mom, but I don't care how old you are—when you live in my house, you *will* abide by my rules. I want to know where you're going, when you'll be home, and who you're going to be with. End of subject. Go to your room."

God, that felt good!

We parents need to stick together . . . there's strength in union—let's continue to stand united.

Let's go rejoin your kids in my living room. If you don't mind, I'd like to discuss a few more issues before we sit down for lunch.

Enjoy your Journal!

OPEN YOUR JOURNAL AND ANSWER THESE QUESTIONS

Journal—Chapter Eight

I'm sure you've had plenty of time to think of how your past influenced you. Although I haven't met one individual in this world who doesn't have some complaint about his or her upbringing and the past, in general, this generation is beginning to understand that we choose our parents and experiences in order to mold who we choose to become. Have you taken the time to see the bigger picture or the events leading you through childhood, to understand that it took all those situations to make you who you are today? Have you taken the time to thank your parents for all things great and small?

Do you know a family or friend who is having problems

raising a child? From your outside perspective, is there any helpful advice you can offer? A word of warning: People don't, as a rule, appreciate unsolicited advice. When people are telling me about their situations, I allow them to say everything they need to say, without interruption. When they finish, I ask them, "Are you asking for my advice?" You would be surprised to hear how many times they say no, because they already know the answer(s)—they're just not ready to take action. They like the drama, and far be it from me to remove what they are actually enjoying.

Ask first before you offer advice.

1. List what you feel your weaknesses are.

2. List how you would choose to strengthen these weaknesses.

3. List three places you could go to get educated on these issues. This could be at a library, through a clergyman, psychologist, teacher, and so on.

4. Do your children make you feel like you're a "control freak"? Have you explained to them that leaving a wet bath towel on the furniture can destroy what you have worked hard to attain? Do they understand that a wet towel, thrown in the hamper, can mildew and cause you (or them) extra work? Are they aware that if they don't check the oil on their vehicles, it can ruin the engine and you're not going to bail them out? Are they aware that if they leave food out, it will spoil . . . which is expensive and unnecessary? If you're a parent and are a "control freak"—you just got another feather.

5. Write a list of twenty things you're doing right now that help you realize *you are a good parent.* In one of your weaker moments, where you feel you have failed, or you're tired and getting bombarded by your children, re-

turn to this section and read, reread, re-reread, and know that you are doing a good job.

Write your heartfelt thoughts in the Journal and state this affirmation aloud. *The power of God's love governs, directs, maintains, and sustains my spiritual family.*

9
Ladies and Gentlemen

Welcome back together as a family.

Ladies and gentlemen, I now come before you, to stand behind you, to tell you something I know nothing about. Next Thursday, which is Good Friday, there will be a men's meeting that only women can attend. Admission is free, pay at the door. Take a seat and sit on the floor and we'll discuss the four corners of the Round Table. I ask you, "With all the fast talkers, double talkers, and smooth talkers, is there any reason why we're so confused?"

When I read different books by the same author, I prefer they don't say the same thing in each one, but I have used the above paragraph in one of my other books. I am repeating it to make a point: People sometimes talk in circles and riddles, and some outright lie. I'd like to teach you how to know if a person is speaking the truth.

You are highly telepathic, right now, and with practice, you will not be easily tricked.

Also, many things you take action on, or agree to do, are not your ideas. You receive a thought, and because it's in your head, you assume it's yours. However, the person ask-

ing a favor of you sent the thought in the request, sometimes without words, and you assumed it was yours.

Until you learn to distinguish between what is transferred and what is your decision, let's practice saying, "I'll
think about it and get back to you with an answer." This
gives you a moment so you can feel the request and know if
it's something you'd be willing to do. This way, you no longer
need to do things you don't feel comfortable doing.

You will begin recognizing these circumstances by recall-
ing something you offered to do for a family member or
friend. When they asked, you accepted, but when the time
came to actually do the favor, you really didn't feel like
doing it. You found you had to force yourself. With no desire or energy to do it, you felt resentment rather than joy in
helping. But you *promised* and you're a person of your
word. Still, you felt forced. You then had to fulfill it out of
obligation, and that never feels comfortable. I'm teaching
you how to listen to your heart. When you do, the outcome
will always be in harmony with your soul.

When you rub your hands together and place them over
your eyes, especially at night when you're falling asleep,
you're going to recognize daily how much more telepathic
you are. You will know when people are lying because "you
can't see/imagine their words in pictures within your mind."
Even if a liar practices a rehearsed lie over and over before
telling it to you, there's no substance or picture behind it,
because it never really happened.

You've been in an uncomfortable position before if
you've walked into a room and found a group of two or
three gathered together. They look at you, join in a huddle,
and "whisper whisper whisper" about you. You don't need
to be a rocket scientist or psychically gifted to know they're
talking about you. (It hurt your feelings, but you pretended

not to notice.) Now think back to a moment when, without body language or a visual picture of the gossipers, you *knew* someone was judging you. You felt and knew it.

Maybe you were standing in line at the theater and could feel someone's eyes on you. All of a sudden, you're feeling embarrassed and uncomfortable about the way you're dressed, the way your hair might look, or concerning your behavior. It's because you're hearing or feeling the judgment of another. Judging is a behavior that almost everyone engages in.

Being judged never feels good, but we all experience it from time to time. That still doesn't make it right. Luckily, we can't be judged unless we've first judged ourselves.

Many years ago I spent an entire day writing personalized fairy tales to be given as gifts for upcoming celebrations. I looked at the clock and it was time to pick my kids up from school. I was in a comfy jogging suit and I'd never taken the time to do my hair, so I had "angel wings'n' tweakers" going every which way. I didn't have time to do anything about it, though, so I slipped my feet into some scroungy old house moccasins and ran out the door.

On the way to the school, I was self-conscious and aware of how frumpy I looked. Having a bit of an inferiority complex, I have to try harder sometimes not to dwell on my imperfections.

So on the drive to the school, I silently and audibly affirmed that I wasn't mediocre cute, but beautiful. Boy, those words almost gag me to say since I can't easily believe their truth. As I drove, however, I affirmed that I am youth, beauty, purity, and perfection.

I ran into the school and down the hall to my kids' classrooms, which happened to be across from one another. As they were getting their backpacks together, three different people stopped to make a point of telling me how nice I looked that day. What an immediate feedback I received from holding positive thoughts about myself!

I never read Emily Post's book on etiquette or manners, but I thought my mom had done a pretty good job of teaching our family manners. I was wrong, as I found out for myself in a Seattle, Washington, restaurant. I had torn my dinner roll into four separate pieces, buttering each and taking a bite. My hostess got the most shocked look of disapproval on her face and remarked, "Oh, Gloria. We *never* do that!"

Innocently, I questioned, "Never do what?" (My elbows weren't on the table, my napkin was in my lap, I wasn't licking my butter knife, I wasn't talking with my mouth full, and I wasn't singing at the table. Running all these programmed manners through my head, and checking that list twice, I didn't have a clue what I'd done wrong.)

She responded, "We *never* tear our rolls into so many pieces and butter them all at the same time." She put so much emphasis on the words, *"We never,"* I felt like it had become a matter of national security.

Attempting to protect my feelings and not embarrass me, she continued, "We tear one piece of the roll off at a time, butter it, lay our knife down, and eat the bread." I must have given her my dumb look about that time . . . my forehead wrinkled and eyes squinted and rolling up to the left, searching my memory bank for the truth and validity of her teaching. She apologized, "I'm sorry, Gloria, to tell you all this. But I'm just doing so in case you ever go to London to have lunch with the queen. I'd hate for you to embarrass yourself."

Well, ol' Dr. Glo-bug had to lighten things up again, so I startled her by saying, "If I ever go to London to have lunch with the queen, we'll be so busy discussing her danged dysfunctional kids, we won't have time to worry about my manners."

I mean no disrespect for Her Highness. And I promise, if I ever go to London to bow before the queen, I will be on my best behavior not to embarrass her or her dignitaries who may dine with us. The luncheon isn't likely, but I'll keep the wisdom in case I need it. (Or I just won't eat the dinner rolls.) In fact, ever since that idea was planted in my mind, when I'm ready to tear a roll in half or quarters, I still look over my shoulder to make sure I won't be offending the queen.

In our home, we live under "Benish Law":

1. No fighting.
2. No biting.
3. No scratching.
4. No kicking.
5. No TV until homework is done.
6. Eat your veggies before the dessert.
7. Call if you're going to be later than expected.
8. Be where you say you're going to be and call if the plans change.
9. If you receive a gift of money or an object, you can't spend the money or enjoy the gift unless you first write and mail a thank-you to the giver.
10. Don't disrespect yourself or one another. (And certainly not in front of Mom.)

I drive my kids crazy, too. All parents do, probably. But imagine having a mother who's spiritually gifted and can telepathically read your thoughts. Whewie. Yikes. My kids know they can't lie to me or I'll know. In fact, Danielle has regular confession sessions because it helps relieve her of carrying unneeded burdens. Plus, she's not quite sure how much I know anyway. Just to be on the safe side, she shares it all.

One afternoon a year or so ago, Danielle asked about the following situation. "Mom, a friend and I went to the grocery store, bought something, and received change. One of the quarters was sticky and when we put it in one of those toy machines, it didn't go all the way through. The machine stayed open. Would it be wrong to take lots of toys for the one quarter?"

I turned the question around and gave her a bigger picture to look at.

"Danielle, the money that comes out of that machine helps some man put food on the table and a daughter through college." She gasped and remarked sharply, "Mom! It's just one stupid toy machine in a grocery store." I patiently replied, "Yes, Danielle. And the man who puts food on the table and a daughter through college has lots of those stupid machines in lots of grocery stores."

Now realizing the reality behind her action, she was embarrassed for her behavior. Taking it one step further, rather than telling her the moral, which she would close her ears and mind to anyway if it came from an authority figure, I asked her to tell me how the situation could have been handled. "Danielle, if you were the man who owned the machine, would you prefer that a kid go back into the store and advise someone the machine wasn't working properly? Or would you rather be the man who came to get the money, to buy more toys to replace the inventory . . . finding no money and an empty machine? How angry would you be if you were the man and someone had taken toys they hadn't paid for?"

As she listened to the multiple choices, she realized the right answers and actions to take in future situations.

As a child, I shoplifted. Insignificant ten-cent rings or candy bars. Just like Danielle, I didn't realize that someone had to restock the inventory and take a loss for the missing items. When you become metaphysical or spiritual, realizing your Oneness with all people, you understand that when you steal, you steal from *yourself.*

The Karmic Law that we all live under in this dimension, expressing two powers in constant opposition to one another, also means, "What goes around, comes around." Cause and effect. If you cause another pain, you will at some point feel it, also. If you steal from another person, you will be stolen from. It may not happen immediately. Time may pass and you may forget that you have done an injustice to another . . . whether it's cheating the government, a restaurant that didn't charge you fully for your meal, or a department store. Karma doesn't always use instant feedback.

When your favorite sweater is stolen at school, when you lose a ten-speed bike—or worse yet, a car, or even a ski coat you just bugged your parents into buying—get audited, or lose your job, it's payback time. God isn't punishing you. The Universal Law is merely being set in motion by your thoughts and deeds.

When you make fun of someone, you will be made fun of. When you do a random act of kindness for another, one will be done for you.

The Golden Rule, "Do unto others as you would have them do unto you," now makes more sense, doesn't it? Whatever you do to others, you are doing to yourself.

When you become aware of this Karmic Law, the "feedback" of your actions comes more quickly as a constant reminder. I tease, "If I spit on the sidewalk, I now immediately look up to see if a bird is flying overhead." (Oh yeah, I remember. *Ladies* don't spit.)

The person you're looking at or who treats you badly appears to be a jerk. But he or she is a mirror image for you, of you. Were you just a jerk to someone else?

Spiritual Law is a level of higher consciousness where we recognize ourselves in others and they perform loving deeds and we experience only goodness. Rather than dealing with health today and sickness tomorrow, clarity and knowingness today and confusion tomorrow, or happiness today and sadness ten minutes later, we experience only God's Will. Our experiences show us where our level of consciousness is. The experiences show us when we rise above Karmic Law. We achieve this state of awareness by devoting a few minutes a day to opening our mind to the violet light; we no longer fluctuate between good and bad human experiences.

In our home, besides living with state, county, and federal laws, Karmic and Spiritual Law, we also live under Benish Law. Benish Law includes the ten things I listed previously, plus no littering because we are stewards of this planet. In this home, if you are being mean about yourself, belittling yourself or another, you must say and/or write ten nice things about yourself or the other person.

It has become too easy, all over the world, to be unloving toward self or others. Teachers, friends, and parents, out of anger and frustration, say things we don't mean. But those who've had their feelings hurt carry that pain until they can learn to dissolve it in the violet light.

One of my friends was called "slut" by her father. She wasn't, of course, at the time. But since he already believed she was, she gave up trying to receive his approval. She said, "I'll show you," and she became a slut. One word, in a moment of anger, changed her life. When she healed that false belief, she found peace and could forgive her father.

A woman came from Virginia to join a group of women

from Idaho for a small workshop at my home. During the day, I performed a private healing for her. She had never felt *any* feelings throughout her life. No love, sadness, anger . . . she felt like an empty robot going through day-to-day and year-to-year experiences.

Her father had molested her nightly when she was a child, and she had totally blocked this from her mind, for self-preservation. Then one day, her daughter and teenage son came to her and begged, "Please make Grandpa stop doing this to us."

Shocked and sickened that her children had suffered, she entered therapy and the stored, secret (even to herself) memories began surfacing. She went to therapy for many years to recall the memories, but still she could feel nothing.

As I took her through the healing process, I asked her to repeat, one word at a time, after me. "I hate you, Dad, for what you did." She couldn't do it. "But I love my father." (I could hear her words, but I couldn't feel them.) Even if there was no feeling behind the empty words, I asked her to repeat, one word, after another, mimicking me. One word at a time, she said coldly, empty, "I . . . hate . . . you . . . Dad . . . for . . . what . . . you . . . did." (*Hate* is such a strong and scary word for most of us to say, but read on to see how forgiveness follows if we'll just honor that real feeling we have, but won't allow ourselves to express.)

As the healing progressed, I knew what would follow as I voiced the question and was prepared to handle it. "How did you feel when you found out he was doing this to your kids?" A literal popping sound could be heard coming from her solar plexus (emotional power center), like the sound a cork makes as it escapes a champagne bottle. Rage came up and her real feelings of hate, along with verbal profanity escaped from her mouth, violently. She began hysterically crying and cursing. I kept my arms around her, promising she was safe.

For a severe and painful emotional healing, for yourself or another, the following can soften it quickly and easily. A crying baby, yourself, or a loved one can heal emotional pain in minutes rather than years of therapy.

Rub your hands together and place your power hand on your forehead, which immediately elevates/raises the consciousness of the situation. Place your other hand on the solar plexus. Within minutes, and sometimes even moments, the painful emotion is purified and dissolved. Not that crying is bad—it's good to cleanse—but it just doesn't need to hurt so deeply.

Following her healing, I asked her honestly how she felt now concerning the situation with her father. She said, "I forgive my father, because someone probably did the same thing to him."

Feel your pain, but don't carry it with you forever. During its tearful release, follow with the hand positions and open yourself to the violet light. Forgive. No longer an empty word, but freedom for yourself and the other person because you are One.

Your homework is placed before you in your Journal. Don't attempt to process a lifetime of pain in just a few minutes or days. Even if the memory seems insignificant, if it comes to mind, write it down.

Birds fly in a V formation, I'm sure you've noticed. The lead bird is strongest and breaks the wind, making it easier for the others to follow. When he tires, another bird replaces the leader. As the birds teach, good leaders are those who are capable of making the way easier for their followers. Once they have served their purpose and know their followers are truly strong and empowered to continue on their own, they take their place at the back of the formation and support the next leader.

Therefore, ladies and gentlemen, I come before you to stand behind you in support. As a temporary spiritual leader and teacher, I will instruct you how to overcome not only your love, esteem, and confidence issues, but also how to become great leaders for this world.

As an individual, you have something unique to do and to give to this nation, and to the world. When others used to ask me what I wanted to be when I grew up, I'd just say, "Tall." What do you want to be when you grow up?

Complete your Journal, maybe having a box of tissues on hand for this exercise and join me so you can to learn to fly those friendly skies with me . . .

OPEN YOUR JOURNAL AND ANSWER THESE QUESTIONS

Journal—Chapter Nine

1. List ten nice things about yourself. The ones that are hardest to say about yourself are the areas where you most need help. Say those ten times silently a day, and when you're alone before the mirror state them twenty times aloud daily until the affirmation no longer feels uncomfortable.

2. List the people who have hurt your feelings and say three nice things about each of them. If it's too difficult to think of three, write ten.

3. List the experiences that have hurt you deeply. Are you ready to forgive these people? Are you aware that everyone is doing the best they can with the level of

awareness they have? If they knew better, they would do better.

4. Write the names of ten people you feel blessed to have in your life. (They may be famous or just folks.) What attributes do they have that you admire and would like to incorporate into your personality?

5. List ten "things" you are grateful for. (These blessings may include roof, food, caring people, opportunities, and so forth.)

6. We all take time to tell one another what we're doing "wrong." Let's take time to tell our loved ones what we're doing "right." Write three nice things about each member of your family. Make it a point to daily say something encouraging and loving to each one from this day forward.

Write your heartfelt thoughts in the Journal and state this affirmation aloud. *I am created in God's image; therefore, I am youth, beauty, purity, and perfection.*

10
What Will Be Will Be

When I was just a little girl, I knew I was going to grow up and do something important for the world. I knew this without asking or being told. I couldn't understand how that could ever happen, unless the world was willing to meet me inside my closet or under the bed. They were my safe refuges, where I went whenever I got scared. And I was easily frightened and often.

I resisted going to college because the only thing I could think of that would mean anything to me was to be a mom and housewife. I didn't need a college education to do that. I had dreams of walking toward a university with books in hand, but I kept dropping them. Every few steps, I'd be picking them back up again, only to drop them. By the time I got to the front doors of the university, I found I wasn't there to learn . . . but to teach.

My mom forced me to go to college so I could "make something of myself." She dropped me off, ninety miles from home, at Northern Arizona University in Flagstaff, Arizona. I was too emotionally immature to leave home and knew it. Her final words were, "Have a good time whether you want to or not." When my grades came out, she saw for herself: I'd had a good time.

Angry I had gotten an incomplete in typing, she barked, "How in the world can someone who types 120 words per minute get an incomplete in typing?" I answered honestly, "It's easy. You just don't go to class." She didn't think my remark was as cute as I did. I took the semester over and got an A in typing.

I dropped out of college and spent the following ten years as an executive secretary in wonderful businesses, but it wasn't my dream. It was just using talents I had and earning a salary. I could type and take shorthand at 120 words per minute, also, and these talents earned me opportunities to get high-paying *jobs*. But they were just *jobs*. Certainly not my heart's desire.

Still, the years passed, and I was finally able to conceive my first child after ten years of marriage. Excited, I began fulfilling the dream of motherhood I'd awaited. My dream wasn't very exciting to friends and family members. They couldn't understand why I would sacrifice evenings out and freedom for kids. It wasn't a sacrifice to me, it was the fulfillment of a lifetime of dreaming for those moments.

My patience with children amazed others. I never talked down to kids. I treated them respectfully. Not that I didn't lose my temper ever, but I had an extremely high tolerance level. There were many times that I had ten children at a time to care for and loved it.

By the way, now may be a little late to be apologizing for my speaking and writing style. One of my friends, upon hearing what I'd be saying to you today, said I should leave out the "baby talk" because not all of you may appreciate it. I'm not talking down to you. I talk this way in everyday life.

At age thirty-two, I finally learned why I'm in this life and the service and role I'm to perform. As I began having mystical experiences, I started realizing other (buried) talents besides parenting, typing, or cooking. Before I fell asleep one night, I asked for a conscious realization of the part I play in God's Greater Plan. That night I dreamed and was shown. I didn't see all the "hows," but I was shown plenty.

I also knew why I was able to type at such an extraordinary speed. As an author, I can sit behind the computer and type full-length books in eighteen to thirty-six hours. I experience those situations I write of, but the Source catalogs them into a flow of inspiration that never forces me to search for a word or phrase.

When you open your mind to the violet light, "It" fills your individual mind. "It," of course, has the ability to purify the belief of disease from your mind. Then physical healing occurs, and we call that a miracle. But when your consciousness is raised to that degree, other miraculous things begin to occur for you.

Those natural, God-given talents that come to you effortlessly—that seem like everyone could do as easily as you—begin to make sense.

If you can see the violet light within your consciousness, you have already met the healer within. There's one talent you may not have been aware of. Although you can see the violet light and can heal your individual pain, you perhaps have no desire to help others heal theirs. So just because you can see the light doesn't mean that you're here to devote your life to that path. The violet light/healing state of consciousness also has other qualities in store for you, personally.

Also, if at first you can't see the violet light, here's a simple exercise to help make it easier. At the base of your skull is what is called the pineal gland. It is the master gland of the body, and if it's open and in balance, all the other glands of the body will behave and be in balance. Through the pineal gland, electricity enters to maintain and sustain your life and health. Spirit told me many years ago that the reason death occurs is because this gland atrophies and the needed energy can no longer flow.

When we get stressed or scared, these emotions tense, like kinking the garden hose in half so the water can't flow. Lean your head slowly back, like you're looking at the ceiling, but close your eyes. Still closed, roll your eyes back in your head as if you're trying to look out the top of your skull. Slowly rotate your head over your right shoulder, down over your upper chest, slowly over your left shoulder, and back to the original position.

Did you hear the sound of "gravel" as you rotated your head? That sound is heard because you are breaking up tiny energy blocks in the pineal gland. As you hear those sounds, the blocks are dissolving and you will find that you can now easily see the violet light. Don't overdo this exercise; a few rotations a day is enough. Also, just so you know, if you had pain (or another person did), rub your hands together, place them upon the pain, and rotate your head . . . the pain will disappear.

Because we are not chiropractors, we do not have the legal right to manipulate other people's heads and necks. However, since we are One, we can rotate our head and they will benefit from the exercise.

The violet light is Christ in action/God's Will in motion. "It" begins to materialize in countless ways. For me, It categorizes matters of importance: how to be an organized and successful housewife and mother. It writes the books for me and counsels people so I'm not just offering human advice or opinions. The violet light also inspires love and Christmas song lyrics through me in about fifteen minutes per song. It has also created three toy lines, along with books. It has also been the spiritual idea and energy behind a divination board game, which I have trademarked and registered, so be watching for it on toy-store shelves.

It's a good thing I didn't know what I wanted to be when I grew up, because instead of seeing the whole picture, I might easily have limited myself. Had I, earlier in life, invested in an education in a certain area, I might have felt obligated to remain in an unfulfilled career.

I certainly would have never dreamed of inspiring the world or being a healer.

When I was a senior in high school, we were playing girls' softball. When I hit the ball, I threw my bat, which gave me a thrust toward first base. I hit my teacher with the bat and she gave me an F for the day. I didn't do it on purpose, but she nevertheless gave me the grade, and I never cared much for her from then on.

Several years after graduation, I saw her at the Elk's Club in the town I'd returned to, to visit relatives. She approached me and we spent conversation time catching each other up on our lives. At one point, she said, "Gloria, you should write a book." Her comment completely took me by surprise. I just wasn't expecting it.

I immediately asked, confused, "About what?" She smiled and replied, "About your life. It's so positive and it could help so many." Sarcastic, I said, "If it's to be about my life, I'm sure it would be an overnight best-seller."

Had I known then that God speaks through others, I would have maybe been more open to listening. When He has spoken to me personally, *aloud*, the sound of the Voice feels like a vibration that rolls through every cell of my being. Perhaps that's because the Voice is "within" me, not far off in outer space. *In inner space.* The Voice calls me by name and I weep when He speaks because the love and energy are so strong.

Many people saved every letter or poem I wrote to them. They said these were timeless and if they just needed to feel good, they'd reread my letters and get a "Gloria fix." Even with all those clues, I wasn't paying attention and accepting the Divine reason for my existence.

If you're an inventor and you open to the violet light, "It" will appear as the inspiration to bring that which already exists in the heavenly state of consciousness to the physical level.

Perhaps you feel drawn to medical science or oceanography because of your love and interest in medical cures or in whales or sea life.

What do you love to do? What stops you from believing you can do it? Not enough money or too many obstacles? Visualize the end result, giving thanks that it has already manifested, and allow the Unseen to take care of the details.

As you continue to open to the violet light, you begin living your life with a new level of confidence. You begin trusting, also, but not falsely. To achieve these attributes of confidence and trust is not something you humanly have the power to do. They become a "side effect" of the Presence of God. Also, as you achieve this level of consciousness and rise above dual opposites of success and failure, and heal your fears, you no longer find opposition as you would if you were humanly trying to manage your life, affairs, and destiny. Without fear, you find yourself taking steps you would never have attempted on your own.

A man who owns a local restaurant near my home brought his seventeen-year-old daughter to me for a healing. She was playing basketball with some girls and she fell. They fell on top of her and broke her back.

Drugged with medication, Nicole arrived at my home with her dad. Even on drugs, each step, with crutches, was hurting her. The medical world had told them she was soon going to lose complete use of her legs.

Thirty minutes later, she and her father, Sam, left my home. On the front porch, she handed her crutches to her dad saying, "I don't need these any longer." She walked to their truck in tears. I joined Nicole and Sam at the truck and held this beautiful girl. She sobbed in my arms; "I felt the love. I felt the love so strongly . . ." she cried. Sam's eyes were misted, also, as he said, "I felt it, too, Gloria, and whatever you want, you got."

I don't mean to be dense. Miracles happen all the time, but human kindness tends to overwhelm me. I asked, "I don't know what *whatever you want, you got* means."

Sam replied, "If you want a healing center built, as of this moment, the financial backing is taken care of." I responded, "Sam, I don't want a healing center. I can't handle one more responsibility. What I want is for the town and world to know I'm credible and only here to help."

He responded, "Gloria, when the town sees my daughter walking, when she wasn't supposed to, *you'll have your credibility.*"

Two weeks later, on the Fourth of July, Nicole was water-skiing, water tubing, jogging, and pumping iron.

On the evening of her healing, I received a call from my new friend Barbara Ann. This was the first miracle Barbara Ann had actually witnessed. She had read my books and listened to me speak at our weekly spiritual group about the miracles that had occurred since we'd last seen one another. This was the first she'd witnessed, however, and she was overwhelmed.

She said, "Now, more than ever, I *know* you're special. You can do this and I can't." I said teasingly, "Barbara Ann, if I have to walk the four blocks to your house and slap you silly and then slap you for being silly, I will. I've been doing this for fourteen years. If you had been 'practicing the Presence' for fourteen years, wouldn't you be at the same level of consciousness I am, if not greater?"

She weakly replied, "I guess so . . ."

I responded, "Well, I don't 'guess so,' I *know* so."

In my younger years, I took piano lessons for seven years. I didn't go to the first lesson and think I should automatically be a concert pianist. Opening to the Presence takes practice, too. I may have a natural talent at loving people, but expanding and raising consciousness takes time. Preparing for the Olympics doesn't happen overnight, nor does being aware as a Master of your soul.

Barbara Ann was heaven sent to me. She moved from Pennsylvania to Montana at a time I needed a friend, too. Nikki had moved to Sacramento and I no longer had a close, daytime friend.

Only weeks before I met Barbara Ann, I had asked my mother, "Would I be a horrible person if I had such a beautiful gift and gave up, no longer doing healings?" I was tired. My mom responded, "Gloria, knowing you, you couldn't give up. It's just who you are."

And so I sit here, telling you of the difference each unique person can make. You have everything you need inside yourself to make a difference, too. Not that you won't get discouraged and tired sometimes. Passion, talents, and gifts are planted deeply within you, and you can't help but be who you are.

You each have many talents and gifts. Some of them are possibly difficult to conceive or imagine until you're actually in the situation. Don't be surprised if you find yourself doing "on-the-job training" as you become conscious of them.

The Bible says, "These and greater works, ye will do,

also." No truer words were ever spoken. Watch, look, and listen. Stay aware. You'll simply be dazzled by your own brilliance!

"Where there's a will . . . there's usually an attorney!" Aw, c'mon, aren't ya tired of the ol' "Where there's a will, there's a way"? Be creative. Be yourself . . . the best and all you can be.

What will be will be: His Will . . . Enjoy your Journal!

OPEN YOUR JOURNAL AND ANSWER THESE QUESTIONS

Journal—Chapter Ten

1. Name those God-given, natural talents you're now aware of.

2. Recall as many times as you can remember, when people have commented on your talents.

3. Other than money, name three reasons why you could never use these talents to provide for yourself.

4. If you perceive a need in the world, trust Spirit will find a way to fulfill it through you. Rather than focusing on all the reasons why you can't do what you'd love to do, list ten reasons why you can.

5. Focus. What is the end result of your dream? Do you want to win the Pulitzer Prize, have your book on the best-seller charts, invent something creative and helpful to humanity? Focus your thoughts and see them as fulfilled. Write down your completed goal.

Write your heartfelt thoughts in the Journal and state this affirmation aloud. *God appears as every person, place, and thing to fulfill my dream and destiny.*

11

Take It to Heart

From the core of my heart, where it beats the strongest, I love humanity. I don't treat anyone any differently than another. Gosh, was that our Creator talking . . . or me? Does it really make a difference? Of course it does. Did you think there are *two* Voices, His and mine? There's only Oneness. His Voice "appearing" as mine, me being the messenger. (The one with skin on, the one you can see and hear.)

During an eight-day promotional trip in the Seattle area, I was scheduled for a TV interview, two author signings, three full-day workshops, a three-hour evening talk, and an eight-hour open house where people could meet me on my final day in the area.

I did everything as scheduled, but by being in teacher mode and in that higher level of consciousness (without a break to mop a floor or do a load of laundry), I was "drunk on the energy" for my evening appearance. I was getting silly and when I invited a man up on the stage, he declined. "No thanks, Gloria. You're embarrassing some of these people and I don't choose to do as you ask."

I crossed my heart and warmly said, "I promise I won't

say anything to you that I wouldn't say to the pope." As the man joined me at my side, I said, "Ho ho little elf! I wouldn't treat the pope any differently than I'd treat someone on the street." The color drained from his face, but I quickly assured him I'd be gentle in reading his energy field.

For my author signing at the Port Orchard Barnes & Noble, during that eight-day extensive trip, I embarrassed myself worse than I can ever remember. The manager of the bookstore made a huge mistake by putting a microphone in my hand instead of a pen. Since chairs were set out for customers who had come to hear me read from my book, I had a small audience to speak to.

If I ever have willing listeners, I don't want to waste my time on words. I take every opportunity to get this message out. I offered to teach a mini healing workshop that evening.

Being near a seaport, I looked danged adorable in my floor-length sailor dress, with heels (sporting my bells, of course). The teachings flowed ever so gracefully, with everyday normal experiences to keep the audience grounded ("in their bodies") while I wove miracle stories every now and then into the speech.

I pride myself that I'm a spiritual Erma Bombeck kind of gal—blending humorous family and friend situations, and adding a touch of inspiration. God rest her soul, I hope my heroine, Erma, is still proud of me after I share what I did that evening.

Enunciating clearly into the microphone, which was being broadcast throughout the store, I heard myself say, "If you fart to steel . . ." And it wasn't like I could cover the blooper, because everyone heard it. Now what are you gonna do, Dr. Glo-bug?

In a slow, overly exaggerated tone, I said, "Oh . . . my . . . God . . . I said the F-word. What I meant to say was, 'If you *start* to *feel.*' " Everyone laughed, including me. The remaining empty chairs quickly became occupied and we all had a great time.

Spending my entire life being nice all the time and saying only what was socially correct earned me an acceptable place in society, but it also cost me a bundle! I experienced cancer twice and severe depression that lasted for years. Later, of course, I realized the blessings of these "lessons," but while I was so lethargic that I could barely move, they didn't seem like blessings at all.

I gave everyone in my midst an opportunity "to take their best shot" to hurt my feelings. I would ask twenty friends a question and receive twenty opinions. They were given *permission* to say whatever they wanted. Without the ability to confront them or disagree, I'd smile and say, "It's okay. Really. It's okay." But, inside me, it wasn't okay.

To be sure, I was a great little actress, putting a smile on my face and another kind word from my lips as *I thanked them* for sharing their opinion. Thanking someone for breaking my heart was about as sick as you can get. Here, why don't I turn around so you can kick me, too?

Don't you just hate it when someone tells you "the truth"? And after they've outright hurt you, they question you—like it's you who've gone crazy—asking you sarcastically, "God, aren't we being a little sensitive?" They meant to hurt you, so why are they acting so shocked that it worked?

I had been through atonement (forgiveness) once before in a two-week period before I received one of my mystical and profound experiences of a Oneness Ceremony with God in 1985. A movie of my life's events played itself through my conscious mind, reviewing all those times I had hurt others or they had hurt me. Fourteen years later, it was time to do it again.

The evening following my Ph.D. ceremony, I returned to the motel with a sore throat. I didn't tell Kirk how badly I was hurting because I knew how tired he was from having so many people around me. Believing I'd just simply rub my hands and place them on my throat to dissolve the discomfort, by opening to the violet light, I found myself disappointed and discouraged that it wasn't working.

I tried to neutralize again and again, separating myself from being the one having the pain, but it still wasn't effective.

Frustrated, I silently said, "God, I could use a little extra help here. What do I need to do?" I was shocked and startled by His unexpected reply: "You must forgive." Get outta here! "Forgive who?" One by one, He began showing me.

Good grief, I hadn't realized how many had offended me. And how many times I'd been offensive. Before I began processing, I remembered the way Nikki had told me she healed while in prison and I borrowed her opening prayer. "For all those I've hurt, I'm sorry. To all those who've hurt me, I'm all better."

To those who had hurt me, in this review of past experiences, I said, "I forgive you. I believe you didn't do or say it on purpose to hurt me. If you had known how sensitive I am, I know you wouldn't have said or done it. I know you're doing the best you can, with the level of awareness you have."

When I watched the past experiences where I had been offensive come to pass, I asked forgiveness. "I'm sorry. If I had known better, I would have done better. If I knew then what I know now, I wouldn't handle it the same way." All through the night, I processed these experiences with others. I felt them, as well. Some made me feel guiltier than others. By morning, the review was over. I didn't have a sore throat. Nor was I tired, although I hadn't slept all night. I felt empowered, no longer heavy like I was carrying a burden.

Our feelings are so important, and yet we deny most of them. Either they're not socially correct if you're religious or spiritual, or we fear we're a bad human if we have them.

Now, I'm not saying that if you're feeling anger or rage, you should act it out and start throwing things or hurting people, or yourself. What is it that occurred that makes you feel the way you do? If it's something to correct or avoid, you know the steps to take to do so.

When my son, D.W., turned fourteen, he turned into a negative butthead. I couldn't understand how someone living in a home filled with so much love could be so hateful. I knew if I nagged him, it would create more negativity and opposition in our household. He didn't have a problem with his attitude. I did.

Therefore, the only place to heal the situation was within me.

I got comfortable and silenced myself. In thoughtful prayer, I silently stated, "God, D.W. is my child in this dimension, and I know he is Your son with whom You are well pleased, but I don't like him very much right now. I'm willing for You to love him, through me, and I just ask for a conscious realization of the child *You* created. And I give my thanks, for it is so."

Now I'd like to say that the clouds gathered, thunder rolled, and lightning cracked, but the shift occurred very subtly at first. I began to notice he was keeping his room clean, homework done, hanging out with healthy-minded kids, and splitting, chopping and stacking wood *without being asked* (which are the key words here!). He was nice to everyone, except his sister. (Which was her problem, not mine. Kidding. Although that attitude is normal, it too began to change.)

A few weeks after this prayer, I went to get the kids from school. D.W. and his friend got in the backseat. I heard D.W. say, "Ya know, I don't feel like being a couch potato today. Let's go do a random act of kindness for the community."

Teasing, I turned to the boys and questioned, "What did you do with my son?" The new attitude was very alien to me; I thought some local galaxy had traded kids with me.

That afternoon, D.W. and his friend Brian put a cardboard box on a little red wagon, going door to door. They collected food for Pantry Partners. This in itself was a miracle, since D.W. normally would have been too shy to go door to door and speak to strangers.

That evening it snowed, so after school the following day, they got one of our sleds out of the attic. Putting the box on the sled, they collected more food for the charitable organization. Day after day, more friends and his entire class joined one another to collect more food than ever previously had been donated. His entire class was rewarded with a pizza party.

There's a big difference between someone hurting you, unconscious of it, and consciously doing it. I had a disagreement with my stepdaughter Jaime one evening and didn't want to win just because I'm the mother. I took her on my nightly walk to discuss it. After we put all the cards on the table and voiced our perceptions of this situation, I asked her, "Were you aware you take these actions and attitudes toward others?" She genuinely replied, "No." I could feel the truth of her response and then replied, "Now that you're conscious of this, if you do it any longer, I'll assume you're doing it on purpose, being outright mean for the sake of being mean." Which, of course would involve another walk around the neighborhood to clean it up.

We have choices: to be and remain unconscious, to be (or not to be) conscious, or to elevate to superconsciousness. I always thought it would be cute for a sweatshirt to have a logo with the words SUPER CONSCIOUS STATE UNIVERSITY imprinted around it.

Spiritual ideas are endless when you plug in Direct to the Source.

The example using Jaime was an unconscious act. I was consciously attacked verbally by a busload of religious kids at a Barnes & Noble author signing in Montana. With Bibles in hand, they approached me in public to challenge me. The speaker of the group interrupted my speech to ask, "What God do you pray to?" I answered, "What do you mean *what God do I pray to?* There's only one." The lightbulb came on inside my head, "Oh. I get it. You mean, 'Do I pray to Jesus as my God?' "

I continued, "No, Jesus is not the God I pray to. He is my teacher, of course, and He's also the only person I've ever personally met who unconditionally loves us all. He's also the only person I've ever met who has individualized the Presence of God. But, no, He's not the God I pray to. I seek to idealize Him, not idolize Him."

Without opposition, the children departed. I could tell they really didn't want to leave. They wanted to hear what I had to say.

As the last teen left the building, a woman in a tone of awe remarked, "*Wow.* I'm impressed how well you just handled that." I responded, "Me, too. But it wasn't me speaking. The words were flowing out of my mouth before I knew what I was going to say."

I told the audience that day (yes . . . they, too, gave me a microphone instead of a pen), "I was always afraid to go public with this information. I was afraid that if someone confronted or challenged me, I would either walk offstage or start crying. But today I didn't feel like crying and there was no damned way I'd walk away."

The intent to embarrass or hurt me that day was a conscious choice to set out, on a bus, to challenge my beliefs publicly. Karmic Law was set in motion by their human actions and judgments; I could only ask God to forgive them, for they knew not what they did.

We're all doing the best we can, at every given moment. We all have knowledge, but it only becomes wisdom as we experience it individually.

Many times throughout the year, I fix a complete turkey dinner, with all the trimmings. The Benish Clan has so much to be grateful for and I see no need to wait until once, each November, to give thanks.

A few months ago, I'd been out doing private, local healings all day. I had just enough time to take a shower before I peeled the potatoes and got them cooking. With wet, flat hair, I stood at the sink and Danielle walked into the kitchen. I could tell something was wrong. I asked what it was and she now, at five feet six, fell heavily into my arms and said, "I just need to cry." I asked what was wrong and she said, "I'm reading *Go Within or Go Without* and I started crying in the introduction and have cried through every chapter."

Shocked, I replied, "Danielle, that book has been off the press for over four years now. Are you telling me you're just now getting around to reading it?"

Through her tearful sobbing, I asked what had touched her so deeply.

"Everything," she hiccuped.

Trying to lighten her heart, I said, "Danielle, 'everything' isn't a very good book report."

Sniffling and trying to speak through her emotions, she said, "I'm just so proud of you, Mom." Agitated because I had so much to prepare for the meal, I thanked her and said, "Danielle, you have to let me go. I need to get dinner ready." Dramatically, she cried out, "Dinner can wait, I still need to hug."

As I continued to hold her, I closed my eyes and placed my right palm on her pineal gland at the base of her skull. I used my left hand to scan her back for hot or cold spots to bring her into balance. With my eyes closed, I watched as the bright pinpoint of light on the upper left hand of my inner vision got brighter and bigger. Knowing she had a strong connection to the Source and was not dependent on me as an individual, I knew it was time to let go.

Just before we released from the hug she said, "Mom, I'm so proud of you. Those who have never felt loved, do . . . after they've read your books, heard you speak, or felt your hugs." Having a Teen Angel tell me that seemed so right on the day we were giving thanks for all things.

I tell people daily, "I love you with my whole, great big heart." Wholeness is holiness. Expressing and accepting all of who we are, forgiving and letting go of all we're not.

Kids are always seeking their parents' pride, but it would certainly make a parent's day if you told them how proud you are of them. Focusing for a change on what they're doing right.

The family unit offers your greatest opportunities to learn from one another. Especially if you all realize you're all the teachers, as well as the students. Parenting didn't come with a guidebook; it's pretty much a trial-and-error profession. What can be done successfully to and for one child may not work for the next personality. Since everyone is individual, with individual needs, I'm going to offer some helpful advice and I hope you'll take it to heart.

Following is your Journal. Continue to be honest with yourself and answer from your heart.

OPEN YOUR JOURNAL AND ANSWER
THESE QUESTIONS

Journal—Chapter Eleven

1. When is the worst time you've felt embarrassed? Give examples of times when you did it to yourself. Also, write about a time when someone hurt and embarrassed you. Was this attempt to harm or embarrass you done consciously, to make you feel stupid and inferior to them?

2. Now, for each person who has hurt and embarrassed you, write down his or her name individually. Remember that the pain, which is so evident, binds you to these people. Every time you think of them or dwell on the experience, you are first giving them energy, which they don't deserve, and second creating another situation just like it. Which is why it's so important to forgive. You are hurting yourself, not them.

Now that you have written their names down, write next to each name, "I forgive you." You may not feel it (yet), but for now, be willing to write the words. It's time to stop giving them power over you.

Here's a story that might help you understand. When Danielle was just a toddler, we were renting a house. On Easter Sunday, I went out early to hide Easter eggs. In the backyard, when I stepped onto the grass, I sank ankle deep in water. The underground sprinkling system had broken during the night and flooded our yard.

On Monday, I called our landlord and he sent a repairman to fix the system. Our backyard was dug up and new pipes replaced. The old pipes were thrown onto our decorator rock garden and awaited disposal.

Days later, I was talking to my friend Robin when we heard Danielle give a bloodcurdling scream from the back of the house. I ran to her side, seeing a neighbor standing near her with a broken pipe in her hand. Trying to comfort Danielle, I asked the neighbor what had occurred. Proudly, she said, "Danielle hit my son with the pipe, so I hit her, to show her how it felt."

Rage filled me. So much adrenaline flowed that I momentarily thought of lifting my house and dropping it on "the wicked witch of the west" and killing her graveyard dead. All I could say was, "That wasn't very appropriate. There's a big difference between a child striking another child . . . and an adult doing the same thing."

I took Danielle into the house and removed her jacket, lifted her shirt and T-shirt, and removed her diaper. An ugly red, raised welt was streaked across her little back and down her hiney.

I placed her, still crying, in Robin's arms and went next door to see the damage to my friend's son, also a toddler. I asked how he was and cheerfully she replied, "Oh, he's fine. Thanks for asking and checking." Through clenched teeth, I replied, "Well, Danielle isn't." I explained the welt resulting from her being hit through so many layers of clothes. I still couldn't believe this abuse had occurred.

Tears came to my eyes as I said, "You could've broken her back or killed her." My friend, of course, realizing she'd taken the wrong action, asked, "Can you please forgive me, Gloria?" With no hesitation, I replied, "Of course I can," and departed.

This occurred on Friday, and I avoided her all weekend. Monday morning, at seven o'clock, the phone rang.

"How are you?" she asked. I started crying and answered, "I'm not doing very well . . ." In a little miss smarty-pants, know-it-all tone, she said, "I knew you didn't mean it when you said you'd forgive me." I barked back, "Oh yes, I did. To me, *forgive* means 'to give up,' and I am definitely willing to give you up as a friend, because no friend would have ever done that."

I counseled her further, "I gave you trust, freely and completely. Because you abused that gift, you will now have to earn it. Because, as of this moment, I no longer trust you around my kids."

3. Name an example (or many) when a friend or family member abused your trust. Did you give them a second chance? (Or a million chances, if you're a slow learner? I was, too, in many other situations.)

4. Did a friend ever betray your confidences/secrets? Name an example (or several). Listing those who have violated your trust and secrets will make you more aware not to tell them your deepest feelings. If you do, you are setting yourself up for another hurt.

5. Allow your mind to show you those people you have offended. Write down their name and experiences, asking them to forgive you. You'd be surprised how many times you've offended through sarcasm, dirty digs, out-right hurtful actions, or unknowingly. Your mind holds a "history record" of this for your entire life. Long-forgotten memories may surface. Be patient with yourself as you complete this Journal section on forgiveness.

6. List the things you've done that you are proud of.

7. List your parents' names along with those of relatives and/or friends who have contributed to raising and guiding you. This may also include teachers. Next to each name, write what they have done that would bless them if they were to know this is how you felt. A simple,

briefly written thank-you card could be sent to each. One simple piece of mail, with heartfelt gratitude expressed, may be just what that person needs to hear the day it arrives. And the note will no doubt be kept and cherished. They'll take that love they felt from you with them throughout eternity. Love never dies; it lives on and on through infinity and beyond.

Write your heartfelt thoughts in the Journal and state this affirmation aloud. *To all those I've hurt, I'm sorry. To all those who have hurt me, I'm all better.*

12
The Circle of (Family) Love

Don't barf, but when Kirk proposed to me on bended knee, he said, "I want to be the father of your children, I want you to be the mother to my girls, and I want to awaken each morning with you at my side." He awakens me daily with loving, heartfelt expressions like he's the luckiest man alive to be married to me. Who wouldn't want to jump her little hiney out of bed to begin a new day, when every morning of her life she's awakened with love?

When my sister Sheila heard of our plans to marry and blend two families, she forewarned me of the impossibility of its success. Hers and others' attempts and failures to blend effectively were proof. Teasing, she said, "And if you prove it can be done, I'll hate you for it." After Kirk and I had been together for many years, I called Sheila and asked her if she hated me. She said, "No, in fact, you just taught me that fairy tales can and do come true, so I'll just plan on having my own."

I didn't give birth to Kerrie and Jaime—their "real" mother did. For saving me all the pain, I give my thanks. I never treated them any differently than my own. Referring to them as stepdaughters seems very foreign to me. Kirk never once showed favoritism toward his girls; he gave my two equal quality time and attention.

Kids will be kids, and I'm sure there may have been a moment or two when they tried to manipulate or test Kirk's and my relationship. But there was so much respect and love flowing from him and me to one another, as well as to the kids, that no one felt left out or neglected.

Kirk and I agreed to be as One in our parenting roles. We stand united in decisions. That doesn't mean we always agree, but we remain open-minded.

Kirk and I have erred by giving too much, sometimes, when it wasn't earned. For Jaime and her first husband, we put a down payment on a new modular home as a wedding gift. The little family was living in a more beautiful home than we were, and enjoyed modern appliances.

Jaime, coming from divorced parents, had another mother and stepfather to give her help, also. Her husband's family and three sets of (local) grandparents added to the constant financial assistance. Both kids worked, but it still took all three sets of parents to maintain their lifestyle.

I provided day care for my grandson, and meals, while other parents provided new tires, an air conditioner, and constant assistance. Kirk cosigned on their car.

We stood back as observers, finally, to see that none of the parents had really helped at all. The children were not committed to one another for their journey in life together. They hadn't worked together or sacrificed for a moment. They were living already at a level that it takes other couples years to accomplish. Budgeting, planning, excitedly awaiting, were transcended and ignored by overzealous parents. We gave too much, too fast, all out of love.

Was it any wonder that the marriage began crumbling? It had no foundation.

When I was growing up and we'd ask our parents what they would like for a gift, my mom always said, "I just want four good girls." I took offense, because she already *had* four good girls. But remembering back to my mother's most heartfelt wish, I brought it forth to my modern-day parenting skills. I wanted to be an example for my children to follow. Then, when I released them to build their own dreams, they wouldn't be a drain on society. Their behavior and personalities would give something to the world, rather than take selfishly from it.

What I hope for my kids and others, however, may not be what they want.

As we watched Jaime and her husband at dinner one evening in our home speaking rudely to one another, I was sad. They were a beautiful couple and I couldn't believe that their marriage wasn't going to last for even two years. Instead of cooing to one another and being affectionate, they were calling one another names and "teasing punching." I said, "Jaime, I can't believe you're treating one another like this. Your dad and I have given you the best example to follow on how to have a loving, respectful relationship."

She replied, "No, Mom, actually you didn't. You gave a very unrealistic example to follow, because every day, when you and Dad awaken, and look into one another's eyes, it's as if it's the first time you ever saw one another."

As I said earlier, different personalities perceive differently. No two kids are alike or will learn the same lessons. Each parent's and child's lessons are different. One kid will push our buttons, urging us to change and grow. Another will be full of love.

Kerrie had set her sights high on a relationship, through Kirk's and my example. We discovered soon enough that she didn't want to settle for just love. She wanted real *spiritual* love.

Kirk and I had gone back to give Kerrie a family fix while she attended Purdue University. She had become engaged after dating a young man for three years. (I'll call him Bob.) We heard, from a long-distance call, about her one-carat diamond engagement ring and looked forward to sharing her excitement.

When we met at the airport, she shined the diamond in our eyes. We picked up our luggage, and Kerrie chauffeured us to the motel. Along the way, we stopped at a convenience store. I remained in the car with Kerrie while Kirk ran in to get a few items. Just having mommy–daughter conversation, me asking questions about the forthcoming marriage, I began to feel empty inside.

The three of us chatted late that night, but after Kerrie headed back to her dormitory, I said, "Kirk, Kerrie's not going to get married." He thought I was being silly and said so. "No, she's more excited in the ring than in the cause behind it." He still insisted I was wrong.

I said, "I can't *see* [imagine] the marriage," and Kirk reassured me that it was because it was scheduled so far off in the distance, following their graduation. For a final attempt to convince him I knew what I was talking about, I said, "There's no love to be felt when she speaks of her fiancé. Also, it's not because it's scheduled in another year that I can't see it, it's because it's not going to take place."

Kirk and I enjoyed our days with Kerrie, being taken around Purdue and traveling in the nearby states. We had just returned to Montana when her phone call came. "I need a mommy–daughter talk." Comfortingly, I said, "I know, Kerrie. I was wondering how long it would take for you to feel safe enough to talk about it." Kerrie, even knowing I have gifts, couldn't believe "I knew" why she called and tested me. "Okay. If you think you know why I'm calling, why don't you tell me?"

Knowing this was her way of having *me* say her thoughts and feelings, because of the guilt and discomfort she felt, I assumed the responsibility. "You don't want to marry Bob, but you don't want to hurt him. You don't know how to stop it from happening and the idea and fear you feel from it overwhelms you. You love Bob like a friend, but not as a mate. He fulfills every need you have, spiritual, moral, financial, romantic, physical, and mental. But your emotional level is empty, and he doesn't make you feel the way you've seen your dad make me feel with affection."

I heard a very heavy sigh of relief on the other end of the line. I finished with, "Plus, you've just met a man, named Chris, at your workplace and you get all twitterpated when you see him or speak with him."

To be honest, I had to admit that part of my knowingness wasn't from any gift I have. During our vacation time together, Kerrie had mentioned his name several times. Each time she said his name, I could see the glow on her face, I could feel the love she was unconscious of, and I heard excitement in her voice. When she talked of Bob, the energy and feeling were flatter than a fritter.

Softly, I asked, "Kerrie, *now* do you want to talk about it so we can get clarity on the situation and take the necessary steps?"

She said, "Yes, Mommy, I do, but first, can I ask *how* you knew all this?"

"First," I told her, "because I wasn't born 'lasternight,' and second, because you have been spinning on all this, and thinking about me, wanting to talk about it. You have been sending me silent messages all along."

It was Kerrie's turn to talk. She parroted everything I'd just said, in the order I'd mentioned, but speaking now in first person.

"*I* don't want to marry Bob, but *I* don't want to hurt him.

I don't know how to stop it from happening." Et cetera, et cetera.

We had a very long conversation that day. It would serve no purpose for her and Bob to marry, not following her heart. How many, in our circles of friends, find themselves wanting to call off a marriage, but don't, due to expenses and fears, or overwhelmed because they don't know *how* to call it off? It's sad, for sure, that people don't trust their feelings and honor them enough to make these choices earlier than after the I do's have been said. One of my sisters married in spite of the feelings she'd had the night before the wedding. Because my parents had spent so much money, she thought she had to go through with it. I don't think any amount of money wasted would have made my parents prefer her to go through with the wedding and suffer the pain that followed this mistake.

There was bitterness from Bob, but he soon found Ms. Right, also. He even recently called me, years after the break-up. He thanked me for being a mom to him, sending him homemade banana nut bread and spiced tea mix in the "We Care Packages" as each new semester began.

Parenting isn't always easy. We can put a Band-Aid on the smallest boo-boo to make it all better, but there's no Band-Aid large enough to fix our kids' broken hearts.

We try to remain consistent, but sometimes we're tired and we falter. Depending on our moods, our "carpenter" kids can just about hammer us to death.

My friend Nikki always called me "Muzzer" and Kirk "Fazzer" when we were in our parenting role, teaching her some of life's basics. One day, seeing my frustration that there's so much sadness and confusion in the world, she said, "Ya know, honey, you have an immense spirit. But you only have one small body, two arms, two legs, one heart . . . and thank God . . . only one mouth." In her own way, Nikki was trying to lighten me up as I looked at how overwhelmingly large the task is of reaching out a helping hand and making a difference in the world. I just wanted to be bigger than earth itself, to place my arms around the globe, nurturing and giving comfort to all of you.

One evening, Kerrie and Danielle followed me into my bedroom and chatted as I put away the day's laundry. Danielle asked me to do something and I said, "I can't right now, Danielle, I'm busy." As I walked out of the room, I heard her mutter, "Oh sure, you've got time to save the world, but you don't have time for me." I started to turn around and go comfort her, although I knew she was hoping I'd just pack my bags and go on the guilt trip she'd just arranged, when I heard Kerrie respond.

"Danielle, don't you ever try to make Mom feel guilty again. Our house is clean, our laundry's done, and we have healthy meals. She takes the time to walk us, individually, around the neighborhood every night, away from phones and interruptions to give quality time and to listen to everything we have to say. She's never missed any of our concerts or field days, and she's always in the front of the crowd at the parades with tears of pride in her eyes. Don't you dare ever do that to her again."

I stood listening at the doorway. It sounded better coming from Kerrie's lips than it would have from mine.

Kerrie returned to Purdue University and sent me a handwritten, homemade birthday card. The day it arrived, I was walking away from the mailbox, and it took me three attempts to read it because my eyes kept blurring with tears. I couldn't get past the first line. The card read:

Dearest Mommy,
A field full of glistening roses could not compare to the beauty you've shown in life. Your warmth and happiness

melt the world into a vision of hope and love. Your strength
and support give others the wings to fly and your unyield-
ing friendship breaks the bonds of time.

You seem to twinkle in a golden light that draws all near,
never questioning, always trusting. You're a beacon to the
world, an undeniable guide. A most peaceful warrior, pro-
tecting, serving, loving. These are the markings of a truly
wonderful being. But you're not just an incredible person,
you're my mom, and the wonders you've managed cannot
be matched. It helps so much to have you cheer me on at
home. I thought I should drop you a note, saying how
much you are appreciated and truly loved.

I'm not telling you about this gift to get another feather in
my cap for a job well done or to break my arm by patting
myself on the back. I mention it only to show that I treat
others, even children, with as much appreciation, respect,
and love as I would choose for myself. If I'm giving it, I can't
help but get it. I can easily express my feelings. For those
who can't, I encourage you to "let Hallmark say it for you."

One of my personal judgments concerns the cost of
cards, which are normally read once and trashed. Add a few
bucks to the amount of a card and you could buy an actual
book. Even though I've been a publisher and know the
tremendous expense of four-color separation, it still fraz-
zles me to spend so much to buy a card. I encourage family
members to make homemade ones.

I would like to show you the card I made for Danielle on
her sixteenth birthday, but I know she'd kill me if I did. I
took her on a "treasure hunt" through the downtown businesses where treasures awaited her and her friends. She
thought it was a "lame" idea until she discovered the final
treasure . . . her sweet (sixteen) cherry-red car.

Not all of my poetry is knock-yer-socks-off and dazzling . . . sometimes it's just very simply said. For Danielle's fifteenth birthday, I got creative and hand-designed, drew, and colored her card. I enjoy putting a little of myself into everything I do and give.

To our dearest daughter, Danielle . . .

> *It was fifteen years ago, oh my!*
> *They placed you in my arms, to lie.*
> *For me, it was complete love at first sight.*
> *You filled my heart with loving, warm sunlight.*
>
> *There's not a day, you don't bring us great cheer,*
> *On every single day, throughout the year.*
> *You're our sunshine girl . . . in all you do . . .*
> *We love you most, for just being you.*

Danielle, there's not a moment I don't feel pride that you're my daughter. When you snuggle next to my side, I can feel your love. I feel such great pleasure that you demonstrate love in so many ways, not only to your family—but also to so many others.

I watch you grow and want so badly to slow time down, and yet I know that before I know it, you'll move on to your "exciting" career and life. Not that I want to keep you as my baby forever, but you have brought me the greatest joy a mother could know. You are the dream I awaited.

I know Dad looks at you with great pride and joy, happy to be your role model and father. I'm grateful I could attract a man who would love you as his very own.

So . . .

> *On this day and throughout your coming years,*
> *May you know acceptance and love from all your peers,*

As well as family, with whom you so freely share,
Knowing how loved you are and how very much we care.

Happy Birthday, Dani Dawn

All our love,
Mom and Dad

As a parent and person, I also demand and command respect, however. When Kerrie came home for the holidays one Christmas, we were buried in snow. She spent the entire day digging her Uncle Doug's house and car out of the drifts. When she got home, I was sitting at the kitchen table, writing.

From the doorway, I could see her and she immediately barked, "Dad's going to be home any minute, and there's nowhere for him to park with the driveway so deep in snow." Her tone just got louder and louder with each word.

Patiently, I said, "I know, Kerrie, that you're very tired. We have shoveled that driveway three times today and we can't keep up with it. It's falling faster than we can shovel. But if you ever come into my house again and treat me with such disrespect, you will never be welcome again. I suggest you use that anger you're feeling and put it to good use. *You* go shovel the driveway."

She stomped out and slammed the door. Don't think I didn't feel bad! She was only home for a few days, but I don't like disharmony in my house. Nor am I a doormat for my kids, mate, friends, or strangers.

Because I am consistent and a woman of my word, I build a trust within others. If I say it, I mean it. I'm sure the ultimatum to Kerrie weighed heavily on her mind and heart. I allow differences to be discussed, but I don't allow mean for the sake of being mean.

Later than evening, I invited Kerrie into the kitchen privately "to clean it up." I never scold a person with an audience. Praise, however, I'll invite everyone to hear. She and I talked, with me once again giving her permission for the exhaustion she felt to be the cause of her outburst. She fell into my arms and sobbed, saying how sorry she was for hurting me needlessly. I, too, was sorry that we had quarreled or that I had frightened her that she could lose my approval or a place in my heart or home.

Unconditional love means I will always love, but that doesn't necessarily mean that people will remain a daily part of my life. I can love and release them to go on to their highest good. That includes a child, if need be.

As a parent, Kirk is an equally strong and honest example and influence for our children to follow. I've never received an award of any kind, but I told him if I ever did, it would have to go to him. Can you imagine a man sitting and patiently listening to every single word this motor-mouth has? And he listens as if it's *all* important. He does the same with the children, sitting for hours and listening and counseling, when asked. If they are sharing their ideas, but have not asked for advice, he has "no opinion."

Like me, the kids sometimes just need to hear their thoughts aloud and need a sounding board. Once they speak their choices aloud, they can hear the truth and make choices.

If we, as parents, offer our unsolicited advice, they tune us out just as we sometimes have to do to them. We attempt to control our children's lives, having already lived through the experiences they're faced with; we know the outcome and consequences. We want to prevent them from hurting. We counsel, based on our own fears.

D.W. got angry once because I wouldn't let him drive to a nearby city on icy highways. Because I couldn't see/imagine him arriving safely home, I wouldn't allow him to go. As I asked him why he was so angry at my decision, he barked, "I just wish you didn't care so much!"

I drove away from the school, where he'd been dropped, and thinking, "How weird. My kid wishes I didn't care so much and other kids wish they had someone who does." Weird. Just plain weird.

Last night, at dinner, I asked Danielle, "For the book I'll be writing, could you tell me what parenting skills Dad and I have that you appreciate?" Kirk jumped to her defense: "I don't think that's a fair question to ask her." Danielle said, "It's easier than the one she asked me the other night in front of my friend Autumn, about the sex chapter." Danielle willingly volunteered the following: "I like that your discipline is equal to the situation; I like when you're understanding when you need to be, lenient when you should be, and not lenient when you shouldn't be. Most of all I like that you're not trying to be my friend and you and Dad guide us all to do what is right."

I'm definitely not a know-it-all; I don't have all the answers to parenting. I'm just sharing what has worked for me so far.

When I was assuming the position of graduating Nikki from ex-con to becoming an asset to society, she volunteered her feelings. "Gloria, you had sent me quarterly boxes in prison, along with stamps and accepting collect phone calls. You've now provided physically for me—a home to come to, food, wardrobe, and giving in so many ways I can never repay. You gave me a life, but in giving so much, I've felt resentment. *You have everything.* There's nothing I could ever give you to equal all you've done." She compared herself to our daughter Jaime, and helped me understand why others don't always show gratitude. Not that Jaime didn't, but I've been in other situations where the kindnesses were abused.

Nikki also helped me to understand that because I have such a tremendous capacity to give—although I never give with a thought of what I'll get out of it—giving to people to the point that they feel indebted can be a burden to them.

The ring made of a Black Hills gold rose that Kirk placed upon my hand is a constant reminder that I'm on the right track and to keep going. But rings are not given to bind one another. We don't possess one another. Nor our kids.

To me, like the shape of the ring itself, this circle of family love is never-ending from beginning to end. Remember: If you want to be loved, be loving. Giving begets receiving, and it is just as blessed, by the way, to receive. Harder to do sometimes, but just as necessary. I hope the truth of this rings loud and clear to you.

Enjoy your Journal!

OPEN YOUR JOURNAL AND ANSWER THESE QUESTIONS

Journal—Chapter Twelve

1. Do you feel resentment toward your family or caregivers? Have they given too much or not enough?

2. What family/marital ideals do your parents express that you want to take into your personal family when you have one? Are "traditions" important to you? Which ones?

3. What family/marital experiences do your parents express that you don't want to take into your personal family when you have one? List these below. You have a choice, remember?

4. Do your parents make holidays and birthdays special, precious moments you can reflect back on someday? Write those memories below.

5. For what purpose, in your opinion, would a parent deny you something you want or something you wanted to do?

Let me give you an example. My mother refused to let me attend my senior class graduating party. "Everyone else is going," I said. Her response: "So I suppose if everyone else was jumping off a cliff, you'd follow?" As a Libra, who has a hard time making up my own mind, hmmm . . . let me see. "Yes. No. Yes. No. Well, maybe. And then again, maybe not." I don't know if my mom ever appreciated my sense of humor.

What? Didn't she trust me? I wouldn't drink underage (even if the beer would be flowing like water). I could even be a "designated driver" for those who would be drinking. I thought if I put on my little ol' "Miss Goody Two Shoes" hat, and the people-pleaser personality, I'd be able to "suck up" and get to go.

She still wasn't going to let me go. I thought she was the meanest mom in the world. The biggest problem about me not getting to do what I wanted was her love for me, standing in the way. "Two big feet (with combat boots on)" as far as I was concerned.

A party and memory of a lifetime—something that could never be repeated. I closed myself in my room the entire night, sulking, pouting, crying, and whispering obscenities.

Mom feared for my safety. It didn't matter if I didn't drink. Others would be, who would also be on the road.

My mom was psychic, too, although that term wasn't

used much back then. I thought she was just stupid. I didn't know until I became a parent, how darned smart she was.

Name something you wanted to do and weren't allowed.

6. Give an example where your parents knew something beforehand and prevented you from following a plan through.

7. Are you aware, when you're thinking of a particular person, that they are receiving the message? Become conscious that this works and practice sending a family member or friend a message. Describe the experience completely once you receive validation.

8. Write your experiences when you consciously attempted to guilt-trip someone into giving you your way. Was it successful? Be aware. Once you're conscious of something, Karmic Law has no mercy, and the Law fulfills itself immediately. Look how quickly Danielle attempted to make me feel guilty, and also how quickly she felt it as Kerrie corrected her. Karmic Law: If you throw a boomerang, it will return to you. It is the same with your thoughts and actions. In order to rise above those we have already set into motion, we must rise above where the boomerang is going to come to rest by opening ourselves to the violet light/Presence of God.

9. Are there any ideals in my family and world that you feel drawn to incorporate into your family and friend circle? List those ideals to help keep them fresh in your mind.

For example, several years ago, I asked Danielle what parenting skills I was weak in. Delighted to think her opinion mattered or could help, she was more than happy to respond. She said, "You're not being consistent.

You threaten and tease that you're going to ground us until we're eighty-nine years old, but you never follow through."

D.W. was on the sidelines, waving his arms and mouthing the words, "Shut up." Danielle couldn't see him from where she sat and kept chirping more bubbly, helpful advice. "You let us get away with too much stuff, asking repeatedly for us to do simple chores." By the time she finished sharing my weaknesses, I didn't feel inept. I felt fortified to be a better parent.

10. Be honest and write examples of your parent's weaknesses. Once you see them in print, discuss them as a family. It will strengthen your family unit, and this exercise will help make you more aware of what ideals you want to emulate for your future children.

11. When your parents are (say) giving you guidelines for an evening out, and aren't being clear by asking the right questions, help them. Ask them to be clear about what your curfew is. If your parents aren't aware of all the stops you might choose to make, or if plans change, let them know. Write about a time when they weren't clear about your directions and rules—and you later found yourself in trouble. "Oh, I thought you meant _____ ; I didn't understand that you meant that."

Although it's silly, I have to share this. When I was married to my first husband, he had poker with his friends every Friday night. The wives decided to have a "Ladies Night Out" at our closest city, sixty miles away, to *party*. Before I left, I was asked when I'd be returning and responded, "Early." When I walked in from being with the women, I was met with one outraged husband. He asked in a worried and demanding tone, "*I thought you said you'd be home early?*" I looked at the clock; it was three in the morning. I gave him my dumb look and said, "It *is* early."

He didn't think it was so funny. He acted like he was my parent. I explained, "The bars closed at one, we went and had breakfast at Denny's, and it's an hour's drive back home."

Be clear with one another and yourself.

Write your heartfelt thoughts in the Journal and state this affirmation aloud. *My spoken word and actions are Law, and the Law fulfills Itself now. I am a clear vessel for spiritual good.*

13

What Is Your Self Worth?

Yesterday morning, as Kirk was driving away to go to work, I held up my hand as I do every morning. Kneeling on the couch, at the picture window, I raised my little finger and index finger, along with the thumb for the universal sign language "I love you" as he drove away. As usual, I sat in silence for a few minutes to devote my life and my day to God. In that moment, many things came to mind that I wanted to remember to say and do with you today. But as excited as I am to share my teachings and stories, I had to discipline myself.

There were things to be done before talking to you today. There was laundry to do, sheets to change, vacuuming and dusting, book orders to fill, e-mails to answer, two business and one personal bank statement to balance and file, and I had to feed the neighbor's dogs (they're away for the weekend).

I promised myself that, although I would rather be talking or writing to you, if I did my chores, I could spend all day with you today. But I felt frustrated inside because I really didn't want to do those things at all. I wanted to do what I wanted and wished I had someone else to do my chores for me. I don't, though. And they needed to be done.

So I just silently said, "God, I'll do it all for You," and the organization of the details and the energy to do it all appeared. As I got into the flow of it all, my thoughts guiding me throughout every step, I realized I was actually enjoying the work. Now, looking back on yesterday and seeing all I accomplished, I feel a pride in myself. Of course, the real glory goes to God, the Source, but I, as an individual, can also feel pride that I allow Spirit to work through me.

I once taught a workshop and met a man who introduced himself as a skeptic. He said, "I only have one question: *Why don't you charge for doing healings?* Other healers charge." I replied that I held no judgments about others charging, but I felt that I couldn't.

"Sir, if I gave you a gift in this hand"—I held out my left hand toward him—"and it was wrapped with ribbons and bows, would I hold out this hand [I opened my right hand, faceup], telling you that it cost me seventeen dollars and expect you to pay me for it?"

I continued, "The gift of healing is a gift, to you from God, that just happens to pass through me." I asked, "Sir, if you had cancer and I (as an instrument) was able to dissolve it, saving you hundreds of thousands of dollars for chemo and radiation, as well as stress and fear, would you want to sign the deed of your house over to me? Because isn't your life worth at least that much?"

I concluded, "I don't charge because I don't know how to put a price on a priceless gift." The man left the workshop eight hours later no longer a skeptic. He had felt the Presence, and learned how to feel It daily.

I also once had a woman ask me, while I was speaking back east, "How do we know you're not a fraud?" I took the attention away from her to answer the question. I did so for two reasons. I didn't want to make her wrong for asking the question, nor did I want to embarrass her.

I asked a man in the front row, "Sir, do you work for a living?"

"Of course I do," he replied.

"And sir, if your company shorted you fifty dollars on your paycheck, would you complain and demand to be compensated?" He said he would. "Sir," I asked, "could you imagine working twelve to eighteen hours a day, for seventeen years, and not receiving a paycheck?" No, was all he could say.

I turned and asked an elderly woman in the audience, "Could you take your retirement money out early, suffer an eight-thousand-dollar penalty for doing so, and publish books, not necessarily to sell, but to donate to the needy and prisoners across the nation?" All of us present could see her fear as she responded, "No, in fact I'm very concerned how I will provide for myself in my golden years. That's what I'm here to learn today."

For my last question, I turned to a woman and asked, "Could you leave your own child at home sick, to go heal another's?" She honestly replied, "No. I'm not at that level yet."

Turning my attention back to the woman who originally asked the question, I said, "I have answered honestly, and if anyone would want to walk in my moccasins, and answer the questions the way I did . . . well, I guess they could call me a fraud."

I'm not a saint, and although some of these stories would either make you gag or convince you I am saintly, I'm just a housewife and mother who has been called by God. Seeing true peace on earth, peace on every level of your life, and to know love, Direct, is greater than any fortune I could amass. Not that being rich is bad, although the media tends to want the poor to hate the rich. Robin Hood and his ideals sounded romantic for taking from the rich and giving to the poor. I'd rather teach the poor *how* to become rich, in Spirit and in the physical realm, as well.

In one of the visions I've been shown, I saw money banded—the way it is in banks—and stacked five stories high, five miles across, and going back into infinity. Abundance already exists. We don't have to create it. As an attribute of God, it already exists. All that the Father has is ours. All He has, He gives to us. He doesn't withhold our good in any form. We need only to raise our consciousness, becoming aware of its already established perfection.

As a healer, with a unique gift and personality, for the last seventeen years I have served the poverty- and middle-class levels and prisoners who could not get help otherwise. Convicts don't have the luxury of going to their local self-help bookstore. Nor can they call in a reliable therapist.

It's not because I'm falsely humble that I don't charge for healings. I truly believe God is the Source of healing, the Source of my supply . . . appearing as everything I need. He, not sick people, will provide me with "things" greater than I could have envisioned on my own. We humans are limited by fears, tunnel vision of only what we've seen or experienced, or what others can do, or have.

If I thought that my writings, or healings, or any good fortune that came my way was due to me, the "success" might be short lived. If I separate my life from God, as people call upon me, I would soon get sick trying to help so many. In one day, ninety-nine people were healed through me. At the end of the day, I was drunk on the energy and walked away singing, "Ninety-nine bottles of beer on the wall." As just Gloria, I don't have energy to do that.

It's not my life anyway, it's God's life that maintains and sustains me. I don't live in a physical house, I live in the consciousness (Mind) of God. I don't eat physical food (or some of it might not be in harmony with me, giving me allergies or making me feel sick, or get fat). Rising above Karmic Law concerning food or anything that touches my life elevates the consciousness of good and bad to Oneness. In Oneness, there is no opposition or competition, only harmony and perfection. Therefore, I don't eat physical food, I eat spiritual food, the Body of Christ/Light. Also, my body appears "physical," but I realize it's truly a spiritual body and no longer subject to anything of a physical nature.

When you seek anything of a physical nature, you are setting the Karmic Law into motion. Be careful, because you just might get what you asked for. Good or bad, who's to say?

Mind is not God, and the reason we know this is that the mind can be used for good and bad purposes. (God is only spiritual good, without an opposite.) Once you devote your individual mind to God, it becomes an avenue of expression for the Divine. No longer are you mentally creating. Only spiritual good will manifest through you.

Money can be used for good or bad under Karmic Law. Fire? Same thing. Water? Yes, we need it to live, but in other situations, it can flood, destroy, and kill.

Anything has good and bad qualities under Karmic Law. But when you rise above the belief in that Mental/Karmic Law, no longer seeking money or any other desired outcome, you begin noticing that everything you need, you already have. Usually before you know you need it.

Don't seek a certain person; ask for a spiritual mate and a conscious realization of Oneness.

Don't seek physical dollars, because you will struggle to get and keep them. Ask for spiritual supply and watch the floodgates open. Seek only Oneness concerning every matter and you'll rise above the constant dual experiences of ups and downs, extreme highs and devastating lows.

What is your present self-worth? In my younger years, I didn't have any. While camping with several family members years ago, we found ourselves on top of a mountain without even a baby aspirin and every one of the six kids was sick. I opened myself to the Presence and by the next morning, they were all as good as new. My niece Brandy, then about six years old, offered to take everyone for ice cream. Proudly, she said, "I have lots of dollars, but I don't know how much 'cents' I have."

Growing up, I didn't think I had any "sense" either, which lowered my self-worth. I didn't have an education to give me the right to put a greater value on my talents. Becoming aware of my healing gift, or writing talents, or a multitude of spiritual ideas all went without repayment. Not because it's unholy to be paid for any talent I had, but because in my formative years I didn't receive since I wasn't willing to accept. Not even a compliment. As we learn to be gracious, receiving—even a compliment—allows more abundance to come into our lives. Each time we negate a compliment, we are closing the door to experience our greater abundant good.

Until it faded and became my "Holy" (full of holes) Sunday-go-ta-meetin' shirt, I wore a T-shirt that said, HUGS: 5 CENTS, KISSES: 10 CENTS, LOVE: NO CHARGE, LET'S JUST TRADE. A Black man approached me in a grocery store one day when I wore that shirt shopping. He walked toward me with a dollar bill on his opened palm. I thought it was cute for a stranger to openly approach me.

I told the man to put away his money and I opened my arms to him and kissed him on the cheek as we hugged. It felt so good. As we parted from the embrace, he quoted aloud as he read from my shirt. He asked, "Hmmm . . . a hug, five cents, a kiss, ten cents . . . if I gave the dollar, what could I get?" I laughed and said, "Change."

What a wonderful life it is. Another favorite shirt of mine said, LOVE ME, SQUEEZE ME, TAKE ME HOME. I had to stop wearing that one in public because I got so many offers.

Do you know the difference between a woman and a lady? Ladies say, "Thank you." When you compliment a girl or woman on her beautiful dress or hair, she has some of the following to say about it: "Oh, this old dress? I got it at Goodwill and I've had it for years." "My hair? God, I'm glad it looks good today . . . because normally it looks like crap."

Women are unable to say, "Thank you," and offer no further explanation. That's the difference between low self-esteem and self-worth.

I can recall the first time I offered this teaching to a broken-spirited mother. I no sooner helped the caller than the universe challenged my belief. Following this phone call, I went to the post office to mail book orders. The postmaster complimented me on the coat I was wearing. I found myself saying, "This old thing?" and giving him much more information than he ever needed, uncomfortable to receive his compliment.

I returned home and telephoned the woman, being honest with her on two issues. I reminded her how quickly experiences manifest once you're aware (only minutes had elapsed following the advice I had given her). Our spoken words and thoughts manifest quicker as we become aware. Second, I wanted her to realize that I'm honest when I say, "I'm still growing, too." I'm not perfect. I live the information to the best of my ability. As I know better, I'll do better.

I realized immediately, however, that "I'd gone and done it again." We don't need to emotionally beat ourselves up, and as we become aware how often we fall back into comfortable patterns, we will begin to make more conscious choices. If we revert to old comfort zones, we must be gentle with ourselves. We'll get there. It just might take a minute longer . . .

As for men, the hungry ones who just hope someone can say a kind word eat up a compliment and glow. Other men become embarrassed and shrug it off in a macho way. "Yeah, I always look this good. Why, hell, I can't keep the women off me." Their insecurity makes a joke out of every compliment. (I recognize this pattern immediately because I've done the same thing all my life.)

Until I created and played my inspirational divination board game, I didn't realize how uncomfortable I felt when a person complimented me. While playing the game, whenever a player landed on the square of our prototype model— "Say something kind to every person playing this game"—I cringed. I would say something silly and uncomfortably wait to hear what they had to say. I played that game for hours before it began to feel comfortable enough to sit, like a *lady*, look the player in their eyes, listen to the compliment, and say, "Thank you."

I believe that somewhere inside each of us, we feel so weak, but our true fear is how powerful we are. If we use only 10 percent of our present mind power and we've gotten ourselves and the world into such a fine mess—think what deep doo-doo we could get ourselves into if we used the full potential we have and are.

And the meek shall inherit the earth. I'd roar about now, but instead, I'll just meow . . . that will help me get to the "catty" part of today's message. We can be so malicious to ourselves, willfully wishing and causing ourselves self-destruction, pain, injury, and distress. Why? My answer would be, because it's our comfort zone. It's so much easier to believe the negative about ourselves than the positive.

But I'm not here to do what's easy, or I wouldn't have forsaken a salary. I would have remained comfortably in a secretarial position just doing my job and getting a paycheck. I could have spent my life just counseling and teaching coworkers. It wasn't easy to trust that all my needs would be met if I did service for God and humanity.

I could have also set myself up as a great healer, built a center . . . which many people have suggested I do. "Build it and we will come." I could have charged large sums of money "for saving people's lives and souls." Part of why I didn't charge for healings was that I believed credibility was more valuable than money in order to be a messenger and be heard. I am confident of my gift, and I am credible. If I choose to charge, that's okay, too.

Is it low self-worth that stops me from doing so? Do I really know how powerful I am? I don't know the answers to these questions, but when I do, I'll be happy to share them with you.

I do know that now is the time for all of us, me included, to learn our true self-worth and to learn to say "Thank you" for every gift—physical, verbal, or spiritual—that comes our way.

Giving is easy for most of us. It makes us feel good. Receiving can be uncomfortable and downright embarrassing. When someone offers to buy your lunch, don't argue and say, "No, no . . . I'll get it." Quietly and genuinely say, "Thank you." You deserve it.

When your mother places your food on the table, thank her. When Dad checks your oil or picks up a needed supply, express your gratitude. When your child performs a random act of kindness for you or another, speak your pride and appreciation.

Oh, I forgot. There's another "Benish Law" we live by. Following the dinner I serve, my kids say, "Thank you, Mom, dinner was delicious. Is there anything we can do to help you?" I didn't need the strokes, but I wanted to know that when they ate at a friend's home, they had enough awareness to give their hostess similar gratitude. I'm not a colonel, raising an army of mechanical soldiers, and they're not punished if they forget or go days without saying it. In the beginning, however, to create the kind and healthy habit, I gave them added encouragement to remember. If they failed to thank me, they got invited to do dishes, empty the trash, and whatever else I could come up with on short notice.

We have such extremes on the planet. Those who are overindulged to the point of selfishness and expecting everything to be handed to them, those who steal to have, and those who have not. Gratitude, as important in life as the ABCs, must be taught. Not only does it show appreciation to the Source, working through the one who showed the kindness, but it also opens the heavenly gates to pour abundance in all forms into your life.

The United States is presently a codependent nation, supporting and providing for many who are capable of being hosted by an Infinite Source of supply. Each person who finds self-worth is one more who has learned how to be independent of governments, churches, doctors, mates, and physical means.

When Jesus stood before the masses with only a few fishes and loaves of bread, He first blessed them and gave thanks. In giving thanks for the abundance *He knew already existed,* He set the Spiritual Law into motion. If you remember this story, after all those present ate until they were filled, he had twelve baskets left over. Giving thanks for those things that *are* seen will become a constant reminder to give thanks for all that has not yet become physical, but already exists. That's faith. Acceptance of your greater good can be so simple.

I owe no one anything but love, and that's all I teach. As a parent and teacher, I have to keep saying the same things over and over until people "get it." The stories change, but the message remains the same. Just as a teacher instructs you in basic arithmetic—two plus two equals four. It's always going to be the same absolute answer. Love is always the absolute answer, also.

What is your self worth? Are you aware how valuable you are? Are you aware what a gift it is to be alive . . . in any age, but especially in this one? It's an honor to be born at this time in our world's evolution as our earth and occupants become more spiritual. You have amazing talents and gifts, and your whole life lies before you to take advantage of opportunities to make a difference. I can't even begin to tell you what amazing and profound experiences await you if you allow Spirit to work through you.

I don't want you to have to go through another day in your life before you understand the potential you hold inside yourself. What a wonderful opportunity is in your hands to begin now.

Children teach their parents where their buttons and weaknesses are (and vice versa). Bosses teach their employees countless skills and lessons (and vice versa). Parents teach their children survival skills (and vice versa), and then, of course, we have the teachers of teachers . . . For those individuals who have devoted their lives to teaching us, I wonder if they'll be ready and willing to learn from you and listen to what you have to say. It's time to learn some spiritual ABCs and 123s.

Enjoy your Journal and I'll meet you within those hallowed halls.

OPEN YOUR JOURNAL AND ANSWER THESE QUESTIONS

Journal—Chapter Thirteen

Greed exists because people think there isn't enough. They want to take from others, whether it's money, energy, or power, because they aren't aware they can "plug in Direct" and have it all. Money is just another form of energy, becoming physical. But energy is energy.

Become aware that it's not always money that is needed to acquire things you'd like to have. Countless things can come to you in the form of gifts, given by others and without any out-of-pocket expense.

Although I'm teaching you how to "plug in" to Spirit where you don't need to ask for your needs to be met, I understand it can take steps of awareness to do that. Therefore, I'll teach how to create on a Mental/Karmic Law level, as well.

See yourself in your imagination, holding the object you desire, surrounded by the golden light. That's it. It's done. Listen to your thoughts and take physical action as you can. You'll be guided to the right person or right place, and the gift is yours.

You don't need to steal or take from others. There's truly plenty for everyone.

On a spiritual level, as you open to the violet light/

Presence of God, "It" flows forth and through you, going before you to prepare your way. Without thinking, asking, praying, or begging God to do something for you—it's already done before you can humanly think to ask. He is our consciousness. He knows our needs before we do (on a human level).

1. Practice holding a picture in your head, holding a simple desire. Surround yourself and the image with a golden glow. Write about your experience after it has manifested.

2. I've learned that it's just as important to remove the word *try* from our vocabulary as it is to remove *want*. Watch when someone tells you they'll "try" to do something for you. (Inside yourself, you can feel they're not going to. Trust yourself. I'm sure you're right.) It won't happen if they said they'd "try," or at least, generally it doesn't. You either *do* or you *don't*.

"Try" to pick up a pen from the table. If you lifted the pen, you *did it*. If the pen remains on the table, you *didn't*. Again, no one can "try" to do anything. You either do or you don't.

Write about some experiences when you or others said, "I'll try." Doing this exercise will help keep you conscious of using that word and help you become more conscious, also, when friends or family members use the term.

We all use the word *try* because we don't feel safe enough to say yes or no to certain requests. We give false hope to the other person, which is more comfortable than disappointing them. It will get more comfortable to be honest once you're aware you're just delaying saying the truth to them, after you're more aware how often you say, "I'll try."

3. If you had a life-threatening illness and someone had the gift to save your life, or heal you and your family's fears so you could pass in peace, what dollar value could or would you put on your life?

4. If you became conscious that you are capable of helping others, would you charge for your services, talent, and/or time? Why or why not?

5. Do you think healers who charge are frauds, or just individuals who are "trying" to make a living, using the best talent they have to do so? Write your thoughts about this, being aware of every judgment you express. Write your thoughts freely and then look back over your words to review and be aware where your state of consciousness is right now.

6. Because imagination is the Source of All Creation, are you aware that you can be or do anything you can imagine? Imagine what you see yourself doing one year from now. Then five years. And then maybe ten years. How are you living? In wealth or poverty? In health? Happy? Content and peaceful? Are you enjoying the pleasures and beauty of this world? What kind of home do you live in? Is there a smile on your face? See each calendar year in your mind as you imagine the possibilities. Write down your images. (Look back on this Journal many years from now, once it's completed, and you'll see that everything you wrote—or something even better—has occurred in your life.)

7. Can you accept a compliment? Without giving explanations following it?

8. Are you afraid of change?

9. Is it easier for you to give than to receive? Name a few examples of times when you freely gave. Name twice as many times you willingly received, without trying to convince the giver they shouldn't. Betcha can't do it. At

least not yet. Write about a few times when you comfortably received.

10. Can you conceive of how you can "have" but not take from others to do so? Imagine your ability to manifest, Direct, from a universal endless Source, without physical means. Get wild and crazy and imagine how this is done, then write down this spiritual lesson. (I'm stretching you, I know, but "Just Do It.")

11. If you owe someone for a bill, write "thank you" on the envelope. Before you cash a check made out to you, write "thank you" on it. Your gratitude creates a vacuum and sets the Universal Substance into motion to fill the void. Your gratitude will open the Infinite Supply. It's not "my bills" (or yours) anyway. I have no personal debts, because my life is not separate from God. My life is God's business to maintain, and as chairman of the board, He is generous and takes care of *all* my needs. Write about what part of your life and affairs you want to take care of and, preferably, how much you're willing to allow God to take care of for you. Your life is God's business. Let go and let Him dazzle you with His brilliance.

12. Are you aware how valuable you are? (If you said no I'm gonna smuck you!) If you did say no, you just set Benish Law into motion; now you have to say ten more nice things about yourself.

13. Are you aware of the gift of life you've been given? (Be careful . . .) You, not knowing what unique purpose you're here to serve, may be the one who kindly talks to someone on an elevator who appears sad. He's smiling by the time you reach the next floor and goes back to his desk. You, not knowing and seeing the whole picture, may be unaware that he was planning to take the elevator to the top of the building and jump. Your simple presence in this world is far reaching. You may not know

how the ripple effect of what you did yesterday is affecting all of humanity today. Write two brief paragraphs about how you have already made a difference in this world. Write two more brief paragraphs explaining how your life has already affected those around you in your circle of family and friends.

    14. If you could do anything (and you can!) to make a difference in this world, what would you do? Write that down.

Write your heartfelt thoughts in the Journal and state this affirmation aloud. *I make a difference in this world, just being who I am.*

14

Reading, Writing, and 'Rithmetic

When I was in sixth grade, my friend Betty and I were rounding the corner of the school street, going toward home, when she asked me a question. A profound question for someone our age to even consider. I don't know if she'd overheard adults talking or if she was brighter than even I believed her to be.

"Which came first? The chicken or the egg?" We discussed it all the rest of the way to my home, where we parted. I have thought about that question my entire life. At age thirty-two, I received the answer Direct from Spirit. "Neither one did. *The thought from Divine Mind came first.*"

Do you remember the "golden sphere" we talked about as we began this day together? Where everything He created already exists? Within the Divine Mind, He holds the seeds of thought (egg), but also within Mind exists the completion of the Divine Idea (the chicken).

Therefore, when you receive an inspired idea, realize that the completion and fulfillment already exist, as well. Most people who have dreams and goals waste energy and lose attention by seeking to figure out *how* each step will appear.

Receiving the idea, seeing the outcome, and releasing the need to know how on earth you can ever pull it off will set your faith in motion. If you can see the already established outcome, it does exist. Just get out of your own way and watch how God will effortlessly align you with the right people, places, and things to express your desired outcome *through you*. You will become aware of serendipity . . . looking for one thing, but becoming conscious of finding something (or someone) you needed more to fulfill it.

As I drove the kids to school one day, Jaime, then a freshman, flipped out. "Oh my God, we're having a test in English today and I forgot to study."

I said, "Jaime, see yourself holding your returned test paper in your hand. See a big fat red A at the top of the page."

Immediately, she responded, "I could *never* get an A since I never studied. And besides, Kerrie gets straight A's, not me."

In Jaime's mind, stretching herself to an A was inconceivable. If she couldn't conceive it or feel comfortable with the idea, it would never happen. We create our experiences at the level of our present comfort zone and awareness.

So it didn't matter if I, as a parent or "eternal optimist," knew that Jaime was just as smart as Kerrie. It didn't matter if I tried to convince her she could get A's. Nagging kids to do better is no more effective than inspiring them, if they don't believe in themselves.

I asked my daughter, "What is the highest grade you could feel comfortable achieving?"

She flatly stated, "I don't know, since I didn't study. I guess I could envision a B, although even that is a pretty big stretch of the ol' imagination."

Just before she got out of the car, I said, "Close your eyes for just a second. See the test paper in your hand. It has a big, bright red B next to your name. Now see yourself jumping up and down with excitement, sharing with me that this technique really works." In as much time as it took to say it, Jaime could see it. Kids' imaginations have not atrophied the way so many adults' have.

You, of course, don't have to be psychic to know the outcome of this story. Jaime got her B. Every year thereafter, her grade point average increased. She was indeed as smart as Kerrie, but she had to discover it herself.

I have used and taught this technique to "alter time" as well. If I had to be somewhere, at a certain time, rather than break the physical man-made law of speeding, I "broke the Karmic Law" of believing and accepting that time holds any meaning in God's reality. Time only has power because humans believe it does.

I would merely see/imagine the time I was to arrive safely, and taking action to drive or walk to my destination.

In Richard Bach's book *Illusions,* my favorite book (which I recommend highly), he speaks of dissolving clouds. Although the book is listed as fiction, I performed the things he wrote of, in my reality.

Looking into an afternoon sky filled with clouds, my attention was drawn to one small cloud. Testing myself with a small cloud seemed easier. With my outer vision, I looked at the cloud, closed my eyes, and imagined it disappearing. I opened my eyes and watched it dissipate immediately.

Braver now, I chose a large cloud. A bigger cloud had no more substance than the small one. They are both just energy.

I then began practicing with cancer and other situations. Seeing the word CANCER on a big black chalkboard, using a huge white light eraser, I wiped the word out of my mind. I saw and experienced this with callers needing my help and then returned to their follow-up calls: "I was just told by the physician, *I don't know what happened, but the cancer seems to have disappeared.*"

Mental healing and imaging works. Spiritual healing purifies the consciousness with the violet light dissolving the error from your mind. Remember, because the mind is greater than humans, something "greater" must be introduced into it. Humans can't heal minds, but introducing God into the individual consciousness can manifest heaven on earth.

We attract what we love, hate, and fear. Remember: We are electromagnetic energy. Human magnets walking around, attracting what we hold our attention to. The electricity/energy is God, maintaining us, and our emotional/magnetic field is the fertile ground where we plant the seeds of thought. Ta da—creation made simple! The violet light will fill us with peace, and purify our minds of fear, and I guess we can all just live happily ever after.

I love to teach, talk, and write. I never get tired of saying the same things over and over. I've done it for seventeen years. Other teachers have said the same things, over and over. Same information, different faces. I believe some teachers have said the same words for so long, they forget you're just learning. They become impatient because you just don't get it.

If you have teachers you love, you might want to gift them with a copy of this book to show your gratitude. (Maybe they're unconscious of the love they project and it's time they became aware what they're doing right.) If you have teachers you especially dislike, maybe your class could take up a donation and get helpful information to them, teaching them how to become more effective.

My dad has three master's degrees; for many years, he

was an English/drama/shop teacher. I was so grateful he changed professions before I reached high school, so he wouldn't be my teacher. He was harder on his own kids than he was others. He expected more.

I was in grade school the first time I heard that a teacher in a Chicago school system had been stabbed by a student. It scared me that my dad could be at risk.

I heard horror stories of drugs and violence in schools many years after I graduated. I was a sophomore before I was even aware of drugs, and only a small minority of kids were involved. Now even elementary schoolkids are introduced to guns, drugs, and violence.

Teachers are paid to teach, not baby-sit, not hand out various medications, not handle out-of-control children even the parents can't control or police the campuses. They're not paid to teach manners or social skills.

Just for a moment, think of teachers as real people. They have families, bills coming in, loved ones going through frightening health situations, and personal concerns and fears. They are expected to put those day-to-day experiences out of their minds and stand before you. Daily, they enter a classroom with thirty to fifty different personalities, boys who got jilted and are depressed, girls with PMS who are overly sensitive, clowns (like I was), kids who are stoned, and kids filled with rage over a family argument before school. Can you imagine how hopeless teachers must feel standing alone, surrounded by such differing needs? And to top it all off, they have to capture your imagination and attention to teach you a boring or difficult subject.

When I told some people I was writing a spiritual guidebook for Teen Angels/Adult Children, their response was, "Whoa. Tough crowd." They actually offered their sympathy on the subject, rather than a "Go, girlfriend." Your reputations precede you. I'm probably too ignorant or innocent to have the same concerns in writing to and for you.

Is your teacher a rose or a thorn? Both are needed. My high school teacher for shorthand and office education was a total pain. On our first day of class, he informed us of his rules. As we learned shorthand and did homework assignments, he was going to call upon us, at random, to read our chicken scratches. If we couldn't read from the text or our assignments when called upon, we got an automatic F. If we got three F's, we flunked the entire semester.

None of us girls thought his rules were fair. We gossiped about, despised, and feared him. Mr. Munoz was tough, scary, and damn . . . he was confident! Some of the girls failed. I was scared . . . straight to the top of the class, which earned me a high-paying on-the-job program at the Northern Arizona Department of Public Safety. I went to school in the mornings and worked the afternoons as a secretary to one captain, one lieutenant, four sergeants, forty-three patrolmen, four dispatchers, two field technicians (and a partridge in a pear tree). I was the only female among all those men.

Mr. Munoz, the scariest, meanest teacher of my life, was also whom I *chose* to teach me bookkeeping. There was a saying around the school: "If you can't learn it from Munoz, you can't learn it at all." Later in life, I wrote him a sincere thank-you letter. If he hadn't stretched me, I might never have done the things I did, had the positions I'd gotten because of my skills, or become who I am. Good or bad, who's to say?

Some teachers who were marshmallows never served me. Their low self-esteem was evident, and wanting to be liked by the kids was more important to them. They were easy to manipulate.

We are all teachers. We are teaching one another all the time. To some, we teach lessons. Other times, we teach love.

Understanding comes from experience. As humans, we have so much to learn—patience, sharing, trust, compassion, to name but a few.

You may not understand until many years later, how a single teacher in school, home, or society has affected your life.

Some of my best friends/teachers have been thorns who forced me out of denial. I would like to say that I'd prefer the rose, the softer touch. But that approach isn't always effective or what forces us to grow. Ask yourself what your troublesome teachers are trying to teach. Although it's painful, maybe they're showing you one of your judgments. Because our consciousness mirrors our beliefs in outer form, perhaps the thorn is merely showing you that you believe a teacher is separate from God. Realize their Oneness and watch the teacher leave your experience *or transform.*

I had been married nineteen years, and we lived in a house of glass and stone on a golf course. The home had thirteen sliding glass doors. As I was spritzing the windows one afternoon, I stated the following affirmation aloud as I did my chores. "Those who are no longer a Divine part of the Plan of my life, leave effortlessly, easily, painlessly, peacefully, and perfectly." I added, "All those who are a part of the Divine Plan of my life come to me now." I found myself in divorce court so quickly, I didn't know what hit me. My mom said it was the most peaceful divorce she'd ever seen. It wasn't that I had a "bad" first husband. It was just that we no longer served one another's highest good.

As you raise your consciousness, some people, things, and habits will leave your life, without struggle or effort. Peacefully.

Those teachers in schools who aren't fulfilled but remain

for tenure or a paycheck may receive a blessing of freedom through your prayers (of opening to the violet light and recognizing Oneness). Oneness: God appearing as the teacher. Twoness/Duality/Karmic Law: a teacher *and* God.

When I am writing or speaking publicly or on the phone, I ask for Spirit to write or speak through me. I want to remove the ego, the human personality, so others can hear the Truth. When I'm looking at a person in my daily life, or listening on the phone, I raise my consciousness of that individual as well. I ask God to speak through him or her. This gets around human wills, personalities, egos, and emotions to be avoided. No more duality, no competition, neither wanting to take from the other. Just Oneness, allowing God to glorify both.

Back to Mr. Munoz for a quick story. Our school was two stories high, and one day I came out on the second landing after his class and headed to my next one. My arms were full of books. The wind caught my full, pleated skirt and whooshed it clear up over my head. There I stood, exposed to Mr. Munoz, who was standing on the sidewalk below me.

At that time of my life, I was always color coordinated with my outfit, so I'm sure he enjoyed the pink full slip that blew up right along with my skirt as I stood before him with bare legs and little pink bikini panties. I tried, with books in hand, to pull the skirt and slip down, but I must have looked pretty lame.

Can you imagine my embarrassment? And do you want to know what Mr. Munoz did? Rather than laugh, which would have added to my discomfort, he smiled softly and compassionately and turned away from me. Not pretending it didn't happen, but giving me an opportunity to compose myself with dignity. It was a great and honorable act of love. He taught love for a student through his actions, teaching me one of life's greatest lessons that comes without a grade.

Life itself is the greatest teacher. So many people call or write me; besides requests for prayers and healings, the number one call for guidance concerns their destiny. Not that they want me to be a psychic and tell them, but they request guidance how to discover it themselves.

Using myself and a handful of loved ones will help you discover the answers to the mystery of why you were born.

My friend Nikki, as a small child, drew a beautifully detailed picture of a cat hanging from a tree. You've seen the poster and pictures of this, with HANG IN THERE written across the artwork. Nikki saw this vision and drew it many years before it became popular. She entered her drawing in a contest and was accused of cheating, tracing someone's work.

Her gift went invalidated, and with no self-worth or pride in her work, she allowed the gift to be misused throughout life and prison. Doing beautiful full-face portraits or original drawings for cards for inmates to send their families, Nikki bartered for a few packs of cigarettes. Although hours were put into each drawing, she had no conception of their worth. For example, she put 180 hours of work into our *Between Saint & Sinner* book cover. It was not unlike her to spend that many hours on a beautiful portrait and perhaps receive fifty dollars, if that.

I recognized her gift and invited her to join hands in a dream. But after she got to Montana, she found she could no longer do her artwork. She said, "It actually hurts me to draw." Too many, for too long, had taken advantage of her. This isn't shared to make her feel guilty for not fulfilling the dream, or to make you angry with her for being unable to, or to make you believe she's a victim. The art was only one of Nikki's talents. She's an exceptional writer, as well, and has countless organizational skills that she now uses in her day-to-day office job. The art helped her to survive on many occasions, and was a single step in meeting me, to take her where she would find herself now.

As a child, her mother recognized her talent, and had events gone otherwise she might have become a famous artist. She was a child prodigy, but that wasn't the talent God wanted to develop within her for this life. It had already been developed in another life, and she had other lessons to learn and gifts that would become developed. She didn't "miss the boat," and was not denied an opportunity by not using that talent. We are never denied the fullness of God on any level. He can and does express Himself through each of us.

As an elementary student, our daughter became fascinated with *Star Wars* and watched it so often she could quote it. Kerrie wanted to grow up and work for NASA. She researched and found that more astronauts graduated from Purdue than any other university. Her goal became getting grades that would allow admittance to this school. Remaining focused, she graduated as valedictorian of her class, one more step toward fulfilling her dream.

Kirk sacrificed so Kerrie could attend space academy, where they put the "trainees" in mock space situations to see how they react under stressful situations. Kerrie read and memorized her job description so she wouldn't fail her teammates. Concerned they might forget their own jobs, she read and memorized their job descriptions, as well. She came away from space camp with every award they had to offer.

She continued to remain focused. She dreamed of designing the first manned U.S. space station. She'd need to go, too; if something went wrong, she'd know how to fix it. Kirk and I encouraged her to reach for the stars. We urged her to have her first child among the stars, rather than below them.

Her first year at Purdue, she wanted to drive home for the holidays. I wouldn't hear of it. She could fly, I insisted. It wasn't until I realized later how silly I was being. I'd allow her to fly to the moon but was scared for her to drive across the United States. Duh.

Not everyone is as fortunate as Kerrie, knowing their destiny. Hopefully, before I finish writing this, you will be able to see the part you play in God's Divine Plan a little easier. The Unseen World is teaching you every day, and as you learn to pay attention, the messages are no longer so subtle.

As early as six, I was being "volunteered" (uncomfortably for me) for lead parts in plays, choir, and standing in the spotlight. As a motivational speaker, I am on stage, and those early years were just preparation.

My hobby throughout life has been writing letters to people. As early as fourth grade, I had a pen pal in Germany. My first husband was serving in Vietnam when I met him on one of his trips home. I wrote anywhere from one to sixteen letters a day in the beginning, and one or two letters daily until he was released from the service. My parents were in Thailand for two years and I wrote daily letters to keep them aware of home and their connections. I wrote to a friend daily, and then two to three times a week near the end of his two Saudi Arabia and one Alaska pipeline jobs.

As long as I can remember, I played house, played with dolls, and wanted lots of babies. After school I would create tests for the neighbor kids and play the role of "teacher." I am now a mother, still playing house, and I am a spiritual teacher.

I was a carhop and waitress during many summers of my life, and I love to serve the public and guests in my home.

My first high school position, as I mentioned, was at the Department of Public Safety. I told Nikki that had I met her earlier in my life, I would have been one to help get her behind bars, rather than later trying to get her released. My earlier focus was man-made law; now, it's to teach how to break Karmic Law and its belief in dual powers, and ascend to live under Spiritual Law of God's Grace. (And don't forget ol' Benish Law, of course.)

I worked for two coal-fired power plants as secretary to managers. Years were spent in acquiring the electric utility background. Now I am a generator of the purest electricity known. I am an individual conduit.

One of you bright lights who hears this information will discover how to put a metal rod into the ground and draw electricity directly from Mother Earth. No longer will gas, coal-fired, steam- or wind-generated, or nuclear power plants be necessary. No more need for outdated or dangerous sources of electricity will be necessary or needed. I've already seen this invention, so it already exists. It's just waiting for its dreamer.

I worked in a bank as a secretary, therefore I have the skills needed to do the bookkeeping and money handling for my ministry and publishing company. In every job I had, I acquired a talent I'd need later. And I was getting paid to learn.

I was the executive director's secretary at a university foundation, where folks researched and wrote grants. Now, as a nonprofit, I'm nearing the step of having a grant written so the Miracle Healing Ministry can charitably get self-help books into 1,104 state and federal prisons nationwide.

Every "job" was preparing me for my destiny. You *do* know why you're here and what you're here to do. You can be confused and think you've forgotten. But though you walk unconsciously, just going through the motions of living day to day, if you will look where you've been, you'll become conscious of why you're here. It's hard to see the forest for the trees if you're standing in the center of the forest. But your destiny is all around you. Every act you have ever performed is a part of your destiny, preparing you moment to moment. And you don't have the power to screw it up. Whew!

You'll be stretched. You will not be stretched to the snapping point—unless you just want to experience that, and then of course you have free choice to do that, also. Trying to figure out all the steps is what winds you tighter than the rubber band. Some people get so twisted, they no longer resemble a rubber band. Relax. Unwind.

God sends you messages and teachers in all forms. A turtle might be telling you to slow down. A deer, to be gentle with yourself and others. You might see a butterfly, and as it unfurls its wings, you will realize that great transformation is forthcoming.

I'm just one spiritual teacher for you. Many more will come and go from your life. Life speaks to you moment to moment and teaches endless lessons.

How wonderful that you have some helpful insight on your destiny. Your hobbies, jobs, careers, daily experiences are all part of it. You don't just wake up one day saying, "Oh, this is my destiny." It's not the final destination that's important, it's the journey along the way. So enjoy it.

The situations you hate the most are the ones that force you to grow. Change isn't always comfortable. When you find yourself in those moments of fear and discomfort, remember that good stands behind that appearance. Don't resist it, welcome it. Not only will you learn the lesson more easily, but the experience will also reveal what new door is getting ready to open. If a door of rejection closes in your face, know that the next door will open. If you are rejected, realize that it's only because God has better plans in store for you. You will always have everything you need to fulfill your destiny.

The teachers who daily stand before you have a great deal more to teach you than simple basics of reading, writing, and arithmetic. Maybe they're teaching you who you don't want to become. Maybe they're showing you ideals you want to incorporate into your life. All ages are always learning and we're going to keep doing it over and over, until we get it right. If that takes millions and millions of years, God is going to be patient with us.

History repeats itself if we don't learn. As teachers of teachers, let's learn the lesson of love. As we demonstrate it, others will learn and live it, as well.

Enjoy your Journal and let's take a break to enjoy a home-cooked meal, together.

OPEN YOUR JOURNAL AND ANSWER THESE QUESTIONS

Journal—Chapter Fourteen

1. Kids—how far can you stretch yourself? What is your present grade point average? Can you imagine being at the top of your class? Can you imagine hitting that home run or being the hero for running the final touchdown that wins the game?

Parents—if you're taking night classes, ask yourself, "Can I imagine being at the top of my class?" Can you imagine living in your dream home and doing what you love? Can you imagine a happy, loving family? Stretch yourself and imagine your dream.

2. Start at a place you feel comfortable. Begin with one

subject or test. Write your vision below and return later to write the outcome. As you feel more comfortable, stretch yourself in all areas of your life and experience.

3. Practice dissolving a cloud or an argument you see occurring. Write about your experience.

4. If you are running late, stop fretting. Stand or sit still, take a deep breath, see the clock on the wall displaying the time you need to arrive. See yourself saying, "I did arrive safely on time." Write of your experience below.

5. Do you know someone who has cancer or another illness? See the word in your mind on a chalkboard. Watch as the giant white light eraser erases the word from your mind. See the person calling to tell you the cancer no longer exists. Tell no one you do this. First of all, they will plant seeds of their doubt in your mind. Second, they'll believe you're on an ego trip, seeking glory, credit, and thanks. Be silent. Write about your experience before and after it manifests.

When I use the word *teacher* below, realize I'm referring to school/boss/society/family/friend.

6. Name the teachers you've loved and why.

7. Name the teachers you respect and why.

8. Name the teachers you disliked and why.

9. Name two or more of your favorite memories of work/school days.

10. Name two or more of your worst memories of work/school days.

11. What were the lessons you learned from your positive and negative memories? What attitudes were inspired within you from these experiences?

12. What was the nicest or best thing a favored or unfavorable teacher ever did for you?

13. What are your first memories of life?

14. What were your favorite toys? Dolls? Blocks? Lincoln Logs for building? Legos, computers, art supplies, or just being highly creative?

15. Were you a dreamer? Did you lie on the grass and look to the sky, filled with clouds, and see shapes no one else could see? What is your dream?

16. What are your hobbies?

17. You are so multitalented . . . but are there one or two things that bring you the most joy to do?

18. What are those things you dislike doing the most? Those, too, are interwoven in our destiny and journey. The things I hated most, I had to keep attracting until I was neutral about doing them.

19. Do you have gifts/talents/dreams that others don't honor or validate? List them. They are important—perhaps only to you. For now, that's okay. But I'm asking you to honor them first.

20. Do you have a gift others have misused or abused, like Nikki, and no longer want others to know of this talent? Many healers "burn out" because they are judged if they charge; "it's not holy" to do so. What makes healing different from other gifts? Why can a superstar charge millions for entertaining you in sports or movies, while one who can heal a life is not paid? What is your gift that you yourself have not placed value on? Write about an experience of being used, the feelings of anger or resentment, and then write what amount you believe you deserve to receive if you choose to use it again. There is no shame in receiving your worth . . . and there's no power in opposition to you preventing you from experiencing payment.

21. How can you remain focused, even if a friend/ boss/mate/parent/teacher/counselor doesn't support you in your dream? What grade point average do you need to attain to reach the next step? What university or trade school offers you the best education to fulfill your desire? Is money a problem? If so, see yourself already there and be dazzled as scholarships and other assistance appears. Money never needs to be the problem, so don't use it as the excuse from preventing you from *just doing it.* (Just see the end result.)

22. If you're at an age when you can already look back, viewing how your steps have been provided, preparing you for where you stand right now, write them down. Did you work as a lifeguard, and receive training... then months later, while on vacation, save someone's life? Look at a message you received just yesterday that someone you were talking to today needed as an answer. Watch, look, and listen. Magic is in the air.

23. Are you a rose or a thorn with your teaching method? Are you patient or abrupt? Do you have a low or high tolerance for people? Are you quick to anger? Is it easy to smile? What's your easiest button to push? You may want to be conscious of that button, because it's going to be pushed (by the Unseen World, acting through others) until it's no longer a button.

Write your heartfelt thoughts in the Journal and state this affirmation aloud. *Alpha and Omega, from beginning to end, I am held perfectly in the Mind of God. My destiny is clear and I am conscious as it is revealed one day at a time.*

15
Soul Food

C'mon in and gather around my table. There's room for everyone. Kirk and I bought a bigger table because our kids would bring so many friends home for meals. Their parents were either working or didn't have time to prepare family meals, and these kids enjoyed coming to our home for a sit-down-get-together-with-a-family-and-discuss-their-day. Many of Kerrie's and Jaime's friends, now graduated and grown, still enjoy the memories of meals at our house.

I love to cook and I love to see people eating and enjoying the food I prepared while whistling or humming. (It's usually the *Addams Family* theme, so if I ever ask you to "name that tune," you'll already have a clue what it is.)

For lunch today, I've prepared spiritual food, with loving hands, to feed your hungry souls. For those of you who eat meat, there's spaghetti with meatballs and tossed salad with every vegetable I could add to it, in all the colors of the rainbow. Radishes, tomatoes, cucumbers, red, green, yellow, and orange bell peppers. Purplish red onions thinly sliced, and shreds of purple cabbage. Carrots, broccoli, and cauliflower, too. Lots of choices of salad dressings, and a nice garlic toast. I've got a wonderful turtle sundae for your dessert.

For you vegetarian eaters, I've got an Alfredo sauce for your pasta, and a side dish of steamed, sliced, and sweetened carrots and broccoli.

Before we eat, I'd like you to rub your hands together. Place your rubbed hands toward one another. You can feel warmth, tingling, and a little bit of resistance as you bring your hands together. Now rub your hands together again and place them toward the hands of a family member sitting next to you. You can't "see" the energy, but you can feel it. For now, while I'm teaching you, rub your hands a third time and place them about an inch above the food on your plate.

I'm not sure if you saw the movie *Like Water for Chocolate.* I didn't, but I heard that it was about a woman who loved a man her sister married. As she was preparing the family's meal, she wept and the tears fell into the food. That evening, as her loved ones ate the meal she had prepared while processing her pain, they began crying. Although they didn't know why, they were feeling her emotion as they consumed the energy of sadness she had felt in preparation.

With your hands over your food for a few moments or minutes, you are dissolving another person's negative energy. Not everyone likes to cook. Think back on a time when some of your food didn't set well, gave you a sour stomach, or made you sick. Was the cook angry or upset when the food was being prepared?

As an exercise, I'd like you to go to your kitchen cupboard, or to a local grocery store. Go to the bean aisle. You can do this with any food, but beans are very dramatic to make my point. It doesn't matter if they are pinto, navy, or white beans. Take a bag of beans off the shelf, rub your hands, and place them over the beans. The energy will feel very erratic on the bottoms of your palms. They will feel like Mexican jumping beans. As your hands continue to rest over the beans, you will begin to sense them feeling "more peaceful."

Now imagine if those beans were cooked in that erratic state and you ate them. No wonder beans make us feel bloated and we "fluffy" (pass gas).

"Raying" your food by putting your rubbed hands over it will dissolve the negativity of whoever prepared it, farmed, produced, packaged, or placed it on the shelf. Everything is energy. Purifying your food's energy will allow it to be returned to its natural state of goodness.

Many people think they have to become vegetarian to be spiritual. I don't agree, because I see all things as One. However, I offer no judgment about what people eat or don't eat. Your bodies crave certain foods. Parents want kids to eat healthy because it's preventive health care.

There are so many restaurants, I wonder how they can all stay in business. But then I realize that cooking at home is becoming a lost art. Parents don't have time to cook, and kids don't know how. And many have no desire to learn how.

I don't force my kids to learn to cook, but I encourage them to join me in the kitchen. D.W. and Danielle made me breakfast two days ago. Eggs Benedict. I was impressed, and the fact that they cleaned up their mess was just as wonderful.

I attempt to teach them every shortcut I can, along with ways to enjoy cooking. During one Thanksgiving dinner preparation, I taught them plenty about what *not* to do! I had gone holiday food shopping and bought a five-pound bag of frozen, tender, tiny peas. While I finished a few errands and drove back home, they had thawed. I refroze them, so when I got ready to prepare them for the holiday meal, the bag had frozen into "one solid pea." Everyone was sitting around the kitchen table, talking while I cooked.

Proudly I said, "Hey, everyone watch this." You know how you break a five-pound bag of ice from the store by dropping it on the pavement or floor? Wellll . . .

I had all of their attention as I dropped the five-pound bag of peas to the kitchen floor. The end of the bag blew out and blasted peas all over the kitchen. My kids said, "Great lesson, Mom." Kirk's brother Doug, as a guest, replied in a tattletale tone, "Kir-rk, Gloria just pea'd all over the floor . . ."

Down-to-earth stories like that, concerning our lives together under this roof, make you realize we're normal people, too. Normal? Well, at least average . . .

One of my dreams would be to write a book for kids to be given the day they move out of their parents' homes. Or to be used while still at home, to prepare the family's meals.

I didn't realize that the ability to cook a turkey dinner with all the trimmings didn't come easily to everyone. Having every meal come off the stove hot, all at once, is considered a gift.

In my cookbook, I'd offer healthy menus and choices, stating what would be needed to be bought in order to prepare the meals, and in what amounts. There would be step-by-step instructions for how to bring the meal from stove to table easily, effortlessly, and enjoyably. (And what to do with the leftovers. I don't like food to be wasted . . .)

Though I'm not a general and don't make my kids toe the mark on every single issue of life, I seem to have a natural-born talent to "cook for an army." I make dozens and dozens of homemade sausage/biscuits and freeze them so the kids have healthy food to eat while I'm teaching across the nation. Dozens and oodles of cookies, all varieties, homemade breakfast burritos, and my specialty, green chili/pork/potato/cheese burritos.

While you're sitting there enjoying your meal, I'd like to offer you some simple teachings. On a physical level, do you understand the importance of balance in drinking water, eating, sleeping, exercising, and playing? And especially eating veggies and things you may not care for, to maintain your physical health through preventive maintenance? Sometimes we have to do things we don't want, just because it keeps us healthy. The physical is as important as the spiritual as we live in this dimension. Also, our spirit must be in balance; if it's neglected, we don't live a full, well-rounded, healthy life.

We drink approximately eight to ten eight-ounce glasses of water daily because we are all natural-born healers. Water is a conductor of electricity/energy and, being electromagnetic energy, we will dehydrate if we don't drink enough water. Many illnesses and pains are the result of severe dehydration. By the time our lips tell us they are dry, we are already dehydrated.

Getting sunshine feeds us natural vitamins, but for me, it also helps burn off negativity I've taken on (purposefully) from others. Since I know how to dissolve it by placing my hands over my eyes at the end of the day, I want to "get it out of another person" who may be unaware how to do this. I encourage you not to consciously do this until you're also aware how to burn off negativity, but too late. Being compassionate, empathic, spiritual, loving beings, you are already doing it. So remember, nightly place your hands over your eyes. Also, when the weather is nice, enjoy daily sunshine, ten to thirty minutes, depending on your personal comfort level.

Sleeping? This is individual, although we're taught in

school that eight to ten hours is needed. For me, it's not so much sleep that I need; I just need to reach the dream state. If I haven't received my spiritual direction in daily quiet time and meditation, through visions or intuition, I hunger for it in my dreams. For example, last night—or I maybe I should say this morning since it was two-twenty—I had to get up. I went to bed at ten at night, but around one in the morning, I started dreaming about writing.

I couldn't go back to sleep, so I opened myself to the violet light. Still unable to sleep, I got up and made a pot of coffee. I felt as if I'd had a full night's sleep. I can ask you to trust your body, and urge you to get the rest you need. Don't get run-down on a continual basis. Bodies grow and heal while you're sleeping.

Playing is great. Some people, any age, find it hard to take the time to do so. It is necessary. Look how healthy and happy you children are when you run and play hard, skip and scream. You rush to grow up and miss out on childhood. Then when you're my age or older, you want to turn back the clock because everything got too serious and you have no time to play. Maybe that's one of the reasons I like kids so much. I'm willing to play with them when I'm around them.

Parents, remember how much fun it was to stand with your arms out at your sides, as a child, and become a human top? You'd spin as fast as you could in a counter-clockwise motion until you were dizzy. That is actually a spiritual exercise that alleviates stress, and it's also "rumored" that it reduces and reverses the aging process. Whether it does or not, it feels good.

You Teen Angels/Adult Children are so grown up these days, but you should find a safe place to twirl (since it sounds so immature and lame). Play, play, play. Work will come all too soon, so *enjoy* your youth.

Work. See how quickly that came? And it's a part of daily reality. Don't be afraid of it. I have to be honest. If you think you'll become spiritual and your workload will become easier, you have another think coming. There's a saying: "What does one do before one becomes enlightened? Haul water and chop wood. What does one do once one becomes enlightened? Haul water and chop wood." One woman asked me, "I'll bet you hate to come down from that level of miracle consciousness to mop your kitchen floor." I responded, "I love to mop my kitchen floor, because I see the Presence of God in everything I do."

As you become enlightened, you will discover you're actually here to be a servant to all, not just the "slave drivers" under your own roof. I just shook my head and heavily sighed as I realize some people go to an eight-to-five job and they're done for the day, and have weekends off.

Now, I'm not whining. Well, maybe I am, but it's okay. You're a great listener and a broad shoulder to lean on for a second. (And besides, I *like* to whine!)

See, I was ignorant when I turned eighteen and moved out on my own. I didn't even know you had to pay for water. I felt such an accomplishment as I paid those first utility bills for electric, and phone, and . . . trash? You mean you actually have to pay someone for coming and taking something you don't want anymore? And you pay *more* if it's really heavy? (I almost croaked the first time I went to the dump and found out I had to pay six dollars to get rid of our trash. I thought, perhaps, it would be more fun in the future to spend that money on a movie instead . . .)

I was so dense. To show you how dense I was, I was shocked when the bills came in for the next month, too. And kept coming in. I guess I thought if I paid them once, I was done with it for a lifetime.

Life is continual growth, so imagine me when I was

forty-four years old and signing a contract to buy a van. It's the first car I bought on my own where a husband didn't commit to the payment responsibility. When I bought the van, I was teaching lots of workshops and doing private healings. The donations went into the ministry and were used for the monthly payment since it was a business vehicle.

I had no sooner signed the five-year note than all those opportunities stopped. Oh dear. Being prideful, I wouldn't ask Kirk to pay for something for which I hadn't sought his opinion or support to purchase. He offered to make the payments, but it was time for me to grow up and be a big girl.

It wasn't until I took responsibility to pay for (or sell) the van that I knew how either my first husband or Kirk—and all men—feel worldwide. Good grief, the burdens they carry to provide financially, the concerns for possible or real layoffs—I hope you can understand why your parents (or mate) may not always be quite as cheerful as you think they should be at the end of the day.

That feeling of responsibility, of a simple car payment, was heavy. I could have easily sold the van. Think of men and single women who carry the financial burdens for a family. My van was not a necessity. Those who are providers don't have that option. The mortgage, car, utilities, food, extras, insurance, car maintenance, income tax, property tax . . . all become heavy to those who are attempting to live a human life without spiritual awareness.

Just when you think you're going to get caught up and have a little extra for a change, ol' Aunt Whatchamadoozie gets sick and you have to spend $850 to fly to her side and nurse her back to health. So much for the summer vacation fund. Better keep working, instead of playing, *just in case* another emergency comes up.

Spiritual reality is great for me to share, but so is physical reality. When I left the workforce to start my family at age twenty-nine, word processors and computers were just beginning to be introduced into the business world. When I rejoined the working world, I hadn't worked outside the home for nearly a decade, and I found myself lacking confidence to reenter that world. My skills were outdated.

As I walked away from the nineteen-year marriage, I felt fear to raise my two children in the style to which we'd become accustomed. For half of my life, my parents had financially supported me. The second half, my husband had. Now I was alone, and facing the world was frightening.

I moved out of the three-thousand-square-foot glass and stone house on a golf course and moved in with my sister Sheila in Aurora, Colorado. Texas had been heaven to me with its friendly, warm, loving people and climate. The Denver area was a "big city" and, my God, where would I begin looking for a job? I'd never left my kids with sitters, except on rare occasions. I was overprotective because I had waited so long to begin my dream. I didn't want a stranger raising my kids.

Sheila and I struck a bargain. She, being a single parent of two daughters, gave me room and board in exchange for watching her kids, cleaning, cooking, and laundry. Her meals were ready when she got home from work, a luxury she'd never had until I moved in.

Our arrangement worked quite well for both of us. My parents, knowing I needed to "grow up," encouraged me with want ads and suggestions. I don't think I was as afraid of work in the modern world of technology as I was at the thought of leaving my children.

My dad asked one day if I'd ever considered being a cocktail waitress, because if I was willing, Holiday Inn was hiring. He thought my personality would rake in big tips.

I appreciated his suggestion, but I needed to make my

dad aware of my fears. I had been so sucked dry of energy, I'd lost all my hair two years prior. Doctors said it wouldn't grow back and I replied, "You just watch me . . ." Never say never to me or anyone on this planet, right? I willed my hair to grow in, along with some helpful Guidance from Spirit.

I had helped countless alcoholics, and couldn't conceive of putting myself (on purpose) into a cocktail position. Bartenders and hairdressers also fit into the "friendly neighborhood priest" classification—the ones to whom lost souls unburden themselves.

I just couldn't counsel one more person until I got my own life back on track. Plus, with my magnetic personality in that type of situation, and my vulnerable state of mind, I'd be setting myself up to attract another alcoholic. I might have used or manipulated a man. I was conscious of my fear of being alone and I didn't think a man deserved to have to caretake me any longer.

Just to be on the safe side, and learning to depend on my own resources, talents, and courage, I would find another way to support my kids and financially help my sister until I could get a place for the kids and me.

My favorite (only) brother, Bill, stopped at my parents' home while I was visiting one day. Teasing, I asked, "Bill, why don't you hire me?" He looked intently at me and asked, "Are you serious?" Seeing the look on his face, I have to admit, I was feeling strange inside. I found myself asking in return, "I don't know, are you?"

My logic was screaming, "Have you lost your mind, Gloria?" But my heart was saying, "Go for it."

At the time, my brother was a manager of the McDonald's in the Aurora Mall. He was also a great troubleshooter, meaning he'd been hired more than once to bring substandard restaurants up to health code acceptance. His personality and ability to gain employees' respect is outstanding.

He said, "Gloria, I've got six weeks to get ready for inspection and with your personality and hardworking ability, I definitely could use your help." I was given a hat and name badge and began working the next day, for minimum wage.

Going from living on a golf course and only knowing high-paying secretarial jobs, I was humbled by the experience. I worked my "taillights" off. Because I'm small, Bill had me cleaning from floor to ceiling, spritzing and shining the chrome cabinets and fixtures.

I waited on customers and was old enough to be my coworkers' mom. I washed down tables, swept, emptied trash, and mopped the dining room. Cleaned the bathrooms, washed dishes, and returned to clean the dining room again and again.

In one shift, I'd mop six to eight times and empty trash, picking up the public's mess. I felt like I'd graduated from two toddlers to hundreds and hundreds a day. I was actually shocked to see how the public disrespected this McDonald's. They left the trash on the floor and seats, and didn't pick up after themselves.

On my final day at work, the six-week agreement with Bill was coming to an end. All the employees had worked hard getting ready for the inspection. Bill, along with the owner of the store, gave us all a pep talk before the doors opened on the day the inspectors would be arriving. The owner promised an extra twenty-dollar bill to whichever employee had the most smiling customers at the end of the shift. We were also prompted to "suggestive sell." Meaning, "Sir, could I suggest some french fries to go along with that sandwich?" We were also advised that the inspectors would time us to see how quickly we could get the orders up. The doors opened, and the race was on.

I needed that twenty bucks. I would be driving back to Texas for my final divorce with the money I earned from working for that six weeks. I needed tires and gas money. Twenty dollars seemed like one of the most important things in my life.

I told each customer who came to my station about the owner's offer. "Whoever has the most smiling customers gets an extra twenty at the end of the shift." Customers left my workstation laughing because they couldn't believe I was so honest.

At noon rush hour, I looked up from my cash register to see the face of the male inspector. I moaned aloud, surprised to hear my thoughts become verbal: "Oh no, why did you come to my station?" He smiled and said, "I heard you were the best." Sarcastic, I replied, "Right. I've been here six whole weeks."

Turning on my charm, I went on, "Okay, sir, how may I serve you?" He started overordering from every category and I recalled how we'd been told we'd be tested. After he'd named off enough items to feed a small army, I also remembered our "suggestive selling tactic." So I asked genuinely, "Sir, could I perhaps suggest an ice cream cone for dessert? And, maybe you'd like to eat it first, while I'm getting your order up." I ended with, "Because if you don't, and you eat all this first, you're going to have heartburn so badly, you won't be able to enjoy dessert."

He laughed and I wondered if I'd gone insane, talking to an inspector that way.

In record time, I had his order on the tray, except for a family-sized order of Chicken McNuggets. I asked him to have a seat; I would bring them to him as soon as they were available.

Three requests to the cook for the inspector's nuggets failed. Other employees kept snatching the order. By now, I was too embarrassed to take him the long-overdue order. Maybe I could pretend I forgot? No. I wouldn't want one mark against my brother's record for the restaurant, due to me.

So, shoulders back, head up, and walking as tall and proud as I could, I approached his table. As I placed the completion of his order on the table before him, I said genuinely, "I apologize, sir, for the delay in your order. I'm so sorry it took forty days and forty nights for you to get it, but I hope you enjoy—and have a nice day."

I hightailed it back to my station, not believing what had just fallen out of my mouth *again.*

At the end of the shift that day, as I was turning in my hat and badge, and saying good-bye to all my newly made friends, the owner and my brother, Bill, approached me. I had actually forgotten about the "deal" by surviving the rush hour. The owner placed twenty dollars in my hand and said, "The inspector said, *Thanks for the smile.*"

Smiles and kindness can and do feed people just as much as physical food.

Spirit provided for me and the children as I took physical action to humble myself and take a position, perhaps one I felt was beneath me. Probably until that experience, I thought I deserved to have the best-paying job, and yet I no longer had the skills to earn me the right to that position. I was going to have to work my way back up.

After my experience at McDonald's, I actually realized something far more important than just the physical money I'd been paid. In fact, my paycheck completely covered the tires and gas to get to Texas. The extra twenty allowed me to buy my kids, and all the nieces and nephews, each a sundae. (We always have everything we need, usually before we know we need it.)

The greatest lesson I learned from working for McDonald's was something that could be adopted into every family and the world. At the time I worked there, everyone was paid the same wage. It was the hardest job I've ever had . . . and it was a pleasure, although it came without "tips" for a job well done.

So here's your tip. The employees cover each other's backs, helping one another to get the food to the trays as quickly as possible. *No one* says, "That's not my job." They believe in team effort (although neither Bill nor the owner states that to the employees).

Think carefully about how well individual family units and the entire world would work, in harmony, if they just incorporated those few ideals in their lives.

I can see you've all finished your meal, so let's have that turtle sundae I promised you. Vanilla ice cream, hot fudge topping on half and caramel (or butterscotch) topping on the other half, whipped cream, a few whole pecans, and don't forget the cherry.

Rub your hands and "ray" the sundae, and enjoy, sweetie.

Following a meal, what do we do? Rub your hands and place them over your eyes for two to ten minutes, to help the digestion and keep your energy field high.

Enjoy your Journal before we continue.

Oh, and you're welcome. I heard each of you say, "Thank you, Gloria. The meal was delicious. Is there anything we can do to help you?" To that question, "Yes, there is. How nice of you to ask."

OPEN YOUR JOURNAL AND ANSWER
THESE QUESTIONS

Journal—Chapter Fifteen

1. When you rubbed your hands briskly together and placed them toward one another, what was your experience? Did you feel the warmth, tingling, and slight resistance as you brought your hands together, toward one another? Write of your experience.

2. If you have a pain in your body and place your hand about an inch away from the discomfort, does it feel extremely hot or cold? Does the energy in that area feel erratic or weak? Describe the experience you feel as you lay hands on, opening your mind to the violet light/Presence. Does the energy feel differently as the pain dissolves? Have you attempted this on a friend or relative, and if so, what was that experience?

3. Did you perform the exercise with a bag of beans to sense their "Mexican jumping bean" erratic energy? Did you sense the energy of other foods and especially on your personal lunch or dinner plate? Write about the experience.

4. Kids—do you like to cook? What are your three favorite meals? Research a cookbook and write the recipes for each. Invite a friend over for "Guinea Pig" night, and make the meal from your recipe. The deal is, "The guest has to eat it anyway, whether it turns out good or bad."

5. If you feel sluggish, drink a glass of water and see the difference you feel. Describe how water reenergized you.

6. Be in the sunshine for a few minutes and write about the difference in your attitude.

7. If you're feeling extremely angry, walk on the grass or lean your spine against a tree. Are you aware how much more balanced you feel, almost immediately? Do you have clearer thoughts? Write of your experience.

8. If you get a headache or migraine, touch a tree or a potted houseplant. In just a few seconds, or minutes, did you notice that your head doesn't hurt anymore? Write your experience.

9. Do you remember your dreams? Have you noticed how much more mentally alert you are after you dream? The subconscious symbols can be confusing. If you dreamed of a dog (as an example), is your belief that he is man's best friend? Or do you dislike dogs? How you feel concerning the symbols you are shown will guide you personally. Pay attention to the feelings you have during the dream, also. Write about and analyze a dream you recall.

10. What is your favorite way to play? Do you make time to play? Describe it.

11. Do you disrespect other people's property, or even your own? Do you lack appreciation for your clothes and belongings? What does your room, home, or vehicle look like? Clean and tidy, or dirty and cluttered? If you live in dirty surroundings, you can't think clearly. Write a suggestion to yourself about tidying up some aspect of your life.

For example, my friend had an inspirational bookstore. I stopped by to visit her and my attention was drawn to a card rack that was messy. I started tidying it as I stood talking to her. She shared her complaint that no one had bought any of the cards she'd ordered, assuming her customers would automatically see and be attracted to their beauty.

The rack, as long as I could remember, had remained

in the same spot. After I straightened the cards and aligned them with their matching envelopes, I asked her to help me move the rack nearer the counter. We watched in amazement how every customer thereafter, went straight to the card stand, read, enjoyed, and purchased at least one. Talk about immediate feedback!

Rearrange the energy in your room and home and see if you don't study and retain the knowledge easier, and enjoy your room and belongings more.

Also, remember this if you'd like to strengthen your memory. *Read it once a day for a week, once a week for a month, once a month for a year, and it's yours forever.*

12. In your family, do you find yourself saying, "That's not my job"? Do you believe in team effort? If you aren't getting enough (or any) quality attention from your parents, maybe you could offer to help them with the endless chores so they have time to spend with you. List some things you could do around the house, *without being asked* (those are the key words here). What three things could you do to make a difference in the beauty and atmosphere of your home?

13. Do your friends enjoy coming to your house? What attracts them?

14. Are you embarrassed to have your friends or boss over? Is it due to your home being messy? What steps could you take to correct this problem?

15. Society and the rising costs of living make it difficult for kids to move out on their own and "get a life." Is it fair to continue living at home and having Mom and Dad be responsible for your expenses into your thirties and forties? If you were a parent, would you be more apt to do the "tough love" thing, or would you selflessly continue picking up the tab? (Parents, you answer this one, too!)

16. Do your family or friends have a "cover each other's back" philosophy? Write an example.

17. Write a brief example of how you could drink water, eat right, rest, exercise, and play. What would your schedule look like to incorporate an organized routine?

18. Were you aware, before you read this chapter, how much stress a parent/mate feels to carry such a heavy financial burden? Describe how you could help relieve some of the burden. Could you get a part-time job, or baby-sit, to earn some of your spending money? Could you show greater appreciation for what you are now being given? Could you beg and demand less and offer more? Could you do helpful things "without having an attitude" or *without being asked*? Write some helpful ideas you could implement to surprise a parent/mate.

19. I tell Kirk often, "I love being your wife." I thank him for financially providing for us, and our meals are blessed by giving thanks for the loving hands that prepared the food, and for Kirk, who made it possible. Everyone enjoys knowing their hard work is appreciated. Our Creator's love is made manifest in the abundance of everything we eat, the clothes we wear, the entertainment and art we enjoy, and even the air we breathe. Saying thank you to those who provide lovingly for us is thanking God. Besides a gift that came to you with ribbons and bows, what other gifts of love surround you?

Write your heartfelt thoughts in the Journal and state this affirmation aloud. *Love appears in countless, priceless forms. It can appear as a (diamond) carat on a hand, or a carrot in hand. I am surrounded and filled with love.*

16
Honest to God

I'm so proud of *all of you!* Look how easy that was. I, like everyone else, enjoy feeling appreciated. But first I had to learn to appreciate *myself.*

Years ago when I was living in Sacramento, a woman came to me for a healing. Following our time together, she offered to pay me. I knew she was living at poverty level and I asked, "Do your kids need shoes?" Blushing from embarrassment, she replied, "Yes." I said, "Then take the money you would have been willing to give to me, and go fill the needs of your children."

Quite often, I asked people who wanted to donate to me to give to others. Whatever amount they would have given to me, I would have them write an affirmation such as, "There's plenty for everyone" or "You are loved" on the bill and place the money, at random, on people's windshields. Imagine a person's surprise to receive such an unexpected loving gift.

One woman, following her healing, called to tell me her cute story. After her session, she wrote an affirmation of love on a five-dollar bill and put it on an old beat-up Volkswagen Bug windshield in a hospital parking lot. When she got home, she was sweeping fallen leaves on her patio. Amid the leaves, she bent and retrieved a five-dollar bill that said, "Thank you."

I also asked people—especially if their Spirit is broken, or find they're financially in trouble—to randomly put coins in parking meters that are about to expire. By taking our attention off our own problems, performing random, selfless acts for others, our personal problems dissolve. The intent and act of helping another removes the blocks preventing our goodness from manifesting. We are One. Therefore, if you withhold someone's good, you are withholding your own. (You are setting the Karmic Law into motion.) Be willing to pay your debts and loans. They trusted you, offering their services for gas, heat, electricity, phone use, or credit cards. Do not attempt to cheat them and act like they *owe you*. *If you think you're getting away with something, you will find yourself angry and upset later, when someone doesn't cough up the money they promised you they'd pay.*

When I first married Kirk, I was forewarned that every year, around the holidays, the employees where he worked were threatened with layoffs. Knowing this beforehand, each year came and went without concern. Late in 1998, it was no longer a threat. The employees would be laid off for weeks, and possibly the paper mill would be closed. I asked Kirk not to worry. We as a family would move or do whatever we needed to, in support.

Actually, I had hit some pretty good sales prior to the news. A new grocery story opened in the area, giving our only local market some competition. The new store was practically giving food away, and it would have been foolish not to take advantage of the sales. We were well stocked with food, and Kirk and I got to spend many hours together, creating gifts and enjoying one another's company. I felt such tremendous gratitude that God, working through Stone Container, had given our family financial security (and without telling Kirk, at first) that I wrote the president, Mr. Stone, a sincere thank-you letter. It follows.

Dear Mr. Stone:

My husband, Kirk Benish, has been an employee of the Missoula Stone Container for ten years. During the last seven years I've been married to him, I have always written a "thank you" (to you) on his check before depositing it. An accounting department may get to witness the appreciation, but you have never been personally made aware of our family's gratitude. Hopefully, this letter will express our thankfulness.

We have been recently advised that the mill will be closing for a four-week layoff. Rather than viewing what we may not have as a future means of employment, both Kirk and I would like to express appreciation of all that we have had. Because of you and your company, which has always been good for industry as well as individuals, our family recognizes that without the opportunity to serve you, many of our goals would not have been met as easily.

Your company scholarship program awarded our daughter, Kerrie, eight thousand dollars toward her degree at Purdue University. She recently graduated in May as an aeronautical/astronautical engineer, graduating fourth in her class and sixth in the nation. With your help, our daughter has succeeded in reaching her dream and has been employed at the Houston Control Center. (I apologize that I never gave you personal credit until now.)

Whether the closure of the mill is for four weeks or forever, I couldn't allow another moment to pass without personally thanking you for all of the above. May abundance, success, and security be granted to you and your family, as you have provided to so many.

Sincerely, with deep respect,
Gloria D. Benish

A merger occurred and the mill did stay open. Only a few weeks passed and Kirk's foreman called him into his office. His supervisor said, "Kirk, a letter has recently come to my attention. In fact, every Stone Container plant, worldwide, has received this letter and it's *required* reading for all upper management." The foreman asked, "Betcha can't guess who wrote it?" Kirk gulped and replied, "My wife?" His boss affirmed Kirk's response and said, "And I don't think I've ever been more proud than I am right now to call myself a supervisor of one of my employees."

Wow, huh? I didn't know the far-reaching results of a simple random act of kindness. I just knew, from past experience, how fear and anger can escalate into insanity and sabotage in those situations. Love, given genuinely, can dissolve those fears and transform situations that effect thousands.

Get creative and think of anonymous random acts of kindness. Especially if you're bored. Maybe you feel tired or depressed? That's the best time to focus on another. Lonely? Go hold the door all day at a local mall and watch how much love, attention, and gratitude you get. Take a neighbor a cup of hot cocoa. Go visit your local nursing home and play them a tune on the piano.

Shovel your elderly neighbor's driveway. Call a shut-in and tell her you're running to the store. Ask if she needs anything and if she'd mind a little company later. If you're lonely, someone else out there is, too. Think of them and you'll find company in one another. I found genuine companionship in writing to convicts. I inspired them, but they also gave me a safe place to talk about my feelings so I could get clear on how I really felt about the topics we were discussing.

As my daughter Danielle wisely informed me, "Not everyone is going to like your writings, and you can't please everyone." Not every person will agree with me that using Matthew's and Nikki's experiences was necessary to help you learn choice making. Those who do agree might think that I deserve a feather in my cap for my good deeds of helping prisoners. I don't need the world's blessings—I have a heart that tells me that what I'm doing is right. I also have letters that confirm these acts of kindness. Nikki and Matthew have told me how important it's been that I "show them the world" through my eyes.

Nikki recaptures our relationship:

In November 1989, back on the prison-go-round, I was inspired to "Please stop!" in my first week in jail, and ended up with a compression fracture of my spine, two broken wrists, no medical attention, and a big dose of humiliation from my attempt to break my own neck.

When my back hurts now or cold weather inspires toothache pain in my wrists, I smile. It all led me to Gloria.

Having no idea who she was as a person, or even really caring at the time, I heaped cold accounts of my life on paper, baiting her to judge me. I fully expected her, even inspired her to see me the way all "straight" people saw people like me.

Well, Gloria was just as incapable of seeing the darkness as I was of seeing the light. The song "Because You Loved Me" by Celine Dion sums up every feeling I've ever been able to place on that unusual beginning and its growth.

I could not see, so she let me see through her eyes. I spoke through her. I believed through her. For the first time, I saw myself. Once I saw myself, I was able to see Gloria. Once I realized that the value my friend awakened in me wasn't a phantom, I was able to trust in it. I could let my friend see through my eyes, speak through me, and believe in herself through me.

It's truly strange, you know. Gloria gave me the knowledge that I wasn't just this thing that could not exist outside of my own darkness. Once I knew it, everything changed. I gave Gloria the ability to see the darkness she'd refused to acknowledge in her need to see only "good." Once she saw it, everything changed. Every change we've discovered together has created these two, separate, awesome women. Every change we discover separately is shared in depth.

We never lost sight of the nurturing love we share for each other, nor the love surrounding us. It was that love that brought two such uniquely different women together and gave them the honor of passing on the magic to others.

If we seem a little disgusting in our hero worship of each other, try not to hold it against us. When you meet us, you'll understand. We are amazing and nothing about that will change. Our appearance as a duo—our experiences— our future; all amazing. We invite you to see for yourselves. Who knows, you may be touched by something magical and delightful. Don't be surprised. We never are.

I've never understood selfish behavior. I suppose, until I became consciously aware, I judged it as "wrong." Which, of course, would attract another user into my experience. I even suppose that if I'm perfectly honest with myself, I'd have to say I'm probably one of the most selfish people I've ever known. I like how it feels to give. I like how it feels to love. And I'm not too danged proud to say that I really don't care where that love goes . . . whether to a next-door neighbor or to the next convict who writes to me.

Matthew shares his perception of our meeting:

It tripped me out when you said that you had a feeling of familiarity between us like we had met before. I didn't know what it was and therefore, didn't know how to put it into words, but that's exactly it. I felt close to you from the start. It was like we hadn't just started, but rather it was more like a continuation. I'm not really in tune with these types of things but just maybe we were brought together once more because we didn't finish something we had started previously.

Maybe this is a second chance. What that something is, I have no idea. But how else can we explain your book finding its way to me and touching me enough to inspire me to write a letter that would touch you enough to get you to respond? Now look at where we're at. And you're right. There has been a "shift" in our relationship. Maybe we are on the verge of finding out what our mission together is. Maybe it's something we are already doing or maybe it's something that we have yet to discover.

I just know that whatever it is, I'm ready. As long as you're beside me every step of the way, as I will be by your side, then we will have no fear. No hesitation. Even though we both help each other understand things and enjoy great communication, I don't think that's the extent of it. Besides, I don't think it's a "learning" process between us so much as I think it's a "rediscovering" process. No. I think in the bigger scheme of things, there is someone or some persons out there that we will make a difference to. There is no other explanation for it. Just look at our backgrounds. How unlikely is it for the two of us to meet, get to be friends, and be able to relate to each other on the level that we do?

I understand about how you and Nikki came to be, but I assure you, even though I know that Nikki went through hell and back, believe me, we are very different. I am not able to tell you the full story right now, but one day I will be able to. You see, my "adult" life story is not so much as what went on in the outside world, but what went down behind the walls.

One thing I wish you would do for me though: *Stop* saying that when the time comes, where I feel like I don't need you anymore or discontinue writing to you . . . blah! blah! blah! . . . Yadda! Yadda! Yadda! Cut it out already! What part of "Ain't Gonna Happen" don't you understand? Let me put it this way. What if one day I said to myself, "Hell, I don't need my eyes anymore! I'll just cut them out!" What would happen to me? I wouldn't be able to "see."

Do you understand? I need to *see*. I need to see from all different perspectives. *I see through you*. Not just the descriptions of snow on the trees that you describe to me, but "really" see. You have your "Aha's," I have my "Ka-Ching" when things register.

And I've had many things register since I've become reacquainted with you. I do understand your hesitation to become fully open with me. I'm also glad that it's a "you're a male" thing. That I can understand and appreciate. It does seem to me, however, that just as I am comfortable and relaxed with you, so are you with me. What do I get out of writing to you? Well, I get a nonjudgmental ear. I get someone who would like me to, and help me to, readjust my life and way of thinking to better find my way down life's path, but at the same time is willing to accept me just as I am if need be.

I get someone who can show me and teach me a different lifestyle from the one I'm accustomed to, one that I knew existed but didn't give much thought to. But most of all, I get unconditional love. Which is something else that I knew existed but thought was for other people, not a guy like me. My life has always been under one condition or another. At the same time, I also was guilty of placing conditions on things. I'm learning from you that life doesn't have to be like that. That not everyone in the world is out to "do you." I'm still learning. I don't think that there is enough time left in this life for me to learn all that you have to teach me. Maybe that's why we were brought together once again.

And maybe that's why we will be brought together again. Maybe we are part of an everlasting learning experience. I don't know or pretend to understand these things, I just know that I'm grateful to you.

Since I've been corresponding with Matthew, he has been moved out of a lock-down prison—something he's waited for, for nearly seven years now.

Well, here it is, the seventeenth of June, the day I've been waiting for—the day my hole time is officially *over,* but it doesn't look like I'll be "leaving" the hole today. Ain't that a kick in the ass! Before I tell you "why" I'm not leaving, first, let me tell you something else: *I don't care!* Of course, I would like to leave, but it's no big thing. You see, this is a significant improvement in my life. If they would have pulled something like this on me, not so long ago . . . Oh man! . . . it would have been a hot time in the town tonight! I'm telling you I would have gone straight bananas on them. Up until today, I wasn't sure how I would act if they pulled this because I knew in the back of my mind that something like this might happen. It always does. But I didn't really know how I would react to it.

I do attribute a lot of my remaining calm about the whole thing to you. I told you before that you've become a very stabilizing force in my life and you've helped me to "turn the corner." I look back on some of the things I've done while in prison and I've got to say to myself, "How stupid was that?" But, see, I never used to stop and think because my mind was always in such turmoil that the slightest thing would set me off. Later, I might have thought, "What the hell am I doing?" but by then, it was too late. I had already taken it too far so there was no turning back. One of the unwritten rules in here is that once you start something, especially with the guards, finish it.

I'm just taking all of this in stride. I don't want to give them a reason not to let me out. If they ever take me to a shrink to try and find out "why the sudden change in attitude and behavior," well, expect your name to be prominent in the explanation.

You know, even though I know that we are friends and that whatever I do in here won't affect that friendship, I still think to myself, "If I do that, what would Gloria think of me?" Even though I know that you would probably never find out unless I told you, it doesn't matter. Just me thinking that you would more than likely frown on it makes me stop dead in my tracks. That's what I mean by you "helped me turn the corner." Now I "think" about what I'm doing and in my mind, I know that I'm tired. I just might live to be eighty years old, so that means that I've already lived half of my life one way . . . now it's time to try and live the other half another way. Time to turn the page and start a new chapter. You helped me realize that. That's one of the reasons that I like to hear about your travels and what goes on in your home life. Makes me know that this is what I want and need, even if it is unobtainable to me, I can still keep the hope alive by striving toward it.

Who knows, maybe one day before they lay me down that final time, I will have experienced it once in my life. That's all I ask. And if not? Well, that's okay, too. You have let me experience it through you. Thank you and I will always love you for that and much more.

In his letter, Matthew commented that he believed our meeting would possibly affect someone "out there," and I believe he's right. The same is true with my friendship with Nikki. Had I not been Divinely drawn to these relationships, my writings would speak only of a happy family life and miracles. If so, my readers would say, "Well, that's all well and good, but none of that fits into my life." With the help of Matthew's and Nikki's experiences, I can easily relate choices, consequences, and reality that I would have had no understanding of otherwise. And to both of them, I once again give my thanks.

Do you realize how many people, places, things, and experiences we judge daily as good or bad? And how we limit ourselves with denials of our true selves and the ability to achieve our dreams?

Everything we judge as (human) good or bad keeps us under Karmic Law. When we can look at an uncomfortable situation we're in, realizing, "This, too, shall pass," we break the resistance and allow the experience to change. Many times instantaneously.

Looking at a person who's being rude and silently affirming the true nature of his or her soul, "This, too, is God" (appearing in form) heals the negativity. A silent "God bless you" purifies the behavior, as well.

We judge everything. We judge apples ("An apple a day keeps the doctor away"), believing them to be "good" for us. Yet that same apple may give another person hives, which would be "bad." An apple is just an apple—without power separate from God for human good or bad—unless we hold a simple judgment about it. Unless we give people or "things" power, beyond that of God, or in opposition to God, they are also God, appearing in physical form. In God, there is only harmony. There's nothing in God that can hurt you.

Your ability to be used as an instrument is not dependent upon anything you do or don't do. This ability is possible because *you now know the nature of God.*

You will become very aware of your judgments now, and you will heal them one by one as they appear, by remembering Oneness. Not God *and* "whatever," but God appearing *as* the "whatever." Healing judgments will become a daily process. "I ask for a conscious realization of Oneness concerning this situation." Or, demonstrating your faith that you have already received it, giving thanks for those things *not yet seen*, "I give thanks that I have a conscious realization and understanding of Oneness concerning this situation."

Don't try to fix or change the outer. *Take care of the inner and the outer will take care of itself.*

Sometimes you'll just want to keep making the judgments. It's human nature to want to do so. And it's okay for now. Changing a lifetime of behavior and responses may not all be fun.

Nikki once made the audience laugh on stage in Boise: "Discernment is the judgments I want to keep." Having "no opinion" about people's behavior, gossip, and actions can quiet the mind and dissolve the negativity quickly. Without "an opinion," there is no mind chatter and nothing good or bad to discuss. Thus, the judgment is healed. Humans feel smart to share their opinions, but opinions are judgments. We have opinions about everything.

Making judgments about relatively simple things, such as an apple and its good and bad qualities, doesn't seem as hard to bring to a state of consciousness of Oneness as the thought of a man serving a life sentence or a drug dealer. And yet both situations have equal need of healing as you rediscover how many judgments you meet daily.

Again, don't give up on yourself, thinking it's too difficult to maintain a constant level of consciousness above the Karmic good and bad beliefs. Awareness of your judgments is a fine place to begin. Don't expect overnight success. (Besides, I've heard that overnight success takes seventeen years.)

If you think you can't do this (or anything), you're right. But do you want to be right or happy? If you think you can achieve this state of consciousness or anything else you attempt, you're right about that, too.

We all say, "I can't." When we do, our belief blocks the flow of energy and ideas to fulfill what we choose to do. *The Little Engine* we read about as children said, "I think I can, I think I can . . ." In today's lesson, *know you can,* because you can.

At the end of our lunch, you offered to do something for me. And this is what I'm asking from you.

No matter where you find yourself, right now, instead of focusing on what you don't have, shift your awareness to what you do have.

You have your health? Many kids lie in a children's hospital, praying for a miracle.

You have a roof? Many street people don't.

You have food? Millions starve.

You have this information in hand. There are countless souls awaiting a helping hand.

How you can help me to help others is in learning to believe in yourself, your talents, gifts, and capabilities. I need you. The world needs you. It's my dream to see peace on this earth in my lifetime.

If you meet selfish individuals, teach them, by example, how to think of another. If you meet people who don't know how to receive, teach them. Demonstrate your love first to yourself, so you have it to give.

Practice what you've learned today. Practice daily and I promise it will be a better world. Your individual world and the world as a whole.

Don't look to "someone else" to do it. You do it. Each one of us, doing our part, will make a difference. (Can you imagine the transformation in individual schools and communities across America as your family and groups open themselves to the violet light/Presence of God? The word *miracle* would become a part of the world's everyday vocabulary.)

We must learn to listen. God talks all the time. Years ago I was working at a coal-fired power plant in northern Arizona as a secretary to the manager. I asked him, "Marshall, at lunch today, can I take an extra half hour? I need to do some errands in town." He immediately said no. No forethought, just no.

So I asked again. "Okay, but Marshall, at lunch today, can I take an extra half hour? I need to do some errands in town?" He looked at me like I was crazy and said, "I just told you no." I smiled and said, "I know. But I'm going to keep asking until you get it right." He laughed and let me have the extra half hour.

We do the same thing to God. We ask, but because it's not the answer we think we want to hear, *we keep asking, hoping He'll get it right.*

If we don't get what we asked for, perhaps it's because it's not for our highest good or something better awaits us.

We *do* get our answers, we just haven't been listening. When Nikki wanted to remove herself from our dream, I decided to pray about it. Silently I asked, "God, I'm asking for a conscious realization whether Nikki is supposed to be part of these businesses any longer."

The telephone rang immediately and I thought, "I can't get the phone right now, I'm waiting for a message from God."

The second ring, I thought, "Shaa! Maybe it *is* God calling." When I picked up the phone, I swear, this is what the woman said: "Hi. My name is Debbie and I live in New Jersey. I'm reading your book, *Go Within or Go Without,* and I'm very attracted to this character, Nikki. I'm wondering if you think she'd be willing to move to Scottsdale, Arizona, and caretake my elderly aunt?"

Nikki's next step was prepared, and my answer came through loud and clear, via AT&T. Not a booming voice in the clouds.

We ask silently. The answer comes through a parent, a child, a TV commercial, a song, a license plate, a friend (or maybe even an enemy). Our answers surround us. *Listen* and *silent* contain the same letters. They are just spelled differently.

I'd like to ask one more thing of you. After you complete your Journal, keep it so you can look back upon it years (or even months) later to see your growth. Also, before you pack it away for safekeeping, read back through it, and everywhere it says the word *God,* replace it with *good.* It was probably just a typo someone overlooked in ancient writings.

Recognizing goodness in everything and everyone in your life will help remove the mystery of God and Its message. Good/God surrounds and enfolds you, and it's easier to understand how every part of your life can be devoted to It now, isn't it? Not a human good that can turn to bad, but a spiritual goodness that has no opposite.

There are some who think our world has no hope; don't let them stand in your way. We'll join hands, hearts, and minds, and stand united, being the nation to teach all nations the meaning of love. And we can teach it, because we *know it,* by experience.

Isn't it interesting that my lifetime dream was to become a mother? Not anything spectacular by the world's standards. Something that comes so easily to others, and I had to struggle for ten years to conceive my first child. Motherhood, not being accepted as noble, honorable, or valued in today's society, has become the key to many answers concerning the world's problems. In 1985, I received a revelation from God: "Write a book, awakening millions and millions of My children from their past slumber of negative beliefs and fears, healing the minds of humankind." Countless experiences with children, adults, and miracle stories led to the teaching of today. Who would have ever thought or believed that I, just being me, a danged ol' housewife and mother, could make a difference and reach a dream?

I spent my life saying, "Why me?" Maybe the rest of my days upon this earth, I should ask, "Why *not* me?" Think about it, family. Why not you, too?

It's time for our day to end, and I do so sadly. I have so many stories to share, but I know you have other things to do, besides sitting here and listening to me. I've certainly enjoyed this time we've had together and hope we can do it again soon.

To close, I'm offering you a poem that sums today's teachings from beginning to end.

THE PRESENCE

With the miracle of life and all that it brings,
Reminds me to recall the truly important things.
And so, as a human, and what I would wish to share,
To let each one of you know just how much I care . . .

I silenced myself, to ask, so that I might know,
What He, our Creator, would want me to sow.
Words of His wisdom were whispered softly in my ear,
And I became aware of a solitary tear.

Down my cheek and to my lip, it rolled,
As I felt His Presence, within me, unfold.

His message of love was given simply, you see,
And I give to you as He gave to me . . .

I have no hands, allow Me to use yours,
I am with you always, He softly assures.
Reach out to loved ones and strangers, in need,
Offer My love freely in each random deed.

"I hold you within My hallowed memory in Mind,
And recall all the moments you were loving and kind."
The message didn't stop with just those few lines,
It continued on with even more Divine signs . . .

"Walk proudly in your Christhood, throughout each and
every day,
Just be who you are and show others the way,
For this earth shall know peace, this I solemnly vow,
Beginning this moment, for My Present is now."

I felt His loving Presence and believed in His Word,
I think it was the sweetest promise I had ever heard.
And when I finally understood His message, life and its
meaning became clear,
And I had to laugh, to myself, for the needless times I'd felt
fear.

By staying in the moment with no fears of future or past,
I realized I had no needs and felt total serenity at last.
If we want to make a difference, we have to be the difference,
you see . . .
And I am willing to be perfect love—for perfect peace just
began within me.
World peace is a dream, yours and mine,
Together, we can make it reality and that's the bottom line.

Give me a hug and don't let go until I tell ya! Thank you all for coming . . .

May peace be with you, today, and

Always,
Gloria D. Benish

P.S. I love you all with my whole, great big heart!

OPEN YOUR JOURNAL AND ANSWER THESE QUESTIONS

Journal—Chapter Sixteen

1. Name three things about yourself that you appreciate.

2. List three of the closest people in your life and write one to three things about each that you appreciate.

3. Name two selfish people you're aware of. Write down something you've learned from this book, if even only one line, that you could share with them.

4. What are some random acts of kindness you could perform anonymously for individuals or the community? Be creative!

5. Name ten judgments you hold against yourself presently. Take one at a time and silently state, "I surrender this _____ judgment about myself. I choose to no longer have an opinion about it. I seek and know only Oneness concerning it."

6. Name ten judgments you hold against family, friend, boss, school, society, and the world. Silently state, "I surrender this _____ judgment concerning

_____. I choose to no longer have an opinion about it. I seek and know only Oneness concerning it."

7. Name three things you would like to do, but fear you can't.

8. Write the above three things in a present affirmation, and repeat each one until you realize you can.

> I can _____.
> I can _____.
> I can _____.

9. Write an experience that appeared negative, a time when you wondered, "Why me?" Perhaps the experience was a blessing in disguise, helping you become aware of a need in the world that needs to be filled.

10. Why not you? What is one of your dreams, and short-term goals? Don't be afraid to dream (big). It's safe to write it down.

11. If you don't have money, do you think you have nothing valuable to give? A gift from your heart is the most valuable. What gift, from the heart, could you give to a parent, friend, or teacher? Write an example.

12. Children and parents: Is there an employer who has supplied you with a paycheck? Although you're being paid for your services, your employer would appreciate knowing that his or her company has been beneficial to you.

My goal was to teach you how to know yourself. We get traditions and beliefs handed down to us, but you now hold in your hand a complete, individual Journal so you know who you are, your likes, dislikes, boundaries, feelings, desires, and attitudes. It was never my desire to have you adopt my beliefs or feelings, becoming a chameleon and changing your beliefs and attitudes to mine just because they might sound good. It was my intent to take you inside yourself, to know you, to know how you feel and to learn to imagine and dream. I choose for you to have the opportunity that I (and your parents) never had: an opportunity to realize—young—how to imagine and know your potential.

God doesn't want you to be another Gloria. He wants you to be you. Let me ask you this: Now that you've read this book, do you know how loved you are? How valuable are you in His greater plan? If you have doubts, I, as a messenger and spiritual teacher, have temporarily failed. But have no fear, because I'll never give up, never give up. I'll write it again and again, and I'll remain patient until you "get it."

He never gives up on any of us. If he has one hundred sheep and loses one, He'll find that one and bring it home, back to the Heart of God. So if you still feel lost after reading this book, be patient with yourself . . . because I know you'll find your way back home. If not through my writings, then through another teacher. There are many paths, but there's only One destination. Be the best you can and enjoy your journey.

Write your heartfelt thoughts in the Journal and state this affirmation aloud. *God must love me so very, very much to surround me with caring parents, friends, and strangers to protect me. I am safe in the arms of God.*

Ask "Dr. Gloria"
Questions and Answers

Dear Dr. Glo-bug:

I'm like your friend Barbara Ann. After reading your book, I feel like "you're special" and that's why you can do the things you do. Are you sure others can do the things you can? I think you are special.

Signed: Hoping I'm Special, Too!

Dear Hope:

You should know me by now: If you ask me a question, I'm going to start talking again. When I was told by a doctor that I was pregnant with my first child, D.W., I was driving back to work, crying tears of joy. I had waited so long to hear those words. I continued to cry as I drove. A "Voice" said, "You are carrying the Christ Child." Not being spiritual or religious at that time, I silently wondered, "Where in the hell did that thought come from?" Somewhere, inside myself, I knew the message didn't refer to the child I was carrying. I was carrying the "Christ Seed" within my consciousness. (So do you.)

Three years later, D.W. crawled into bed with me during the night, crying because he was having growing pains. I snuggled him to me and groggily said, "D.W., just take a deep breath and relax." I knew there's nothing anyone can do in this situation. He cried harder, saying, "I can't, Momma, it hurts too bad."

An inner Voice asked me to place the index and middle fingers of my left hand on his forehead and state aloud, "Peace be with you." Being awakened from a sound sleep, I didn't have any prejudgments that it wouldn't work. I did as asked. Immediately, D.W. stopped crying and fell asleep in my arms. I silently said, "Thanks, God" and fell back to sleep.

The following morning, when I awakened, my first thought was of what had occurred during the night. I thought, "Wow. Think of all the possibilities." I recalled the experience off and on throughout the day.

Later than afternoon, I was driving through heavy rush-hour traffic in Sacramento to meet a woman at a restaurant. She was going to interview me as a possible guest speaker for an AIDS group. Along the way, I continued to have a thought hammer me to stop at a metaphysical bookstore along the way. I didn't need anything from the store; also, if I stopped, I would be late for my appointment. I had only met the owner of the store, and her daughter, one time. I continued to rationalize all the reasons it would be silly to stop. Maybe on my way back from the meeting? The thoughts continued to urge me to stop.

As I stepped over the threshold, I met the owner and gave her a quick hug. Not even knowing why I said what I did, I asked, "Is your daughter here?" The mother said, "Yes, she's in the back room." As I approached the back of the store, I could hear her crying. I asked if she was okay.

Gina replied, "No, I'm not. I burned my little finger and it's throbbing. There's no ice available and it's killing me." As she stood there before me, crying, I started sharing what had occurred during the night with D.W. I said, "Here, maybe I should try to do it on you, too."

I was being silly, as usual of course, and was pretending I was one of the Three Stooges and that I was going to use the middle and index finger of my left hand to poke her in the eyes. But at the last moment, I gently reached up to her forehead. I touched her softly and said, "Peace be with you."

Before I could even take my fingers away from her forehead, she startled me, which made me pull my hand away quickly from her face. "My finger doesn't hurt anymore!"

"You're kidding? Cool." I hugged her, and made it to my appointment on time.

There I was. Not having a clue what was happening in my world. Sometimes with a slight touch, or no touch at all . . . tasting and smelling purity as people were healed through me. Danielle was only a baby then, and nearly three years later she taught me "how to lay hands on" and give others a little extra love.

I'm not any more special than anyone else. I'm just a teacher. Once you have the awareness, and open yourself to the violet light/Presence of God, you'll be dazzling yourself as you see these kinds of experiences occurring. You are (acting like) an ordinary person, who in reality is an extraordinary Spirit. And don't you forget it, buddy.

You are special; here to be and do something unique that no one else could do quite the same way. You may not be aware yet how even a kind word, a smile, or your presence can affect another. Or how your personal and special gifts can and will touch humanity. But trust me, if you will just practice the Presence, you will find out. That's a guarantee.

Dear Dr. Glo-bug:

I seem to freeze when I am met with someone being negative. I feel immediately intimidated by their tone and feel "bitten." I don't know what to say. I walk away feeling angry, with myself, because I handled the situation so poorly. Do you have any advice?

Signed: Frost "Bitten"

Dear Frosty:

Chill out. Help to warm your heart, as well as theirs, is on its way. Before I share the answer, I have to tell you a simple lead-in story. You know I wear bells on my shoes, but many of my sneakers have "lights" that blink as I walk, also. On top of that, I had an angel charm hooked to one of my shoelaces. My sister Sheila asked me one day, "Gosh, Gloria, you have an angel, bells, and lights . . . do you also have a horn, for when you're backing up?" I laughed and said, "Now, wouldn't that be a little childish?"

The bells have come in handy for other things. I was invited to lunch at a barbecue restaurant while passing through Denver to see my family. I don't care much for barbecue, and don't like to waste food. I asked the man behind the counter (unaware that he was the manager) if I could choose something smaller from the children's menu.

Clearly, the sign said, CHILDREN'S MENU'S—12 AND UNDER ONLY. When I asked this permission, the manager got a growl in his voice and barked, "Why don't you just give me one good reason why I should let you do that?" I raised my foot, clear up to the counter, and softly replied, "Because I wear bells on my shoes and I'm very childlike?"

His voice softened immediately, also, and in a tender way, he asked, "What can I get for you today?" He came to our table three times to make sure we had everything we needed.

When you meet these situations, people's first reaction is to bark back, which just creates more resistance. We don't see the whole picture. Maybe they just had an argument with a loved one or got some distressing news. And maybe they're just buttheads. At any rate, I normally speak my thoughts aloud, seeking any one loving, good, positive thing about the person and sharing it. Love can dissolve negativity in a heartbeat.

As you continue practicing the Presence daily, you will find a level of confidence, love, and peace that radiates from you. You don't have to do anything to achieve it, because it's just who you are. People will be able to sense this, and you'll be surprised how often someone opens a door for you, smiles sweetly, or randomly compliments you.

You're not doing anything "wrong" in the way you are presently handling the situation, other than *thinking* you're wrong. Be honest with your frustration if you fall back into the old pattern, but watch, look, and listen as you see that experience changing.

Dear Dr. Glo-bug:

I have a question and confession to make that I'm even scared to ask about or tell you. I feel so ashamed, I can't even talk about it with my closest friend and would die before I confessed it to my Heavenly Father through a local priest. I find myself attracted to the same sex. I'm so afraid to act on these feelings, but I think my greatest fear is, if anyone found out, I would be rejected totally by my parents and friends. "It says, in the Bible, it's wrong to be homosexual/lesbian." Can you please help me understand?

> **Signed: One of Many Who Don't Know How to Handle This**

Dear One:

First of all, I hope you're never frightened to talk to me about anything. Many adults were sometimes afraid to talk to me of their "shadows" and found comfort in sharing them with my "con" artist, Nikki. They were afraid they would lose my approval, but Nikki assured them that if she could be accepted and loved by me, anyone could. Many other adults, knowing I smoke, 'n' drink, 'n' cuss, feel safer sharing with me than with a minister of their faith, whom they feel is "too holy" to express their real feelings with. So, rest assured, Dear One, I am a safe place to say anything you want and need to.

I agree with your signature; there are many who don't know how to handle this. As I was flying to California last year to speak in a women's prison, I was surrounded by a college girls' basketball team. Since anytime I'm asked who I am or what I do, I share as gently as possible, hoping I won't overwhelm, that's what I did. As our conversation unfolded during the flight, they, of course, heard I was telepathic (and so were they).

When we landed, one of the girls approached me privately at luggage pickup and started "testing" me. "Yeah, right, if you're so telepathic, why don't you tell me what I'm thinking?" I begged her, "Please don't make me do this." I knew she was testing me, but I didn't want to be the one to take the responsibility to say the words (as I had for my daughter, Kerrie, when she wanted to end her engagement).

Again and again, this college kid kept asking, and almost daring me to tell her what was going on inside her head. I asked several times, "Please don't make me say this." I've been hammered by the best, having four kids, and just as they are able to do at times, I caved in.

Without judgment in my tone or making her wrong, I softly said, "You are a lesbian, and you're on a big guilt trip. You fear if your friends and parents knew, you would lose their approval. You have such strong desires for a young woman and you're so torn, you can't stand it. You're confused, *but mostly you're frightened to come out of the closet about who you really are.*" There. I said it. I heavily sighed, while watching her jaw hit the floor that I knew her deepest secret.

She asked how I must feel—since I'm a minister—about

this situation? I only had a few minutes to talk to her, because the busload of girls would soon be leaving the airport.

I explained briefly that I have no judgments about homosexuality. I attempt to teach others not to judge, also. They may just discover, through the judgment, that they, themselves, a mate, child, friend, or grandchild will give them an opportunity to experience the situation.

As I hugged this tall young woman good-bye, I whispered, "*When* you can learn to love and accept yourself, your loved ones will, too."

The first lesbian I counseled found acceptance and unconditional love from me. Following her visit, a dear friend of mine was shocked "that I had let a queer in my house." I said, "You're alcoholic and I let you in my house. Alcoholism is not *who you are,* it is just *one aspect of who you are,* just as her situation is just *one aspect of who she is.*" He was upset with me that I would allow someone *like that* into my home and love her as much as I would him. Sad, isn't it? He couldn't accept himself and his condition; therefore, he can't accept another's.

As for you, my Dear One, you must feel so much better that you finally got to relieve yourself of the guilt and fears you carry. Perhaps, once you start practicing all I have taught you through this book, you will be able to heal your fears concerning this. Maybe you'll find someone you really love and will feel comfortable and excited. You'll accept your experience and go on to help others, in similar situations, to find peace in their hearts, too. Good or bad, who's to say why we choose certain situations? It is a soul choice . . . you are loved by your Creator and have His approval. (And remember, He's never going to change His Mind about you. That's an absolute certainty, or He wouldn't be God.) If you open yourself to His Will to express through you, and He judges you not, do you really want to judge yourself?

Dear Dr. Glo-bug:

There is so much teen suicide. I have used this fear to manipulate my friends and parents in order to get what I want. Other times, I have thought of hurting myself, or "walking out of the movie early," because I hurt so badly. I know you talked about your experience of wanting to dig a deep hole and jump into it after Nikki left, but I was wondering if you ever considered doing something like this seriously?

Signed: Too Chicken to Do It, or Am I?

Dear Chicken Little:

I have counseled many people through this feeling, successfully. Thank God, no one who ever called for help took the physical action to follow through. I know exactly how you feel. I'm sure, if (practically) everyone on this planet would be honest, at least with themselves, they'd admit they've had these same feelings. At least once in their life. Sometimes our burdens get so heavy, we can't see any other way out.

I don't believe we "go to hell" if we commit suicide. If there's a hell, it's right here on earth. I do, however, believe that if people choose to take their own lives, they will reincarnate and pick up where they left off, having to deal with the same situation anyway to learn it. Not as punishment by God, but as growth for the soul.

When I was in college, I called my sister Vicki one evening. I had been using her car and I thought it was extremely gracious of me to call and forewarn her of my plan. "Vicki, I'm going to run your car off a cliff tonight, with me in it. I'm just telling you this so you don't feel guilty that your car had anything to do with the accident. And, besides, your insurance will replace it." Thinking I was teasing at first, she laughed. I told her I was serious.

I explained that I had just looked at my check register and realized I didn't have money to cover the checks I'd recently written. The thought of bouncing checks or having to ask my mom for money to cover them was totally inconceivable. I thought there was no other choice but to kill myself. I was being completely serious. It seemed like the end of the world to me.

Vicki tried to comfort me and would have given me money, had she had it to give. She would give the shirt off her back to help another. But she didn't at this time, and was feeling very frightened by my behavior. She begged me to call Mom and discuss it. (I would have died first.)

We hung up and the phone rang immediately. My mom said, "Vicki just called me . . . and stop talking like an ass, Gloria. Go to the bank tomorrow and explain the situation. If you find out how much money you need to cover the outstanding checks, I'll take care of it." God, could it be that simple?

The next day, I went to the college bank branch and explained the situation uncomfortably. The teller looked at my check register and, tickled, said, "Oh, look here. On this deposit, you subtracted it out . . . rather than adding it in." *I did have the money.* I realized I would have killed myself for nothing and apologized to Vicki and Mom.

I know when you're going through a moment of the deepest pain and confusion you've ever felt, leaving sounds a whole lot better than staying. A simple phone call, even though you're embarrassed or scared, could give you the simplest solution.

When individuals called me to say they were going to commit suicide and had a bottle of pills in their hands and were ready to do so, I interrupted their hysteria with shock value. "Then just *do it.*"

"Excuse me?"

Immediately the tears stopped as I repeated, "If you're going to do it—then just do it. Stop manipulating your loved ones and friends. If you don't really want to kill yourself, then go flush the pills down the toilet and get a life. Stop being so selfish and put your thoughts on someone else. Help me to help others b'cuz, God, I could certainly use a helping hand."

As a personality, I would never say those words to someone. As an instrument, allowing God to speak through me, I'm totally amazed at times what comes out of my mouth.

If you consciously know you are manipulating your loved ones and friends, then be honest and knock it the hell off. If, however, you find yourself entertaining the idea seriously, I beg you to get counseling and begin practicing what I'm teaching in this and my other writings. Stay in touch with me and let me know how these helpful hints work in your present experience.

Dear Dr. Glo-bug:

Can you tell me why anyone should develop the gift of telepathy?

Signed: I Can't "See" Why It Makes Much Difference

Dear Vision of the Future:

When I was living in Sacramento, I was driving to a dentist appointment in the rain. The roads were slick and everyone was being very cautious. Traffic in front of me had stopped. My attention was drawn to my rearview mirror, where I saw a car approaching. I could see that she wasn't paying attention that traffic had halted.

Still looking in my mirror, I screamed silently, *"Look up now."* She did and immediately slammed on her brakes, skidding and fishtailing out of control. Luckily, there was no oncoming traffic as her car whipped back and forth in both lanes.

She came to a stop behind my car as the two bumpers nearly "kissed." Still looking in my rearview mirror, I silently asked her, "Are you okay?" She nodded her head yes.

I'm sure when her adrenaline wore off and she had time to think about it, she probably questioned how we had a discussion without words.

I could tell you countless stories just like this. I believe it's more important for you to trust yourself, however, and write to me . . . telling me the reasons why developing telepathy is so important.

Dear Dr. Glo-bug:

I feel ashamed of myself, but I don't know how to change the way I react when I see someone who's handicapped. My mom tells me to treat them with kindness, but they scare me. I don't know if I should talk to them or look away. Sometimes when I think they aren't looking, I find myself staring. Everytime I notice someone in a wheel-chair, missing a leg, or retarded, I feel so uncomfortable. I get embarrassed and act more retarded than they do.

                    Signed: Watches from Afar

Dear Watches:

I am so proud of you that you have the courage to see a real problem of the world and address it so honestly and simply.

Do you realize that adults (yes, even parents) feel the same discomfort and fear you do? Parents of these children are aware that others feel uncomfortable, and it hurts them to see people (of all ages) shy away from their child. Their feelings are hurt to see their child or loved one rejected or judged by peers and society.

I had no idea I'd get to address this situation in this book. I'm so grateful to have an opportunity to talk about it today. Your question needs to be answered.

I was flown to Los Angeles to help a three-month-old baby who had been given her last rites. She had been diagnosed as severely brain damaged due to oxygen deprivation. The doctors told the mother that her first child would never see, hear, speak, swallow her saliva, eat normally, or sit up (if she lived). During the flight to California, the infant began telepathically talking to me so quickly that I wished I had a pen and paper to take dictation.

The infant said, "Gloria, I don't need eyes, ears or a mouth to talk to my mother. Teach her and other parents how to talk, telepathically, to their loved ones who are in comas or brain damaged."

Infants, of course, can't speak, but baby Rachel could talk to me from mind to mind. All babies can, all ages, even those society terms "deaf, dumb, and blind." No one in the world is limited if they don't have a voice. Everyone has this ability, of course, once they're aware of it.

Baby Rachel asked me to teach her mom, Lyn, how to access and trust her talent so they could speak to one another. Which I did.

Now, anyone else might believe I was "just using my imagination" and making this all up. But Lyn directly experienced "hearing" her baby. They had five weeks to talk to one another and express their love before baby Rachel chose to pass away peacefully in her mother's arms.

One of her messages to Lyn was, "I'm so tired. I need a new body." The "vehicle" she would have needed for this life was damaged beyond repair. Lyn thought she was flying me to Los Angeles for a miracle healing. She had an expectation of me being used as an instrument. I, as a healer, never know how the miracle will unfold, but I believe it will be in Divine Order and the Will of God, relieving me humanly of the responsibility.

Rather than baby Rachel living, and her body restored, the miracle was far reaching. She asked me to teach her mom how to telepathically speak to her, so Lyn could go on to teach others. Baby Rachel also told me, "I don't want you to write a book about this. I want my mom to write the book." (I was actually being used to heal Lyn, not the child.)

Through Lyn's grief over losing her first child, she could see no way to fulfill her little angel's request. But God could. One month after baby Rachel was laid to rest, Lyn came to me for a private healing, and she received her miracle. Proud of her and happy for her, I felt drawn to invite Lyn to stay for my seven o'clock appointment with a young man, seventeen years of age. I didn't know why I invited her to remain. I don't normally do that. I trust my thoughts and guidance, however, and the experience changed Lyn's life forever.

Due to a surgical error, D.J. had known chronic pain since he was three months old. Morphine and powerful drugs could not bring relief for the child. D.J. was also born with other defects that made him appear retarded. He lived in a body that didn't work. A body that baby Rachel would have experienced, had she lived.

Seeing this sad mother–son relationship, and having so recently lost a child who would have also known this same frustration, was more than Lyn could bear. She began crying. Although D.J. is sadder than words can say, he (being empathic) felt her sadness.

He momentarily thought her tears were his fault and

reached out a hand to touch Lyn. She heard his thoughts and exclaimed, "No. This isn't your fault."

He attempted to nod his head, unable to speak. She again remarked, "No. It's not *because of you* that I'm crying." Touching her heart, her tears flowed as she softly whispered, "*My heart hurts, too . . .*" She verbally spoke to him, telling D.J. of her recent loss. He looked at her with such love in his eyes; it would have melted a heart of stone within a hundred-mile radius.

For seventeen years, he had been trapped alone in a body that wouldn't do what he wanted and needed it to do. He was frustrated because he couldn't tell others of his needs.

D.J. telepathically told me to speak to him verbally, not mind to mind. He was cherishing the time we had together, because all he'd ever known was hearing the verbal and silent cruel judgments and comments of others. He "said," "Gloria, all I've ever known is people talking about me—in front of me—but never to me."

Because he "appears" retarded, others talk in front of him (rather than to him), thinking he can't understand. In fact, he's very bright and understands completely, but is verbally unable to express himself. He's a very sensitive young man.

Lyn, beginning immediately, taught D.J.'s mom, Vykki, how to communicate with her son. Fulfilling baby Rachel's request and guidance, Lyn will go on to write a book to help countless people. We don't always understand what situations will force us to grow.

D.J. didn't want to leave our company that evening. He was so afraid that "*This was all too good to be true.*" But it was true, and we vowed he could begin meeting regularly with Lyn, to teach him how to heal. We each carried on a complete and meaningful conversation with D.J., but he was far more attracted to Lyn. Their love had been made in heaven, and on earth they had met again.

Not once did any of us "talk down" to D.J. or treat him as less than he was. He is also a great spirit trapped in a broken body that can heal, too. But first, his miracle came in the form of healing his broken spirit. In fact, I had a mystical experience while with D.J. His face, which appeared "re-tarded," softened for a few moments into the face of a handsome young man. I *saw* his true spirit.

These people teach us courage, many times *showing* by example how not to allow life to keep us from being all we can be.

When you meet another situation such as your question conveyed, look beyond the "appearance." Look the individual in the eyes, the windows to the soul, and see their bright and shining spirit looking back at you. Even if they can't speak, whether it's an infant or aged person, a stroke victim, or "deaf, dumb, and blind," realize they *can understand*. (And you don't need to shout. A simple thought can be projected by you and received by them.)

I believe your mom was correct. Treat them kindly. If you're willing to be their friend, you have an opportunity to learn far more than you could have ever imagined. And you'll experience an unconditional love you had never dreamed possible.

Even when the medical world says a person is brain dam-aged or in a coma, that simple limitation does not interfere with the Voice of the soul. When Jesus talks to me, or others who have departed, this is the vehicle of communication they use. A person's consciousness never *dies*.

Imagine the possibilities. An infant, or toddler, who can't speak, lying in a mother's or father's arms, or in a hospital, who can't tell another where they hurt, or what's wrong, can share silently through telepathy and our gifts of empathy. You, who already are telepathic, could help the medical world diagnose and treat more effectively.

As you become friends with these individuals, you'll grow beyond your present fears. Teach them how to open themselves to the Presence of God. And then just watch to see what other miracles are in store for both of you.

Epilogue

I get calls from parents whose children are afraid to go to school. School is a place where a child, teen, or college kid should feel safe, and yet they just aren't sure anymore. Maybe it will take groups of you, joined together, before school boards or before Congress, to reintroduce God into the schools in the form of courses on meditation and self-esteem.

As you practice what I've taught in this and my other writings, you'll see the difference you can make to help yourselves and one another. How will you know that your practice is paying off?

- Do you see more random acts of kindness as you daily walk through life?
- Do you see the beauty of nature?
- Do you feel harmony in your life and workplace?
- Do you feel loved in the presence of family, friends, and strangers?
- Does it feel like magic is in the air?
- Do you witness the brotherhood and sisterhood of those you meet, no longer concerned about color, race, and creed . . . but seeing all in the wholeness created by All That Is?
- Have you given and received love today?
- Have you hugged and been hugged today?
- Do you walk in love, rather than in fear?

- Do you feel greater compassion and acceptance for all creatures great and small?
- Have you noticed that you and all others are focusing and speaking more about all that's good and right in the world, rather than what's all wrong?
- Have you noticed yourself smiling, humming, and whistling more and that you no longer seek love, for it seeks you?

If so, my writing is a success.

I play a game in my workshop called "We always have everything we need, usually before we know we need it." To get everyone in the workshop on the same wavelength, we rub and place our hands over our eyes for two to ten minutes. If you play this at home, in a club, or can convince a teacher to allow you to do it during a class, you'll be amazed at the results.

In a group, count off 1, 2, 1, 2, 1, 2, all through the people present. Ask each person to remember which number they called off. All 1s write the word QUESTION on a piece of paper (or notecard) at the top. All 2s write ANSWER on the top of their paper or notecard.

All 1s now write whatever question they want answered. It may be a personal question: "Am I liked?" "Should I tell Mom why I was so angry the other night?" And so on.

Or your question may be a question about the world, or for the group as a whole, or concerning your spiritual journey. "Will the world know peace in my lifetime?" "What do I most need to work on or become aware of?" What do I need to do to further my spiritual growth?"

All those who have ANSWER on their paper will write an individual answer, which may be as simple as "Yes." "No." "In three days, you will have the answer through a trusted friend."

Or the answer may be something inspirational: "With God, all things are possible." "Ask and you shall receive." "Go Within or Go Without."

Choose two people, one to pick up all the QUESTION cards, and one to collect all the ANSWERS. Shuffle and count to make sure you each have the same number. Read the question, followed by the answer. You can shuffle again and again and your questions and answers will reveal some startling facts for you. The game is almost eerie as to how it gives the players the answers they seek.

In the introduction, one of my questions to you was, "Do you need someone to talk to, someone who will really listen?" I am offering to be that someone, if you choose. My ministry Web site is www.miraclehealing.org, and I will be creating a chat line so the public can reach me for questions and continued guidance. I would love for you to stop by and visit.

If you enjoyed the day we had together through this book, please watch for my next book, *Spiritual Security Blanket*. In it, I'll be meeting you at the trailhead and leading you up the mountain of transfiguration, heightening your consciousness from human to Divine. This book will explain, simply, how to achieve financial security, emotional security, security in decision making, and security in God and all spiritual matters.

In understandable language, you will achieve the full awareness that any of life's imperfections aren't "in the body" or "in the experience," but *within the mind*. Because they are in the mind, and we know that thoughts themselves have no power, illnesses, pains, problems, have no reality, no substance, and no power because God is the only Power.

Once you become aware of this simple spiritual teaching, your life, of course, will never be the same. So plan on meeting me at the trailhead in that book and "be on the lookout" for new opportunities to bring you peace of mind.

It's time to close the longest love letter written in the history of humankind. So from a *child at heart* . . . to you, another I'll hold in my heart, it's time to release this book into the hands of those it can serve. Until we can meet again . . .

Always,
Dr. Glo-bug

May the Source be with you!

Acknowledgments

Through my writings and teachings, I have received thousands of acknowledgments for my contributions of taking the time to care and to serve. Most of these efforts, however, would not have been possible or successful without the help of those I have listed below. My editor teased me that she thought I'd just taken a telephone book and copied names from it, because there were so many to receive credit. I believe that you should see your name in print—you have been the wind beneath my wings, giving me the support that was required to do what must be done.

To my teenage editor, Kristen Lynch, who agreed to be the first to read this manuscript chapter by chapter and give feedback. I appreciate her willingness to help make this book the best it could be and am anxious to meet her and physically hold her in my arms. Until we can, I'll just hold her in my thoughts and heart (forever).

To my siblings, Terry, Vicki, Sheila, and (favorite/only brother) Bill. Terry is my favorite person to watch classic movies with, especially movies starring our archetype (perfect example to follow) Doris Day. Sitting around, eating popcorn and chocolate, and drinking iced tea gives me fond memories. Not only is she a good friend, but I'm also fortunate to have her as a sister.

Vicki was and is my hero. I looked to her in moments of fear, as a child, and as an adult. She would give the shirt off her back to help another . . . and quite often, did.

Sheila and I are playmates, and she makes me laugh. Bright and witty, she sparkles and just makes life more fun for everyone around her!

Bill once said, "Gloria, having you as part of our family is like having our personal Goddess. Every time you come to town, *everyone* wants to spend time with you. You're so loved and admired." Yeah, well, I admire and love my family, too, and Bill, get ready for that trip to Hawaii.

To Cynthia Vaughan. She asked a simple question and I wrote this book as its answer. To Chris Nelson (age ten), who shared his vision of how I could help all kids, nationwide. Countless parents and myself will be eternally grateful. To my friends and supporters, those who have freely helped me to help others, asking for nothing in return . . . the board of directors of the Miracle Healing Ministry, Mr. and Mrs. Ken Tritz and Mr. and Mrs. Dale Evenson.

With deep respect and appreciation to our dear friends Bob (the "builder") and his wife, Julie, who are always on hand to help others build their dreams.

To my world's greatest cheerleader, Barbara Vital. To my spiritual group members, Deborah and Laura Goslin, Sandy Kenyon, Sandy Coyle, Claire Trauth, Jill Myer, Tom Herak, and June Nelson.

To my "keepers": Lee Rust, Rondi Wright, Nancy White, Debbie and Randy Bennett, Debbie Lewis, Cheyenne Peck, Debbie Dillon, St. Michael and Laura Kakuk, Diane Johnson, Johnny Patton, Kimber Webb-Fierro, Debra Jones, Terry and Jay Moyer, Susan Liepitz, Jim and Joan Rhodda, Judy Twentyman, April Carter, Carol and Robert Larson, Richard Berry, Eleanor King, Katherine Weiger, Robert and Marianne Peck, Alex and Deborah Kolb, Link Fountain, Choy-Lang Bontrager, Wynona and Kevin Martin, Patricia Ingram, LuAnn Stallcop, Fred and Dorothy Pfeiffer, Jayne Lynch, Lisa Smith, Barbara Wagner, Lee Daly, Evelyn Preece,

Bea Jackson and her daughter, Leisha, and so many others. If you don't see your name in print, don't think I have forgotten you. I have a memory like an elephant, and I'll never forget where and how it all began.

To Emerson Theological Institute and its board of directors, for the opportunity to serve in a doctorate capacity, to be a more credible voice to the world. To Dr. Angelo Pizelo, Bob Hand, and Jack Gyer . . . thanks for another danged title!

About the Author

One of today's fastest-rising inspirational authors, Gloria D. Benish is a mother, wife, dynamic speaker, spiritual healer—and one-woman powerhouse. She travels the United States giving talks and healing thousands of people each year. She lives in Stevensville, Montana, with her husband, Kirk, and their four children. More information on Gloria's work is available on her Web site, miraclehealing.org.